THE DEVIL WEARS CLOGS

THE DEVIL WEARS CLOGS

JENNIFER BURGE

WORLDWISE PUBLICATIONS
QUEENSLAND, AUSTRALIA

2nd Edition ©2016 Jennifer Burge
WorldWise Publications
www.worldwisepublications.com

Cover Design by Todd Cronin
Categories: Travel, Biography & Memoir,
Business Travel, Women in Business

The right of Jennifer Burge to be identified as the author of this work has been asserted by her in accordance with the *Copyright Amendment (Moral Rights) Act 2000.*

This work is protected by copyright. Apart from any use as permitted under the Copyright Act 1968, no part may be reproduced, copied, scanned, stored in a retrieval system, recorded, or transmitted, in any form or by any means, without the prior written permission of the author and publisher.

1st Edition Published 2014

ISBN 978-0-9942449-0-1 (Paperback)
ISBN 978-0-9942449-1-8 (eBook)

WorldWise Publications
Queensland, Australia

Dedication

This book is dedicated to my husband, without whom there would never have been a story to tell. While life hasn't always been a fairy tale, you are my happy ending.

Acknowledgments

I would like to thank my circle of believers, strong intelligent women who stood by me during this story and in the re-telling of it. You know who you are. Todd Cronin, you translated a daydream into a beautiful work of cover art, thank you.

Contents

PROLOGUE 1
LIFT OFF 3
SPRECHEN SIE ENGLISCH? 9
EUROPE'S CHANGING FACE 21
AMSTERDAMNED 29
THE BLACKEST FOREST 37
FURTHER AFIELD 41
LEARNING TO FLY 47
PROVING GROUND 53
LAYING THE GROUNDWORK 63
WHAT LIES BENEATH 71
FIRST DATE 81
TICK TOCK 93
GOEIEMORGEN ALLEMAAL 101
THE DUTCH DAILY GRIND 115
SILVER LINING 123
HOLIDAY CHEERLESS 135
REALITY BITES 141
BREAKTHROUGH 145
OUT OF THE FRYING PAN 151
INTERVIEW WITH THE DEVIL 161
ALTERED STATES 167
THE ROAD LESS TRAVELED 189
HOW TO LIVE IN A DORP 197
OPPORTUNITY KNOCKS 215
CHOOSING SIDES 223
BREAK IN THE CLOUDS 233
FAIRYTALE 239
KNIGHT IN SHINING ARMOR 251
SWITCHING TEAMS 255
ABOUT THE AUTHOR 267

PROLOGUE

I cleared my throat. "You're wrong," I said. Quietly.
"What was *that*?" the CEO growled from the other end of the phone line.

"I said you're wrong. That isn't going to improve the situation in Paris. It will make things worse," my voice was even. As the only person present who understood both the American and European viewpoints of this business equation, it was my obligation to clarify the delusion of Team USA. No one was more surprised than me.

Twice every month, I sat at the conference table. We, in the Netherlands, had begun the call. Updated agendas in hand, we had waited while the phone line choked with the noise of hasty positioning across the Atlantic. Flanked by experienced colleagues representing the Dutch, British, French, and Belgian views, the speaker-phone claimed its usual position of honor in the center. No American apologies for lateness or for wasting our time. Only the barking of orders, which our lowly European team was expected to summarily execute.

The purpose, for the American CEO and his team members, was to review all large mobile computer deployments in progress in Europe. Project plans were dissected, documents analyzed, decisions scrutinized. Always, raised voices brought the temperature in the conference room to stifling, regardless of the season. Rarely, an agreement with a clear action. Praise was an endangered species.

The lone American on the European team, I was often embarrassed by the arrogance spilling from the phone line. A Scottish colleague had the best description: "cringeworthy," or "the tendency to cringe upon hearing statements which contradict what is known to be reality." This day, however, my cup ranneth over.

What did the American team know of conducting business in Europe? They. Knew. Nothing. Yet, here we sat bi-weekly listening to the Gospel According to America.

The cringeworthy suggestion was that the American CEO was to show up at our largest French client, *my* client, unannounced and uninvited, to glad-hand, kiss babies, and throw around sales propaganda that lacked supporting facts and figures.

That a female would display brazen insolence by voicing a dissenting opinion was cringeworthy in upstate New York.

CHAPTER 1
LIFT OFF

On September 7th, 2001, I dropped my bags on the floor of my townhouse, corneas still cauterized by the snow-capped Canadian Rockies where I'd fled for weekend serenity. At the start of the year, I'd joined this firm of 100,000 employees worldwide to boost my chances of taking my life and career abroad. Calgary was step one of The Plan.

The high of blending work and travel, jetting around the country and points abroad with someone else picking up the tab was intoxicating. When the request to move to Europe for a one year assignment in a German software firm landed in my mailbox, I was already addicted.

On my last return flight from Calgary to Cleveland, I didn't realize how lucky I was to get home. Four days later, no flights were permitted to fly in U.S. airspace. Four days later, the world was a hostile place.

I am positive that I watched the plane that eventually crashed in Pittsburgh, fly far too low past my nineteenth floor window. My legs shook violently as I ran down nineteen flights of dimly lit stairs, our office tower closed by order of the Federal Government. It was no longer possible to ignore the stopwatch looming over each of our lives. We never know how many minutes are left on the clock.

The United States was in a state of shock after the collapse of the Twin Towers. Disbelief lingered for days and very little made sense. By late afternoon of that terrible Tuesday, my best friend Karla and I had drained several glasses of wine. Later that night, when President George W. Bush finally addressed us, Karla and I heard his message through the big-screen TV at the neighborhood pub. President Bush, unfortunately, had little to say after his long delay. It was far from the powerful, reassuring speech we expected from the leader of the free world after the brutality wrought on our country for the first time.

The tears, which flowed like waterworks every time a new revelation hit the news, made the rest of my week unproductive. I owed final documentation on service level agreements to my Canadian project leader. Since I wasn't maimed or killed, there was no excuse to be late in concluding business according to him. Eventually, I switched off the blaring non-stop media coverage and tried to focus.

The email that changed my life arrived the following week. Someone with my technical background was needed in Germany. The message, from my former manager on a New York project who I'd shamelessly begged to help me get to Europe, said that if I was interested, I'd better get my ass into gear and contact the decision maker.

Germany? In my many dreams of a romantic life abroad, Germany wasn't the setting. It's obvious now that much was missing from the picture I created in my head. At thirty, I'd traveled enough to know life overseas would be far from easy, but I didn't often stroll on that sidewalk for fear of falling through the cracks.

I didn't ask the immediate question: Was I living in a dream? Absolutely. Nor the visionary question: Would those cracks eventually overtake the entire pavement? Almost. Not the obvious question—How long does it take for the dream to dissolve into a stark reality of life without friends, family, or professional support? Nor the ultimate question—Can a successful female American career and personal life truly be transitioned to another country?

Was I looking for an escape? For adventure? For purpose in my life? Yes, yes, yes. I was young enough to jump the gun, but suitably well-traveled to know that what I was doing wasn't for the faint of heart. My teenage years in small-town Ohio had left little question that my thirst for world knowledge was greater than most. So when the dubious reactions began to pour in, I pushed them aside. Whose life was it anyway? The Twin Towers had just been leveled. In a world where that could happen, where was the baseline for measuring "crazy"? Opportunity may only knock once and who cared if it knocked with a German accent?

The Devil Wears Clogs

I started tossing things in suitcases: my giant fluffy leopard coat, books, every pair of shoes and boots I owned, makeup, clothes–*wait!* What do women even wear in Heidelberg? *Screw it*, I thought, and shoved it all in. I glanced at my shelves full of photos. What would I do without my friends? *They can visit*, I shouted back at the whimpering voice in my head. The devil on my other shoulder knew this was my chance.

Surveying my eclectic two-bedroom Cleveland townhouse, I said a silent farewell to the vintage furnishings I'd managed to collect. I was lucky to have such a beautiful home, but the cliché that you can't go home again has truth in it. Living in the sprawling city of Phoenix, Arizona after university had put life in perspective quickly.

Two years after returning, I'd outgrown it. As an IT consultant, my job had taken me to Dallas, New York, and Calgary before the invitation to Germany arrived, and I knew I wanted to live life on a bigger scale. My Arizona beau often remarked that I had "wheels on my ass." I guess that's one way of putting it.

I would have been equally enthusiastic about going to Luxembourg or Malta. It was Europe! For a year! On my own! That's exactly how the thoughts came to me: short, emphatic, and positive. When the role to assist with a new version of German customer management software was officially offered ten days later, I pounced. I asked how much I could pack and sadly flew my cat Bijoux to her temporary home with an Arizona friend. So few planes had returned to the sky. It was unnerving for both of us.

My life was reduced to the contents of a sea container when I flew the unfriendly skies in the first week of October 2001. After witnessing tragedy of epic proportion, I was convinced that playing it safe would get me nowhere.

* * *

The day before I left, I said good-bye to my landlord and grew bored listening to his drawn out stories of Germany during World War II. He was certain I'd be home by Christmas because, in his words, I would hate it. Clearly, the normally overflowing well of optimism shared by most Americans had run dry.

My Lufthansa flight connected through Washington Dulles at 6 p.m. The airport had a distinct military feeling. I thought maybe I ought to be marching. Walking for what felt like miles through the beige beehive of uniformed travelers, I found the connecting gate. I leaned against the window watching black clouds roll past one another with alarming speed. Outside, the screaming wind made me wonder if we were going anywhere. Standing in line to board, the gravity of what I was about to do finally hit home.

With the rush of packing and logistics behind me, panic appeared for the first time. Beads of sweat lined my brow. As I dragged my heavy laptop bag, overflowing purse, and backpack to my cramped economy class seat in the back of the plane, I promised myself I'd see as much of Europe as possible. Seatbelt safely fastened for the eight-hour flight and a cursory smile to the guy next to me, my body went into shutdown and I promptly dozed during takeoff.

The respite was short lived. I was jolted awake by the plane bucking beneath me. In slow motion, I lifted my window shade and double-checked my seatbelt. A blinding flash of white light, followed by a deafening crack on the opposite side of the plane, made its skeleton shudder. My seatmate and I exchanged raised-eyebrow glances while waiting for the pilot to explain. We all considered a possibility too frightening to be spoken.

Goosebumps rose on my arms when the first address was made in loud halting German. In my head, Captain Schmidt was shouting that we'd been hit by enemy attack and I'd silently prepared to die before he repeated his address in English. Lightning had struck the left wing, but there was no cause for concern. Wanting nothing to do with the situation, sleep took her leave at that point. Several glasses of wine eventually brought my heart rate back to normal. Hallelujah for those hardy blonde German angels and their clinking drink carts flying up and down the aisles.

I watched two movies and read until the pilot announced that he was preparing to land in Frankfurt. My subconscious worried about finding my way through the maze of German customs, luggage, and rental cars, but, more than anything, I was pumped. My adventure was on. I would have to find my way without the benefit of a roadmap from those who had been before me.

I was Magellan.

* * *

Germans are true to their stereotype of efficiency. They are organized and succinct. Clear English signs lead you through the airport. Within an hour of arrival, the immaculate glass airport doors swished shut behind me and I held the keys to a gleaming white Mercedes Benz, complete with sunroof. Though the vast number of buttons and dials of the luxury automobile were a mystery, I found the radio with no problem. Panic reappeared when the English signs vanished outside the airport. Magellan knew it was up to him, so I collected myself with several deep breaths and drove out of the parking lot at grandma speed. Relief permeated my being when I discovered that although the signs were unfamiliar, it was easy to reach the autobahn. Hitting the entrance ramp, I could finally exhale.

Evening European flights from the U.S. arrive in early morning. The sun was beginning her ascent in the cloudless blue sky as the airport gradually disappeared in my rear-view mirror. My hands gripped the leather steering wheel of this beautiful beast of German automotive excellence and I drove for the first time without concern for the speed limit. Paradise was an open sunroof and the crisp autumn wind teasing my hair. As the sun increased her intensity, October's frost-covered fields surrendered their armor. Germany was a fairytale landscape of golden wheat and castle spires poking through the misty hillsides.

Ninety minutes later, I entered the mammoth campus of VDS, the software company where I'd work for the next year. Crushed by sleep deprivation, I stuck around long enough to meet my new boss and co-workers face-to-face. As they headed to lunch, I escaped to my temporary home, a hotel 20 minutes from the office. It was an American chain hotel where the staff greeted me with a warm cheery "Welcome!" for which I was grateful. I was less enthusiastic about tackling the German language than I'd been about driving the autobahn that morning. In a haze, I followed the bellman to my room and collapsed onto cool white cotton sheets. Peeling off the clothes I'd been wearing for more than twenty-four hours, I was asleep in minutes and slept like the dead.

The shrieking alarm destroyed the silence. Three hours felt like three minutes as I dragged myself out of bed to the zombie-like existence I would become intimate with. Squinting and taking in the view from my third story window, I found the sun getting ready to call it a day.

I bolted into the bathroom for a quick shower before the sun disappeared, but the apparatus in the tub was alien. I turned one knob with no result. Then another. Still nothing. I scanned the bathroom for some obvious indication of how to turn the water on, but not one clue appeared. In desperation, I called the front desk to explain my dilemma. Two things made me grateful: one, they didn't laugh directly into the phone and two, a woman was sent to my rescue. Taking hardware lessons from a man would have been far more humiliating. The tall sturdy *frau* smiled kindly, lifted a ring on the underside of the faucet, and water flowed like the Mississippi. I couldn't remember feeling quite that stupid in the past year.

Rushing, I showered and bee-lined to the hotel's executive lounge for a courage-enhancing drink before meeting the team for dinner. The lounge wasn't luxurious or outstanding in any way. Two worn brown leather couches lazed against one wall like an old married couple. Haplessly strewn Formica tables and chairs mingled in the room's center. Cheap snacks littered the bar. What caught my eye was the winding corner staircase leading up to what I imagined was an outdoor deck. To avoid making polite conversation with hotel strangers, I poured a glass of chilled dry Riesling and went straight for the stairs.

My reward was a picture-perfect, windswept autumn view of the medieval city. The hotel sat on the banks of the River Neckar in Heidelberg's *altstadt*, and towering oaks guarded the riverbank, brushed with every conceivable shade of fiery red and golden orange. Minutes before the sun took her evening bow, her last bittersweet rays extended like fingers grasping the storybook landscape. My eyes welled with tears. The extraordinary gift of living here for twelve months almost overwhelmed me. Luckily, I held it together and didn't give anyone cause to wonder why the strange American woman was weeping outside the executive lounge.

CHAPTER 2
SPRECHEN SIE ENGLISCH?

The week of my arrival, a soft-spoken German woman named Regina collected me at the hotel to show me the vacant apartments leased by my company in Heidelberg.

Methodically, she rattled off the pros and cons of each, giving me my first insider glimpse of the city.

I knew it the minute I laid eyes on it. The apartment beneath the brooding ancient castle that reigns over the town center, the *Schloss*, was the one. It fit my romanticized ideal of the Continent perfectly. I christened my comically small apartment the "shoebox." The kitchen contained a sink, a hot plate, and a mini-fridge. The bathroom was consumed by a disproportionately-large bathtub, and the combined living and dining area held a double bed and a table that I converted to my dressing table.

Later, I learned that the narrow cobblestone street I lived on, Eselspfad, meant literally, "donkey path." It was the path used to carry loads of flour to the castle residents of the 1600's. Miniature apartment or not, I had a roof, a bed, and a job in old Europe. Dream come true? Check!

Customs was an even deeper bureaucratic swamp after the 11th of September, but eventually my shoes and coats were allowed entry into Germany. Once I created organized chaos out of my belongings in my tiny new home, I ventured out to explore and complete essential business. A German bank account and mobile phone couldn't wait much longer. Tri-band phones hadn't been invented yet and my American cellular phone was useless. I felt naked without it.

German shopping was one barrel of laughs after another. The best one is the total absence of convenience. If you combine the Metric system, language barriers, and parking garages a ten-minute walk from home, a few simple errands equate to one exasperating afternoon. Dealing with the apartment's washing machine and dryer was as successful as taking that shower in the hotel my first day. All instructions were in German. I had no idea how hot 40 degrees Celsius was, and the clothes I retrieved from the dryer looked and smelled as though they'd been electrocuted. I know my taste in clothes may leave something to be desired, but I don't think the penalty fit the crime.

On my first weekend living in the altstadt, my sole mission was to stuff the tiny fridge. Combing the rainy narrow streets to find a supermarket, or a market of any kind, another surprise: ancient trade laws keep most stores closed on Sunday in Germany. For the *entire* day. Let's face it, I was already out of luck in the grocery department by four o'clock closing time on Saturday afternoon. The only places with lights on were cafés and shops selling gaudy whatnot to tourists for a small fortune. By a stroke of what appeared to be luck, I found a corner shop that combined souvenirs with a small deli and grocery selection.

My next hurdle was the currency conversion from U.S. dollars to German *deutschemarks*. Stupidly, I hadn't calculated the exchange rate in advance, so I had no warning I was about to be ripped off beyond belief. Even if I had known, the only other option was eating my Sunday meals in cafés, trying to decipher German menus, and hiding from the famous *Deutscher* stare.

The intrusive gaze of locals is capable of penetrating walls a foot thick, a flimsy paper menu or newspaper held up were nothing to deflect it. In my book, overpaying was a small price to pay to escape being placed under the microscope.

The human brain becomes a supercomputer when it comes to language. The programmer inside realizes that English isn't an option and throws the lever to change to the next available track. In my case, this resulted in a very puzzled young German girl. Without realizing it, I had greeted her and asked a question in Spanish before her face alerted me that something was amiss. Flushed with embarrassment, I

The Devil Wears Clogs

quickly paid and fled the scene before further conversation could ensue. Having had sufficient Sunday adventure, I retired to my shoebox to spend the rest of the day with my books and the one cable television channel not dubbed entirely in German: CNN. No one could call me uninformed this year. Later expeditions were similarly successful. Having fellow Americans on my team at work meant the opportunity to seek advice with each new mission. Rumor had it that there was a Deutsche Bank employee who would come to your home to set up a new bank account. Uncomfortable conducting business in the shoebox, he kept late office hours for me one afternoon, so I could meet him after work.

As I mentioned, Germans are organized. They will happily tell you exactly what to do and how to do it on any given occasion. I was instructed to bring my passport and fill out the appropriate forms, all of which went swimmingly. My contact, Herr Mueller, was formal, but at the same time gave the impression he understood how confusing it felt to land in a foreign country. Perhaps he was merely taking pity on an ignorant American female, but I saw it differently because I was desperate for *someone* to understand how difficult I was finding the adjustment. At the end of our meeting, when he was locking up his briefcase, his patience and calm demeanor evaporated. In their place, the tone, which would surface over and over again in my travels, made its first appearance: *incredulity*. Europeans are forever amazed at the depth of your ignorance.

"And how much do you need for a minimum deposit into my new account?" I asked.

"The bank is closed, *fraulein*. You cannot make a deposit after bank hours," he said, peering at me over his wire rims like a schoolteacher, emphasis on the word "closed," since I clearly didn't understand its meaning.

"Right. Oh, sorry. I'll just deposit money into the ATM outside then."

"No. You can take money out of the machine, but you cannot put money in. You will not be able to make deposits to your account unless you come back to the bank during bank hours."

Was he joking? I didn't know then that Germans rarely joke. Why was I bothering with an after-hours appointment when I would need to come back again during business hours? It was the stupidest thing I'd ever heard. How could the supposedly superior German mind even conceive of a *one-way ATM*?

He wasn't joking. How silly of me. How fortunate for me that Herr Mueller could illuminate the error of my ways. This was the attitude of The Enlightened One. My logic wasn't applicable because it wasn't German.

Deutsche Bank wasn't exactly a funhouse, but it was nothing compared to the Great Mobile Phone Incident of 2001. In the U.S., Americans choose a service provider and are given a selection of phones, which can be used with the chosen contract. In Germany, the process is the opposite. A phone is selected first and then the options of different service providers are given. I had already been given a head's up on this and was convinced I had my bases covered. Armed with the "right" answers, my passport, and a bank account with actual money in it, I headed to the phone shop on Heidelberg's Hauptstrasse.

A middle-aged, grim-faced sales assistant, Dirk, was the suspicious judge of whether I was a real prospect, or a member of the American military that had infected neighboring Mannheim (his surly demeanor made his opinion on the local U.S. Army bases abundantly clear). Sweating through his intense interrogation, I was sure I'd be walking away empty handed. Irritated that he couldn't find a reason not to, Dirk ultimately granted me phone privileges.

Dirk: "If you choose this provider, you get cheaper calls at your home."

Me: "I'm sorry; I don't know what you mean."

Dirk: "The calls you make at your home will be less expensive if you choose this service."

Me: "So the rate you pay on your cell phone is variable, based on where you are calling from?"

Dirk: "*NO!* The calls! At your house! You pay *less!*"

Me (pissed off at having been spoken to like a three-year-old): "In the United States, the contracts are different and I just don't know what you mean."

Next, our man Dirk takes to the battlefield. Whipping a cheap pen from his front pocket, he draws a picture of a house and a telephone. My temperature instantly rises ten degrees. Calmly, without raising my voice, I pointed to a specific calling plan and suggested he forget about calls from my home—whatever the hell it is he's trying to get across to me doesn't matter now that we've entered kindergarten art class. My new buddy Dirk agrees with a thin, tight-lipped smile and I select a phone, which is less traumatic. After making a copy of my passport and checking my payment method, he tells me to come back in four hours. I glance at him in disbelief.

Dirk: "The phone takes time to be prepared!"

Of course it does. What was I thinking, expecting to leave the store *with* the phone I'd just purchased. Had he been able to open the door and shout "*Raus!*"–German for "Get out!"–I believe he would have. He seemed dangerously close to the edge for a man that sells mobile phones for a living.

Walking outside, the crisp autumn wind, which cooled my red face and eased the tension in my shoulders, was a gift. Becoming aware of my surroundings again, a bewitching ancient city on a day that isn't a Sunday or rainy, I resolved to make the most of it. Heidelberg has no shortage of indulgence. Handmade chocolates and liqueurs, artfully arranged flowers, and all manner of expensive treasures peek out from Hauptstrasse storefronts. To forget about Dirk's treatment, I ordered *eine Tasse kaffe* at a nearby café and settled in with an English newspaper.

At the designated time, I returned to the scene of the crime. Dirk tells me to wait, *tells* does not *ask*, while he finishes the phone setup. Ten minutes later, he shoves a Nokia box at me and rattles off my new phone number. Exiting the store with a great big smile and friendly wave, I say "Thank you, Dick. I really appreciate your help today, Dick. Bye bye!" I have no idea whether Dirk caught my improvisation of his name and I didn't care. It felt good to exact a little vengeance.

Later, it dawned on me that he was trying to explain that if I were to change my home service to the same one as the mobile phone, I would receive a discount on calls from the shoebox. American cell phone providers hadn't moved into landline services, and I just didn't get it. Honestly, let's just add this to the growing list of things that I did not get. With more German shopping experience under my belt, I finally grasped their superbly simple concept of customer service. "Take it or leave it."

* * *

More surprises came my way during my early days as a *Heidelberger*. The day a *strassenbahn* appeared in front of my car out of nowhere comes to mind. Who has the right of way? The letters, which invariably arrived in our mailboxes with grainy black and white mug shots from the city speed cameras, were a definite highlight. The day Regina screamed bloody murder when I turned right on red (*oops, verboten!*) cost me an eardrum temporarily. The party just never ended.

Another fine example of German customer "service" presented itself when a colleague and I literally ran to the Heidelberg train station to buy tickets to Paris one evening before closing time. As soon as we walked in the door, the frumpy matron behind the counter stared in shocked disbelief. "*Seine fünf minuten bis neun!* We close in five minutes! Please leave!" Unbeknownst to us, the last five minutes of the evening are the safety buffer against dumb tourists and complicated transactions which require one to stay past quitting time. Brilliant. I'll remember that the next time my phone rings at five to five.

In the last days of October, my colleague and I did manage to buy those tickets to Paris. My maiden voyage on the legendary European train system was a thrill. My colleague, Nancy, had arrived in Germany a month before me from Portland and this was her first visit to Paris. We'd only known each other a few weeks and I wasn't sure we'd make great travel mates. She struck me as a little naïve, despite taking on the twelve-month German challenge. Wanting to see Paris again, I crossed my fingers and hoped for the best.

The Deutsche Bahn system is a model of German locomotive mastery. The seats are comfortable and well structured. The train travels at over two hundred miles per hour, making the three-hour ride to Paris Gare du Nord a breeze. The bar car was at the end of the train. More out of curiosity than hunger, Nancy and I decided to investigate.

The Devil Wears Clogs

Despite literally bouncing from side to side, we made our way through several cars without incident.

Many details of train travel intrigued me, but the food and beverage selection did not. The disappointing menu consisted of potato chips and soggy white bread sandwiches. We handed over our deutschmarks anyway and sat down at the larger of two tables in the dining car. Our table had room for at least 6 people, but there was no one else in sight.

Shortly after we sat, a mature stylishly dressed French woman approached. *"Est-ce que cette place est libre?"* She asked, indicating one of the empty seats at our table.

"Oui, s'il vous plaît," I replied. Of course we didn't mind.

I glanced at Nancy, but she was engaged in a fierce struggle with the plastic, keeping her from her sandwich. Her open soda bottle sat precariously between her right hand and elbow.

Picture it: Doe-eyed American blonde is victorious in freeing her sandwich from captivity in plastic triangle container. Pulling ridiculously hard, the hand with newly-freed plastic makes direct contact with large open bottle of cola, knocking the contents from here to Provence. With horror, I watch Elegant French woman with newspaper experience a slow motion train wreck. Sticky brown cola dripped from her glasses.

She delivered a grave look and said, "Don't worry. It isn't so dramatic." She followed with, "I'm going to sit over *here* now," indicating the only available seat in a tiny corner table. Mortified, we fled the car after numerous apologies in both languages.

Several cars away, the unbelievably humiliating faux pas was relived several times in hushed tones. Finally, a bout of uncontrollable laughter cleansed us of complete embarrassment. Dear Elegant French Woman, wherever you are today, *"Je suis desolée"* once more.

* * *

Paris, sophisticated and alluring as ever, invited us to stroll along the Seine and discover the treasures tucked away in St. Germain de Près. Despite initial appearances to the contrary, lady luck accompanied us. Autumn clung tightly that November before giving way to winter. Nôtre Dame and the Champs-Elysées donned glittering outfits of falling golden leaves, and pink-cheeked Parisians capped with colorful berets.

We entered Nôtre Dame so Nancy could experience the exquisite, Gothic interior for the first time.

The three-day trip was possible because of a holiday in Germany. The first of November is All Saints Day, but I didn't need to be Catholic to enjoy the sublime pageantry inside the church. As we walked through the massive wooden entryway, a parade was just beginning.

Laughing French children, barely older than toddlers, carried huge wooden banners decorated with solemn saints on eggshell-colored canvases. These little angels struggled to hold their heavy charges upright, but they smiled nonetheless, pleased to have been bestowed with such great honor. The afternoon sunlight penetrated the ethereal rose window and again I was struck by my tremendous good fortune.

Nancy clearly enjoyed being in Paris, but I wasn't thrilled repeating every tourist activity from my previous visit, and she claimed to have "no interest" in The Louvre. I agreed to accompany her to the Eiffel Tower because it is such a spectacular view and the weather was much warmer this time around. Standing on the viewing platform, my heart was gripped by icy fingers of fear. *What if a bomb strikes this tower?* the voice in my head whispered. I shivered, despite the warm evening, and noticed how far it was down to the ground. The next day we parted company, which gave me free reign of one of the world's most impressive museums. It was better company than Nancy.

Mercifully, our return trip to Heidelberg was uneventful. One last moment of 2001 hinted that Americans weren't the only ones on edge. On a November afternoon, when mercury had dropped considerably, another American colleague, Dora, called to ask if I wanted to check out the demonstration. Demonstration? Her boyfriend, an American Army lieutenant stationed in Mannheim, had been told of a "political demonstration" taking place that afternoon. All members of the U.S. military were under strict orders to keep their distance. They were not to be in attendance and they *definitely* were not to engage in any disturbance taking place.

Clearly Dora and I had to investigate. I liked Dora immediately and, despite the short time I'd known her, we were fast friends. She spoke German like a native, was also from Ohio, and was several notches higher on the savvy scale than the doe-eyed Portlander. Agreeing not to carry or wear anything that would identify us as American, we walked down the Hauptstrasse toward Universitätplatz, the main viewing area.

It wasn't easy. Winter was beginning to show her hand in Germany, and the ground was covered with a thin layer of frost. I've come to believe that European cobblestones possess magical powers. No scientific theory exists to explain how sub-zero cold transcends thick leather soles, and winter walking becomes literally bone chilling. It's very different than walking down a frozen cement sidewalk.

We quickly determined we weren't the only ones with an overdose of curiosity and the size of the crowd mystified us. It was clear that the clandestine message of the demonstration had struck a chord. By the time we wove slowly through the crowd to get a look, everything was in place. The entire square, all four sides, was lined with a hundred *politzei*, the meticulous forest-green clad German police force. Each one stood with one hand on a riot baton, and a demeanor steely enough to send a chill down your spine—cobblestones or no cobblestones. I was already nervous about being there and the show of force did not exactly put the brakes on my racing heart.

The post September 11th world had grown paranoid. Regardless, we waited, side by side with the tense German crowd, to see what the fuss was about.

The ten minutes we stood there felt like an hour. Before they rounded the corner, we felt the vibration of booming speakers and saw eight flatbed trucks approaching. Finally able to get a good look at the people on the trucks, we found the "demonstrators" were twenty-year-old kids brandishing beer bottles and shouting about freedom of speech and religion. There was zero "anti-American" sentiment in this unruly display and we were immediately bored by it. As soon as we could extricate ourselves from the crowd, we disappeared into a local bar to warm our hands and faces by the crackling fire.

Talking through it, Dora and I wondered aloud why so many politzei had been present. The only reasonable explanation was that the Germans were also on edge and weren't taking chances. It was obvious that these kids were not a threat, but the show of force alone was enough to make you think twice about sudden movement of any kind.

Normal life resumed after the "demonstration" excitement, if German office life can be considered normal to an American. The physical location I worked in was as non-descript as any other office building in any other country. It was the people I encountered that colored my experience. The office location is a massive concrete campus and a sea of ten thousand employees. The first adjective that comes to mind to describe Germans is "aloof" or maybe "restrained." I would have said "cold" before I knew any of them.

My workstation was a shared office with my client, Hanna. She was responsible for prioritizing my work and issuing requests for me to follow up on to support their new customer software. Hanna and I became fast friends and I immediately recognized that I could learn much from my witty, well-traveled new office mate. Hanna had long golden blonde hair that reminded me of Rapunzel. Although she would often ask me to double-check the grammar of a document or an email, she was fluent in English. She was friendly and patient when it came to my lack of German understanding. Unlike others I'd dealt with, she never made me feel ignorant for not knowing how things worked in her country. On the contrary, she was eager to explain.

As for the 9,999 other German fish in the sea, I hadn't a clue how to relate to them. The most obvious difference I noticed in the office is that Germans do not display emotion or feelings to strangers. Casually, I walked down the office hallway all smiles, and after passing ten people, I wouldn't get a single one in return. It's not really a problem per se, it's just unexpected. Until I was around long enough to see that it was the norm, I thought maybe I smelled or had something in my teeth.

As for me, I am generally open and friendly with people, whether I know them or not. It was no easy feat to train my face not to smile when someone passed me in the hall. I should have practiced it in the mirror at home. I didn't want to seem unfriendly, but I wasn't wild about looking like the village idiot either. Wiping the reflexive smile from your face sounds easy, but I assure you it is harder than you think. Unless, of course, you are the ultra-serious type, then it will be no issue and you should submit your resume to German businesses post-haste.

Another helpful hint on German behavior is that they prefer to work independently. Your project might have a deadline twelve months away, as was the case for me. It is your decision how to execute it. Americans have a more iterative working style. We schedule regular meetings and checkpoints at which we receive feedback before a large project is finalized. When Americans working with Germans seek a similar relationship, Germans find Americans too needy. If the differing viewpoints are never discussed, the German may continue believing the American is unable to work independently.

Americans are coached to collect feedback from their manager or customer throughout the process. This ensures that considerable effort isn't wasted pursuing the "wrong" direction and accommodates changing circumstances. We would rather know that we are on the intended path than fumble through the dark. It's that simple.

Germans are often surprised when you want to discuss a project frequently or at length before it's handed over. My assignment to complete a complex implementation strategy document in twelve months was a good example. It was difficult to coax information out of my German colleagues besides Hanna. They were "too busy" to waste time talking to an American about the same topic more than once—even when that topic had numerous variables and potential scenarios. Once was enough. Hanna, on the other hand, was full of information. The only problem was that often I didn't have enough international perspective to get the message.

Despite differences in working styles and the lack of visible friendliness, there are goodies in store for Americans working in Germany. Every American feels shorted when it comes to vacation time. My discovery that nearly every May weekend was a three-day weekend due to the abundance of bank holidays practically made me giddy.

Given their astonishment at the number of places I talked about visiting, I'm sure my U.S. friends thought I wasn't actually working in Germany at all. In their minds, I was enjoying an extended vacation with a glass of Riesling permanently in hand. My tales of the office Christmas celebrations didn't help much. I enthusiastically described carts overflowing with wine, candy, and pastries rolling through our offices in the latter half of December until I realized that my friends didn't really want to hear about all the fun I was having.

I'm not here to tell you that work life in Germany is a permanent vacation or a constant party, quite the contrary. My experience consisted of long hours supporting business activities around the world. My point is that there is still fun to be had in these offices in addition to hard work—the fun that has disappeared from so many American offices because many people would rather sue one another, instead of taking personal responsibility for their actions.

I felt lucky to be part of a fun and friendly mix of Americans and Germans. The final days of 2001 delivered an unexpected crescendo of holiday cheer in my world. In December, I was introduced to the German Christmas tradition of the *Weinachtsmarkt* or "Christmas Market." I roved these rustic outdoor markets on the coldest of evenings with my gang of international co-workers. As tradition dictates, I drained more than one glass of gluewein, warm mulled wine, to fight off the chill. I tried, unsuccessfully at times, to keep the sticky red potion from ruining my gloves when I was jostled by the crowd.

With a steaming mug to warm my hands, I visited every single display of decorated gingerbread, handmade jewelry, colorfully-painted glass, and a confusing array of marzipan shapes and colors for sale. My first German Christmas was a real life winter wonderland. Fresh pine filled the air and snowflakes landed in our hair.

All the while, ruddy-faced Germans laughed heartily, providing background music. For once, I hardly felt the cold, but the memory was frozen in time.

CHAPTER 3
EUROPE'S CHANGING FACE

Like everyone else, I went back to the United States for a Christmas break. On the way, I made a hair-raising discovery. Changing planes in Newark, I nearly collided with a guy in military fatigues carrying a machine gun. September 11th had cut deeper into the souls of New Yorkers and inhabitants of metro DC than the rest of the United States, but it was alarming that these serious measures were the "new normal" of American airport security. You could cut the tension with a knife. The last drop of joy left in travel went down the drain, especially during the chaos of the holidays.

My trip home that December was my first experience with the Olympic decathlon of fitting my nearest and dearest into the harried, and all-too-brief, schedule I'd committed to. I will never get used to cramming friends and family into miniature timeslots, and the accompanying guilt when I inevitably disappoint someone because there simply aren't enough hours in a day.

I found this the toughest adjustment to my new life abroad. Long phone calls replaced face-to-face conversation. When I was in Ohio, perfunctory obligations devoured every minute, never leaving enough time to go deep. My friends and family understood that I was only human, but that did nothing to alleviate the profound loneliness and intense isolation that stalked me in the slower moments of my year in Germany. Three months into my shiny new dream coming true came the undeniable realization that dreams are empty without loved ones to share them.

Germany, a world away, was pummeled by several intense snowstorms while I was home. It barely registered. I spent New

Year's Day flying the red-eye to Frankfurt. Racing along the snow-free autobahn, I noticed the surrounding countryside was covered with a thick blanket of sparkling white snow. *How pretty*, I thought, continuing south to Heidelberg.

Twenty minutes into the journey, the radio announcer reported that the Red Cross had been out distributing blankets to stranded motorists the night before. As I listened, I felt a stab of empathy for the shivering stranded who had undoubtedly missed out on New Year's Eve celebrations. I didn't think about it again until I reached my Eselspfad driveway.

Squeezed into my trunk were two overstuffed suitcases, bursting with everything I couldn't find in Germany. American toiletries, over-the-counter drugs, and fashionable clothing that were non-existent in Heidelberg. Combined with Christmas gifts I'd not wanted to leave behind, the result was an accident waiting to happen.

Unfortunately, Eselspfad, my beautiful romantic donkey path of a "street," was on a steep hill. It was too narrow, hence the name *path*, to drive to my doorstep. Normally, this was no problem. The climb was an annoyance with arms full of groceries, but not a major obstacle. On January 2, 2002, however, these thirty feet from the base of the hill to my door were equivalent to summiting Everest. Over a foot of snow covered the ground and I wore black leather boots with three-inch heels. Of all the euro days which have come and gone, it is this day more than any other that I regretted my choice of footwear.

Parking at the base of the hill, I yanked my suitcases from the trunk. Without a shot in hell of bringing both up at once, I began to carefully extricate one. The thick wet snow was as slick as ice. Too bad I didn't take five seconds to notice because three seconds later –*whoosh!* My feet were out from under me and my face smacked the frozen snow. For my follow up act, the sub-zero surface was so smooth that I couldn't regain footing to stand up.

Sprawled on the ground, dazed, with snow-covered knees looking every bit the *esel* that I felt like, I could literally feel the Deutscher stare in full force from the windows above. Nothing happened on Eselspfad that escaped the attention of my neighbors. Eventually I spiked one stupid heel in the ground and managed to stand up gripping the open trunk. Dropping one suitcase into my apartment, I prayed it was one that contained flats. The Shoe Gods thankfully smiled upon me. Quickly, I traded fashion for function before returning to the car for the other bag. Finally, I left the car in my parking garage three blocks away. Over an hour later, physical exhaustion joining my jet lag, I peeled the dripping clothes from my body, collapsed onto my bed, and could not have been raised by the Devil himself.

Instead of melting into a steaming hot bath and snoozing the day away as I would have sold my soul to do, I had no choice but to forage the village for food. After the morning I'd had, I looked forward to this as much as Marie Antoinette looked forward to the guillotine. Swearing under my breath, I put the flats back on and trudged into town.

Despite the calamitous start, the day was historic. The euro entered circulation today. Before making a visit to my favorite bakery, I had to get some new currency from the ATM. Holding the brightly colored notes in my hand for the first time, I entered. The mountain of golden baked goods created in this hallowed hall is a gift to all mankind. Shelves of thick crusty bread with crunchy sunflower seeds, dark salty soft pretzels steaming from the oven, and berry-topped layer cakes vie for attention as far as the eye can see.

If you bake it, they will come. And I did, weekly without fail, more if I could. The smiling silver-haired bakery ladies were always kind. I knew enough German to understand a menu, say *bitte* and *danke*, and inquire about the location of the bathroom in any given establishment, but we understood each other just fine. In fact, our wordless exchanges became so routine it's a wonder I ever evolved past pointing and holding up the appropriate number of fingers.

The introduction of the euro, however, threw us a collective curveball. In my rush to get home, I'd forgotten to check the euro's valuation against the deutschmark or the U.S. dollar. I just handed over the requested amount. The new currency was only in use for a few hours and making change required the equivalent to a UN Summit meeting. Locals were still using German *marks* to get rid of them.

The law allowed for the use of two currencies for six months to allow old currency to be spent, but bank machines were loaded with euro starting today. Mine, most likely the first euro notes to cross the bakery counter, were met with wide eyes and a conference to discuss the proper change. Not having the German words to reassure them that I was not in a hurry, I stood grinning like an idiot while they engaged in an animated discussion. *Danke! Auf weidersehn!* We all smiled and waved, proud of our mutual accomplishment.

* * *

The first quarter of 2002 was dark and quiet. Each day provided a fleeting glimpse of daylight before the sun returned to its lair for a fourteen-hour sleep. While the sun played hide-and-seek, temperatures were brutal. Midway through the Hauptstrasse a digital time and temperature display stood at attention. One particularly polar day, I was forced to do some shopping and read -12º Celsius on the display. When I got home, I converted it and discovered this was equivalent to 10º Fahrenheit. As a Clevelander, I was surprised because it felt much colder. The cobblestone chill factor had to be the culprit.

The bright spot of my first European winter was a January business trip to Copenhagen where a required software training class was being held in English. Bonus! I added a weekend and a day off to the four-day class schedule when I booked my flights, excited to lay eyes on Scandinavia for the first time. If I thought Heidelberg was cold, I knew nothing about the true meaning of the word. January in Denmark would enlighten me. I didn't care. New territory called my name and I ran to answer.

Just as I'd ignored the temperature, the potential challenges that can accompany a trip to another new country went right past me. I hadn't yet made a habit of investigating the vast differences between European nations. Crossing borders means all bets are off. There are the obvious clues of unique language and dress, but much more lies beneath the surface.

Attitudes in general are different, and attitudes to women in business are dramatically so. Foods are distinctive to each nation's palate. Climates can be radically different and the level of spoken English varies from "fluent" to "survival." I was in perpetual observation mode, ever watchful for what I couldn't discern with language. Thankfully, my initial frustrations with life in Germany had begun to wane and I understood the universal truth that no matter what the situation, "please," "thank you," and a broad smile take you a long way.

An unexpected passenger on my ride into Copenhagen was panic. The sky was already jet-black when my plane touched down at 5 p.m. I handed the driver a printout with the hotel name in Danish and we drove off. I knew Denmark had a good safety reputation, but as we drove into nothingness rather than a bustling capital city, I found myself at the mercy of the driver. We didn't understand one another's languages. What if he drove into the frozen tundra to rob me and leave me stranded and freezing? Or worse?

For twenty-five minutes, my heart raced until I could see the city lights lighting up the distant sky. I relaxed my grip on the door handle when I realized the airport was further from the city than I'd expected. I scolded myself for being paranoid, but added this to the list of items to check on future trips.

If I thought the shoebox was small, my Nyhavn hotel room was a broom closet! As a graceless five-foot-ten American, I couldn't move an inch without knocking something over. My Copenhagen guidebook had warned me that the rooms at this hotel were small, but I had no frame of reference of what "small" meant in European vernacular and that "small" in Germany and Denmark could be so very different. My suitcase consumed 99.9% of the available free space.

I decided to explore by jogging. Full of adrenalin, I put on my running shoes and covered in warm layers to hit the streets. A quick overview of my surroundings and a second look at anything interesting enough to warrant closer inspection. Otherwise I would waste precious time wandering aimlessly.

Five minutes at a steady pace brought me to the harbor and the succession of seafood shops displaying their specialties packed in ice at every entrance. A bit further down the main road, I found the pedestrian zone of the city center, wonderfully crowded at 6 p.m. Light snow fell and glossy fur coats topped with striking blonde heads glided between shops. When I reached my hotel again, forty-five minutes later, I was on a high, filled with optimism for my week in Copenhagen.

Finally remembering this trip was business, I snapped out of my Scandinavian daydream and began my class preparation. The first night, I savored delicate seafood linguine in a Venetian restaurant while reading technical documentation. Unfortunately, my ability to concentrate had stayed in Germany. I was tingling with the possibilities of this new, exciting city. I read and I re-read several chapters before calling it quits.

Scandinavia is well regarded globally for its positive attitude toward women's equality and, for once, I wasn't the only female in the room. The class size was small—only ten people—and the instructor was a wry Scotsman, quick with a joke. The material itself, about software used in utility companies, doesn't lend itself to excitement, but we created our own by going for drinks after the second day. Pleased to have people to socialize with, I suggested a nearby pub specializing in Belgian beer and Scotch whisky that I'd spotted on my reconnaissance mission as the meeting point.

Liquid courage eventually got the conversation flowing, as we were strangers of differing nationalities. Before long, we were into an intense discussion about September 11th. I was still searching for answers as to why such brutality was leveled at innocent office workers, and everyone had an opinion. The rest of the group was European. While I'll never claim to understand terrorism, I gained more perspective on it that night.

Europeans have been living with terrorism for decades. By definition, attacks are nearly always on innocent people. The faces surrounding me had long since stopped trying to comprehend why terrorists do what they do. To them, it was cowardice combined with weakness. Other than hunting down those responsible and rooting the guilty from society, there is little to be done. A Swede recognized my desperate need for answers. His opinion was that jealousy of American life had a lot to do with it. In many countries, including that of the attackers, you can work to the bone year after year, but reaching the standard of living enjoyed by most Americans is out of the question. By its mere existence, America reminds its tormentors daily of their unrealizable dreams.

The Devil Wears Clogs

Later in life, I would better understand radical religion. On this particular night however, these people who seemed so knowledgeable on the subject were like a drug. The Swede and I talked late into the night. During the course of the evening, I became incredibly attracted to his mind and his Nordic good looks. Our connection was electric and undeniably shared. Inevitably, the conversation became personal.

Before class ended, the Swede and I exchanged information and agreed to keep in touch. Despite my fascination with him, he took second place to exploring Copenhagen and I did not linger over long good-byes. By Friday afternoon, I was shopping and taking photos to send home. For Christmas, my parents had bought me my first digital camera, which received an intense workout. My flight to Germany wasn't until Sunday, which left plenty of time to browse the shops for new treasures. A glittering antique ruby ring could not be left behind and against my better judgment, a knee-length, red fox fur coat was going to Germany too.

As a little girl, I loved looking at glossy black and whites of fur-clad Hollywood movie stars. The feel of this silky coat on my skin made me feel glamorous too. After all, I had made the transition to international businesswoman; didn't I need the matching outfit?

CHAPTER 4
AMSTERDAMNED

No snowstorms prevented my return to the German shoebox, but the analog connection to my laptop sounded like a cyber tornado. Anxious after being away from the office for a week, I fought with it to connect several times before victory resulted in an email avalanche. Scanning the subject lines, I didn't see anything that required immediate attention until six words leapt out.

Subject: FW Utility Conference Amsterdam, Please Confirm Attendance.

The email was from Hanna, inviting me to join her at a software conference in the Netherlands. I read the details in a blur, my eyes focusing only on the words "hotel in Amsterdam city center." I couldn't believe my luck to achieve another European dream so soon. I snapped to it and typed a quick reply to Hanna that it would be my pleasure to help. The same afternoon, I learned that my boss's boss, an American exec named Matthew, was also speaking at the conference. We had a group reservation at the renowned Hotel Krasnapolsky in Dam Square.

Two weeks later, I was relieved to be flying with co-workers familiar with Amsterdam. Sitting in the airport lounge before boarding the short flight to Schiphol Airport, I listened to their animated chatter about returning to Amsterdam. I didn't ask why, but I heard something about "coffee shops," which increased my confusion. Was Dutch coffee really something worth raving about?

I remember the early days of high school. When the "cool kids" talked about sex or partying in terms that I, as a lowly freshman, had no clue about, I bluffed understanding so I didn't appear the hopeless social outcast I feared myself to be. History was repeating itself in the form of a discussion about Dutch coffee shops. I have no idea where the term "coffee shop" originated and how it came to refer to a place where you can order marijuana legally from a menu, but as the cool kids talked, I got the picture. The Germans couldn't wait to visit coffee shops so they could smoke pot, which is illegal in Germany and everywhere else in Europe.

This revelation was news to me. I decided on the spot that I would tag along. But what about the senior American exec meeting us in Amsterdam? How could I keep him in the dark? Who would have ever imagined *this* to be a dilemma I would face on a European business trip?

We gathered our bags, grabbed a taxi, and piled in. The ride from Amsterdam's airport to the city center is roughly thirty minutes without traffic. Rush hour doubled it. We exited the motorway to a blur of one-way streets. Canals flew by one after another for ten minutes until the cab lurched to a halt in Dam Square. Darkness had descended by the time we arrived, so I couldn't make out the texture of the landscape.

The Dam, as it is affectionately known, is Amsterdam's true center. A sizable, grey concrete World War II memorial, obviously phallic in presentation, commands your attention, and the surrounding buildings consist of the former residence of the Dutch Royal Family, several tourist bars and department stores, and the Grand Hotel Krasnapolsky.

In an incredible stroke of luck, we arrived three days before a rare occasion would transform all of Amsterdam into an orange frenzy—the marriage of Crown Prince Willem-Alexander to Princess Máxima of Argentina. Several wedding guests were staying at the Krasnapolsky. Reading this in the English newspaper, I patted myself on the back for hitting this jackpot of euro-culture. As an American, I never imagined witnessing a royal wedding.

When I checked-in, the clerk handed me a scribbled note from my American colleague. "Call Me Matt" wanted to meet for dinner that evening. The Germans had other plans, so I hedged my bets and prayed that, if I met Matt on my first night, he would busy himself with more Important People for the remainder of the conference. Fingers crossed, I'd be free to explore the den of iniquity that is the red-light district with Hanna.

Suited, six-foot, salt-and-pepper Matt stood waiting in the hotel lobby. After the obligatory handshake, he flashed his winning smile and asked if I was ready to go. I was taken aback by the combat zone that is Amsterdam's city streets. Heidelberg's sleepy streets pale in comparison to what lies in wait for pedestrians in Holland's largest city. If you manage to jump out of the path of speeding buses and Heineken's Clydesdale buggy, the huge turbo attack pigeons will spot the bullseye on your head. If you survive all that, you may yet meet your demise by a screeching tram.

Matt had spent his entire career at the firm and had a reputation as a Casanova. He'd been working in Europe for years by then and was considerably more adept than I as we flirted with certain death to locate a restaurant. Ducking into a dimly lit pizza joint near the hotel, he quickly ordered a bottle of Chianti and a *pizza capricciosa*.

My palms began to sweat and the room grew warm as Matt turned his gaze to me. I don't know what made me more nervous, knowing that I had to figure out how to rid myself of Matt for the rest of the conference or the gut feeling that he was going to hit on me. How the hell I would handle that? Matt's good-old-boy Arkansas charm was turned on strong. Losing him would be as easy as removing Maple syrup from a stack of pancakes.

Painfully self-conscious in a one-on-one situation with someone so senior, my saving grace was that it is difficult to linger over pizza. He refilled my glass more often than his own as I fought to keep the conversation impersonal. After squirming through a few slices, I feigned exhaustion and used the excuse of an early morning wake-up call. Walking back to the hotel, it was impossible to escape without a promise to meet for breakfast. Finally alone in my hotel room, I emailed friends about my unbelievable luck to be in Amsterdam. When my head hit the pillow, I'm sure I fell asleep with a smile on my face.

At 7a.m., I walked to breakfast in the opulent Winter Garden. Here, for the first time, "grand" made an appearance. Taking in the vast solarium with its cathedral ceiling, my eyes wandered hungrily over buffet tables jammed with every imaginable variety of international cuisine. I looked over smoked salmon, a rainbow of sushi, marinated mushrooms, and glistening bottles of chilled champagne. The volume of cheeses staggered the imagination. I sipped strong Dutch coffee in fine china and inhaled my surroundings. Savoring breakfast in this exquisite dining room was an experience in itself. If only I'd been alone to enjoy it instead of being held captive by Matt's continual down-home monologue that he used to ingratiate himself with clients. *Check please!*

When it came to the conference, my work was finished before leaving Germany. Smartly dressed and smiling, Hanna spoke confidently into the microphone while I sat in the audience taking notes. My first interaction with Dutch businessmen taught me that the level of political correctness, guiding interactions between American men and women at the office, had not crossed the Dutch border. Men openly commented on my skirt and heels as if they'd never seen such an unusual costume.

I went out of my way to avoid prying eyes and interaction with two particularly relentless Dutch colleagues of Hanna's. My hands were overly full negotiating the puritanical rules of American business practices with the Matts and the Germans in a place where these rules did not apply.

I went from one presentation to the next taking in the varied levels of spoken English and the various types of business dress. We regrouped for the ever-present cocktail hour and networking at the end of Day One. I was drinking a glass of wine and relaxing casually with Hanna and the other Germans in the hotel bar when Matt crept up out of nowhere to inquire about our dinner plans. His question was met with a decidedly pregnant pause before I admitted that there were none. Hanna deftly dodged the bullet by vanishing in the direction of the concierge to inquire about vegetarian restaurants nearby, and I changed the subject.

Never verbalized, the plan was to go to a coffee shop after dinner. The red-light district was ten minutes' walk from the Hotel Krasnapolsky. Over a hundred coffee shops can be found there, each with cheesy themes like fast food chains. Never had I experienced anything remotely like this, let alone had the opportunity to hang out with the cool kids who knew its ins and outs. No one could make me give up this chance, not even someone as senior as Matt.

After another round of drinks at the hotel bar, Hanna announced there was a Thai restaurant that she wanted to try. Conveniently, it was one street over from the Red Light. Matt sealed my fate by offering to treat everyone. Heads nodded the deal was done.

Lana Thai served colorful spicy dishes and enjoyed a perfect location overlooking the canal and Amsterdam's massive Centraal Station. For two hours, I sat sweating it out and making polite business chat until everyone, except clueless Matt, was restless and eager to enter the legendary mystique of the Amsterdam night. Not one word had been uttered about after dinner. By the time Matt paid the bill and our coats were collected, time had run out. I finally summoned the courage to say something to Matt.

Matt, looking me straight in the eye, asked "Where to?"

"I was planning to go with Hanna and the others to check out the town." I mumbled, praying he would take the hint and leave.

"Sounds good!" says Matt.

Damn! says the voice in my head. "Ummm … well, it's fine if you want to join us, but I don't know exactly what kind of trouble we'll get into." I delivered another obvious hint that our further activities should remain unknown, but he feigned ignorance.

"No problem. I'm up for anything," says Matt and off we went en masse.

From the door of the restaurant to the entrance of the coffee shop was less than three minutes' walk. Anyone who didn't realize there was a plan all along would have to be an idiot, but Matt said nothing. An awkward group, we walked through the red-beaded threshold of the Stone Mushroom with its tarnished Indian brass lamps and smiling, glassy-eyed patrons. Dense sweet-smelling smoke hung like indoor smog as we creaked across the heavily-trodden wood floor.

What do you call the person who sits behind the bar and rolls the joints before passing them? Is she still a "bartender"? Anyway, the twenty-year-old brunette with long braided hair smiled over the counter as Hanna perused the glossy black and white menu as you would a wine list. Trying to keep my insane curiosity under control, I refrained from reading over her shoulder. With fake nonchalance, I pulled out a heavy wooden chair by the window. Matt followed suit and sat across from me. Hanna and the German guys sat on bar stools behind us. Fat aromatic cigarettes were passed and smoked. I had smoked pot occasionally in high school, but it had been years ago. Nothing would have prepared me for the swiftness of this powerful high. Inhaling once or twice was all it took to render me numb and intellectually useless.

Uncontrollable giggles steamrolled me as I looked around:

I was sitting across from an exec who ranked high on my company's ladder, and I had just passed him a joint.

The rest of our party was laughing and telling stories in German. We didn't even understand one another anymore.

I was on a business trip in the middle of the infamous red-light district surrounded by shops that specialized in sex, booze and drugs.

Considering all that, the dancing gold dildo from the sex shop next door should not have been a surprise—but it was. It bounced up and down in the window like a hypnotist's charm, sending me right over the edge. Pulling myself together an hour later was my cue to exit. The Germans disappeared deeper into the Amsterdam night. Matt and I exchanged few words walking to the hotel. Neither of us ever spoke about that night.

On Friday, the program wrapped up early. Anxious to escape the stuffy Krasnapolsky, I quickly grabbed my suitcase and bolted to freedom in another hotel. The Swede was flying in to meet me for the weekend. We had separate rooms, but there was no mistaking our attraction to one another. My heart thumped at the possibilities of where the night would take us.

By the time I arrived at my room, the Germans had departed and the Swede was waiting. We met, both flushed with nervous anticipation, in the hotel bar for drinks before taking on the city. It was a spectacular, orange-drenched scene, a fitting tribute to the House of Orange. The wedding of Willem-Alexander and Máxima was the next day and every Dutch citizen was celebrating. Giant posters of the fair-haired grinning couple were plastered on every corner. We drifted from one bar to the next, soaking up the frenetic atmosphere, and wound up back at the hotel very late. By then, I'd had sufficient booze to expose the elephant in the room. The party ended that night with the Swede's revelation that he was married.

The news was crushing. He was funny, intelligent, and handsome. He worked for a competitive firm, which meant he understood the demanding job and loved to travel. I didn't bargain on him being married. I didn't plan on falling in love with him in Amsterdam either. It just happened. The Nordic blonde hair and piercing blue eyes were irresistible to mere mortals and that night I joined him in mortal sin.

To avoid the intrusion of reality, we shopped and ate most of the Royal wedding day away until the city's undertow pulled us in. Resistance to the intoxicating wedding revelry was futile. We stood hand-in-hand in Dam Square while the newlyweds kissed on the balcony of the Koninklijk Paleis and cheered them on to a lifetime of happiness. Inside, the irony of celebrating marriage while I might be destroying one was not lost on me.

Shame filled me from head to toe.

CHAPTER 5
THE BLACKEST FOREST

Sitting cross-legged on my bed later that week, I poured over the map of Germany for new places to explore. The autobahn and I were friends now which made me bolder. Armed with an atlas, I decided to drive my new rental, a cherry-red Alfa Romeo, out of Heidelberg. The name alone stirred my imagination. The Schwarzwald, which doesn't sound as intriguing as the evil "Black Forest," lies in Germany's southwest. Legend claims it to be haunted by werewolves and cross-dressing sorcerers, so I had to investigate. I settled on a hotel in Freiburg at the end of February.

Between Amsterdam and my trip to the Black Forest, the Swede came to visit. The rabid crowds of the Royal wedding weekend in Amsterdam had left a great deal unspoken. My mind reeled. Did he want to stay married? Did he have kids? What's it like living in Sweden? I'd put off asking any of these until there was a serious need to know. We were now seeing each other for the third weekend in the span of a month and the "need to know" stage was long gone. Without realizing it, I'd fallen for this man in a way I'd never fallen for anyone else.

I have no words to describe the feeling because I never admitted it to anyone. The taboo of an affair with a married man was overwhelming. If I kept it a secret, I wouldn't be judged.

I have never been a serial dater. I had boyfriends in college, but I never let them get too close. There was a mile high fortress around my heart. (Thank you, Sting, for the ultimate metaphor.) I believed I was content, and I probably was, until I understood how much more there was to a relationship than going through the motions.

My intention was to live and work in Europe, and I wouldn't let that go for anyone. The fortress kept this damsel safe from troublesome rogues who would carry her away and make her a barefoot housewife. The plan went awry once I was living my dream and dropped my guard a little. When I met the Swede, it crumbled. At the tender age of thirty-one, I fell in love, with a deafening *thud*.

The Swede made only one trip to "darkest Germany," as he liked to call it. The reference amused me because Sweden has a burning match of a summer compared to Germany. We stayed in the shoebox for the better part of our three days together, insulated from reality in a cocoon of sex and Moët et Chandon. I was determined to keep him in my arms for as long as I possibly could. Needless to say, this was much easier naked.

Time ran out late Sunday afternoon. Just hours before his flight to Stockholm, we went to a small intimate restaurant on the banks of the Neckar. The crackling fire nearby should have been comforting, but it was impossible not to feel an impending chill.

My hands shook as I summoned my courage. "Do you have children?"

"Yes, two." His devastating reply was a stake through my heart. Kids were a deal-breaker. Someone unhappily married without children might consider divorce to make a new life. Like glaring overhead lights suddenly thrown on in a dark bar and a shout of "Last call!" there was no hiding from reality now. I would never have an ounce of respect for someone who would abandon his family for me.

Shaken to the core, I struggled to maintain light conversation as these thoughts pounded on my subconscious like patients in an asylum, demanding to be let loose. He told me he'd married at twenty-three and there was discussion about how people change with time. He, of course, said given the opportunity he would not marry so young again and would advise others against it. I wasn't listening. I just filled my glass to its golden rim.

By the time our meal was finished, it was undeniable that we were too. By the time we left for the airport, I was sobbing uncontrollably. Too much truth had been exposed, and the illusion lay shattered at my feet. I tried unsuccessfully to console myself by pretending my sadness was because I didn't know when we'd see each other again. Deep down, I knew it was checkmate. Even if it hadn't been said, we were over.

Because I was so good at lying to myself, when he did eventually end our relationship later—via email—I was devastated. I transformed into the typical, hysterical ex-girlfriend who cries her undying love one minute and vows revenge the next. I was disgusted by my ugly desperation and couldn't bear to be around anyone. It was in this pathetic state that I began my Black Forest road trip. How appropriate.

It didn't take long to get to the Schwarzwald. The Black Forest High Road was just past Baden-Baden, ninety minutes' away. Without having laid eyes on the Black Forest, you might imagine it as I did: towering majestic pines, dense undergrowth of ferns and toadstools, and perhaps a cabin or two dotting the landscape. Factoring in the mythical reputation of this land, you might also expect to see ghosts and serious paranormal activity.

Perhaps you'll understand my surprise when the majority of tall pines I saw were on the backs of logging trucks. I did not expect to see vast stretches of logged forest and entire cities within the confines of the Black Forest. I kept thinking that I was just at the entry of the forest and would eventually find my way to nature, but, after another hour, hope evaporated. While you can indulge in the rich dark chocolate cake of this region or savor their meaty smoked ham, the "forest" is very much like the rest of Germany and very, very populated.

When disappointment faded, I managed to enjoy the ride. Along the way, I found villages with medieval castles and church ruins, and I had the road largely to myself on this February Friday. I meandered through two small towns on foot before I decided to get to Freiburg and rid myself of the car. I'd expected to stroll into town, enjoy simple meat and potatoes washed down with too much wine, and lose myself in deep sleep.

Freiburg is the Black Forest "capital." I picked my destination specifically to distract myself with restaurants and shops the entire weekend. Imagine my disappointment upon discovering that the most remote part of my journey to the forest was the hotel itself. There was nothing nearby to walk to. There were open fields. Lots and *lots* of open fields.

While some might find this romantic, it reminded me of the fields surrounding my grandparents' farm. In over twenty years of visiting the farm, I was never once moved to explore. The website described the hotel as a "spa retreat" where one could have a healing respite in the forest sunlight. To me, it was an unwelcoming, uninviting, ugly yellow dump in the middle of acres of dead brown fields.

Unable to tear my eyes from the withered crops, my excruciating sadness returned. I no longer had the distraction of deciphering German road signs or deciding where to stop along the way. Me, myself, and I and were a very unhappy trio. I flung myself onto the hard bed and resumed sobbing where I left off the night before. I never left the room on Saturday, and I never found the town, which was probably around the corner. What I did manage was to comprehend, in unyielding clarity, why it is called a "broken heart."

Before this visit to the true "darkest Germany," I had no idea that physical pain is a symptom of the broken heart phenomenon. Some things you have to experience for yourself, like it or not.

CHAPTER 6
FURTHER AFIELD

The sharp edges of life in a dramatically different culture were dulled by the team of American transplants at work.

We were remarkably similar, which led to a lot of fun outside the office. I saw first-hand how small the world is when this Ohio girl sat down at a restaurant one night in Heidelberg and met Dora, and her military boyfriend. They were from Ohio and Michigan respectively. There was also my doe-eyed Portland colleague, Nancy, who made *me* look like an experienced traveler. During my German year, I met other colleagues from various parts of the world when they had project work or software training in Heidelberg. Whether they hailed from Brazil, Belgium, or Chile, I was consistently amazed at my firm's ability to hire the same personality type. This revolving cast was outgoing, intelligent, and willing to push the limits—with few exceptions. Some ran with the bulls in Pamplona, while others snowboarded in the Alps. Being a part of this adventurous crew served two purposes: it reduced my anxiety about living abroad and provided instant travel mates. We took turns researching hotels and cities and readily joined one another's excursions.

One of these long weekend jaunts was a St. Patrick's Day celebration in Dublin. We were already on the plane by the time I figured out that the rowdy, green-beer-infused celebrations of "St. Paddy's Day" are an American bastardization of Ireland's religious celebration. Dying the Chicago River green and the drunken lunacy that accompanies it have little in common with the Catholic procession in Ireland. Nonetheless, seated on a crowded Aer Lingus flight packed with U.S. military from Frankfurt, it was clear I wasn't the only one expecting a three-day party.

My first visit to Dublin didn't leave a tremendous impression. I was still in mourning over the Swede's departure. I moved through the city in a daze, luckily with much to distract me. Freezing on the banks of the River Liffey, we watched an elaborate parade that included a shocking amount of large flames leaping from small boats, and loitered unnecessarily in surprisingly empty Temple Bar pubs.

Saturday, Nancy and I walked roughly thirty blocks out of the way trying to find the Guinness Brewery visitor entrance. Sunday was spent in the Jameson Distillery. By 11 a.m., I was performing the hard core Whisky Taste Test—Scotch versus Irish. Call me a walking cliché, but my preferred method of dulling relentless pain was to consume mass amounts of alcohol wandering Dublin's streets. I pretended to enjoy myself, but it was a front.

Depression didn't loosen its grip until two weeks later when Dora and I took off for Sicily to meet Jo, my good friend from the U.S. She intended to trace her Italian father's roots and had invited us over. Neither Dora nor I knew the first thing about Sicily, but that had never stopped us before. Dora had at least *been* to Italy. In our minds, that was sufficient preparation. Thankfully, Jo, the master event planner, had mapped the route.

Sicily is a different world from mainland Italy, cut off from its sophisticated major cities. This is dual-sided. On the plus side, the subtropical weather is enhanced by the magnificent emerald Mediterranean Sea sparkling from every sunlit sandstone cliff. Also in the pro column, we found few tourists in Sicily. On the downside, locals who speak English are rare. We quickly learned to play Charades to communicate. Guessing games can be fun in hotels and restaurants, but are a lot less fun on Sicily's labyrinthine roadways.

Dora and I landed in Catania on a breezy, balmy March afternoon. Waiting in the car rental lot was a Fiat Punto, bearing a striking resemblance to the car owned by Fred Flintstone. I was certain we'd end up pushing this thing at some point. Dora agreed to drive.

Sicily's verdant hills and sweeping valleys have their tranquility occasionally disturbed by psychotic Italian drivers for whom road signs and traffic signals are mere suggestions. The one-hour trip to

The Devil Wears Clogs

Taormina shouldn't have been challenging. And it wouldn't have been if it weren't for a) the stupid Punto and b) what passes for a Sicilian road often resembles a sidewalk.

As we drove away from the tiny palm-lined airport, the sun hung low in the azure sky. On the way to Taormina, we were treated to golden olive orchards and rustic farmhouses. Snow-capped Mount Etna hiding in the distance made us wish desperately for more time. Despite the ancient web of one-way roads that tried to snare us, and the mad Italians who turned even sidewalks into speedways, we kept moving forward. Eventually, we brought that Punto across the finish line in true Fiat style. The literal translation of "Fiat style," by the way, is "reaching one's destination in a lurch with the engine gasping for each strangled breath." We were relieved to check-in, exchange hugs with my friends, and talk late into the night about our plans for the days ahead.

To say that Sicily is beautiful is like saying that the *Mona Lisa* is well-known. For next four days, we wined and dined in Taormina and Siracusa. Always, we were the loudest table in the most crowded of places.

Our group of four women climbed and photographed Roman ruins, and dined on marinated octopus salad atop cliffs overlooking the sparkling Mediterranean. We met beautiful dark haired men in strange bars and attempted conversation. People were kind everywhere we went, even when they couldn't understand us. They gave us gifts of pastry, and directions, while marveling at our shining blonde hair. Somewhere, in the middle of all this, my heart began to heal, and I couldn't wait to experience more of Italy.

* * *

Long weekends with my co-workers increased my confidence about traveling alone. My first step was after another business trip with Hanna and her boyfriend Adrian, to a conference in Prague. I extended my stay for the two days following the conference to see the sights.

Prague wears a heavy overcoat of mystery. Traces of former Communist rule are everywhere and the comrade-era buildings are unmistakable. Our conference, another on topics surrounding the utility industry, was held in a "modern" (read "gray and drab") convention center, and every nearby building was a carbon copy: gray concrete smothered with black coal soot. There was one exception.

Across the city, just visible from the immense balcony, was the crown jewel, the hilltop castle Pražský Hrad. From where I stood at our meeting venue, I wondered about the enigmatic core under the Communist veil shrouding the city. Secretly, I was thrilled I had the weekend to uncover it.

The Czech Republic national anthem kicked off at a deafening pitch to signal the conference opening. Impossible to ignore or to speak over, each participant stood stoically with hand upon heart. The principal players were introduced with grand formality and the audience applauded for eternity. I snuck a glance at Hanna to see if I could read her thoughts. Her wide-eyed stare told me this officious ceremony was not typical by German standards either.

The conference itself was as exciting as a meeting about the utility business can be. There *were* interesting topics, such as cross-border operations for European utility companies in the newly liberalized energy market, and the announcement of Japan as the meeting venue for 2003. Beyond that, I observed people interacting and tried not to embarrass myself while practicing my networking skills. From my American perspective, there was a disturbing amount of kissing going on. How did they know which cheek to go for? Or how much contact was appropriate? With great relief I discerned that this normally occurred when people knew one another from past experience.

At the formal reception the first evening, I felt like Cinderella at the ball. The National Theatre in the heart of Prague is old-world European opulence at its finest. Glittering crystal chandeliers decorated the dining salon and thick red carpets reached out to greet invited guests. Cliché as it may be, the evening had a fairytale quality. As tokens of appreciation for our attendance, we were each presented with small Czechoslovakian crystal vases. It wasn't a glass slipper, but I held it tightly anyway.

Throughout the two-hour dinner, we drank deep glasses of Burgundy and listened to welcoming speeches and introductions.

The Devil Wears Clogs

The heavily-accented English was sometimes difficult to understand, but I was impressed by the capacity of the presenters to demonstrate humor in a second language. Having studied two additional languages, I admired their dexterity. Without proper grammar and vocabulary, a good sense of timing, and true knowledge of another culture, jokes will fall flat every time. I realized then, and still believe, that the pinnacle of bilingual speaking is making a good joke.

Hanna and Adrian stayed one day after the conference. Together, we went sightseeing and shopping when the meetings were over. Our first tour was a bus ride to Pražský Hrad. Before this one, I hadn't seen many castles. Heidelberg has its schloss, which is uniquely beautiful, but is mainly ruins. Walking through the grounds of Prague Castle, my Cinderella fantasy waned but my imagination ran wild. I considered that, while castle living was the summit of medieval social strata, it was certainly lacking the creature comforts of a three-bedroom American colonial.

With unsealed windows in the frosty Czech winters and cold stone beneath, a deep chill would be your constant companion. Forget having hot meals because the kitchen is a half-mile away and warming plates will not be imagined for centuries. While not the stuff of medieval romance novels, I couldn't help but visualize the reality of such a life once I was no longer knocked out by the Gothic beauty. Remembering that Bubonic Plague had decimated Prague and cities all across Europe in the 1300's when much of this castle was built, I felt blessed to live in the modern age.

America is a young nation, so walking in the footsteps of people who lived hundreds of years before is surreal. Despite my modern perspective, Prague Castle left me wanting more.

When Hanna and Adrian flew back to Germany, I was left to my own devices to discover the rest of the city. Prague's Old Town fascinated me. Seated in the three-hundred-year-old St. Nicolas Church, I listened to classical piano. Walking until my shoes held my swollen feet prisoner, I finally stopped for a magic hour of street performers on the Charles Bridge at sunset. Jugglers wowed the crowd while a flute player provided lilting background music. I soaked up the atmosphere like a sponge, wishing for someone to share it with.

With every centimeter of new territory, my appetite became more voracious. My already terminal case of curiosity intensified. I became a more intrepid traveler when my initial gang of ready travel mates ultimately disbanded. Time marched on and colleagues left Germany for new assignments elsewhere or returned home. When my dream destinations didn't match those of new teammates' or their available time off, I was left with two choices: miss out or go it alone. I chose the latter.

Throughout my German year, one worry accompanied my every step. I feared my luck would run out and I would be on a plane back to the States. Assignments were often changed at the last minute, so I was in perpetual overdrive. Weekends rarely passed without a tour or trip. It was April, only six months remained until I had to return to Ohio.

My first solo trip was to Vienna, a one-hour flight from Frankfurt. It was a pleasant surprise that Vienna's architecture is every bit as elegant as Paris. Before this trip, I assumed the French had cornered that market and was thrilled to be proven wrong. The stately Vienna Opera House and regal Schönbrunn Palace are a mere drop in the architectural bucket. Schönbrunn is as stunning as Versailles and fewer tourists allow a more thought-provoking experience. To my amazement, a small zoo existed on the garden grounds behind the palace. I imagined Empress Sisi keeping tigers and polar bears the way I'd kept my cat Bijoux.

Multi-faceted Vienna has a long history as a Mecca of intellectual thought and artistic performance. Visiting the Belvedere Museum, I admired Gustav Klimt's *The Kiss* and considered how differently the artist mind functions. I took the subway to the former residence of Sigmund Freud, where he lived and worked for forty years, and marveled at the overwhelming task of challenging society to think differently. In my new role as independent traveler, Vienna was a great choice. It is logically laid out and had fewer meandering one-way streets than many of the places I'd visited. Later, I discovered that this was because Vienna was bombed fifty-two times during World War II and it has been reconstructed with the benefit of modern vision.

I found new freedom in lingering as long as I wanted at any given place. My only disappointment is that the Danube is very far from blue.

CHAPTER 7
LEARNING TO FLY

The common denominator on every trip was how different each country was from the next. Without personal experience visiting these places, it's easy to assume "Europeans" are fairly monochromatic and "Europe" is a collection of similar states. Americans can often cross three or four states before seeing dramatic change. In Europe, radical change barges in the minute you cross the border: food and drink are different, languages are different, and driving styles are distinctly different. My biggest mistake, however, was assumption that the European mentality is similar to American mentality because we are both "Western," and similar in appearance. There is no truth to that assumption.

In Germany, the difference that hit first and hardest was driving. Germany is home to the best automotive engineering in the world and people take their driving very seriously. When you decide to scrap the speed limit, you had better be master of your game. Often it felt like I'd been warped by the Starship Enterprise while driving north to Frankfurt Airport. I still have occasional flashbacks of the construction zones on German motorways, the narrowest driving confines I've ever seen. Unconsciously, I sucked in my breath and held it every time, as though making myself smaller would make the driving easier.

In America, I took these things for granted: that there will be a massive parking lot outside any shopping mall and that the road construction won't make you hold your breath. Driving in Germany is a precision sport. Germans drive fast, but they drive precisely. It is actually illegal to run out of gas on the autobahn.

To add to the long list of differences between Europeans and

Americans, I will mention something else we all do each day: eat lunch. Only the largest plants and offices in the United States have what we would call cafeterias. In Germany and other European offices I visited, having a *canteen* is common. American office workers often go to lunch with friends at a nearby restaurant or run errands they can't get to on weekends. Germans have lunch together. Seriously, everyone eats together every day. At first, I enjoyed it. Having someone cook for you, especially on the coldest days, was a plus. Later, as I learned more about what was happening in the office and got to know people, the constant togetherness felt too much like a high school lunch period and I avoided it.

While we ate, I listened to the opinions of people who know relatively little about how America works while they discussed "Americans." My German co-workers couldn't comprehend why my teammates and I took off every weekend to visit a different country or only spent three days in another. They found it simply hilarious that Americans come to Europe on enormous coach buses and stop in ten countries in two weeks.

Comments like these rubbed me the wrong way, but I learned an important lesson. It illuminated the value of keeping your mouth shut when a subject arises on which you have no personal experience. Spouting off about how things should be done differently, and more importantly, in the way that *you* are used to, makes your ignorance hard to ignore.

My new colleagues had no idea that, on average, the American worker is lucky to have two weeks of annual vacation. Their only frame of reference was the German holiday allotment of five to six weeks per year. They didn't consider that for many Americans, a two-week tour might be the only trip to Europe they ever take. Even though I didn't appreciate these uneducated views, I saw no value in trying to alter the worldview of people who had no interest in changing. It was easier not to participate.

* * *

My responsibilities at the office increased as Spring made her first appearance. It was my job to support the software newly developed by my German client. Slowly, the software was adopted by large companies in different regions of the world, and I worked with the developers to raise issues and facilitate problem solving. Company-wide software implementations are multi-million dollar projects, which cannot afford to be held up when a problem rears its head. Hanna and I participated in development meetings where I brought "real world" examples to the attention of people who could solve them. I, in turn, took the solutions back to the project leaders in my own firm.

Acting as a conduit, I learned about operations in a Chilean gas plant, an Italian energy exchange, and a Dutch waste management utility by the questions posed–complex, but fascinating. Although I will be the first to admit that between the thick accents, varying commands of English, and my grasp of the technical problems, I fully understand the phrase "lost in translation." Nonetheless, what struck me was how much the Germans appreciated this direct feedback, and in turn they put much effort into developing solutions. When I missed something in recounting the details, they did not hold it against me.

International colleagues from my firm often came to the VDS headquarters where I was based. They attended training classes or participated in joint meetings regarding large software projects. As the local team, we made our coworkers at feel at home by recommending the best hotels and showed them around in the evenings. Often we had large groups for dinner and all of us knew the best Heidelberg hotspots for after-work drinks.

In May, a training class at our office was scheduled in my specialty area. When registration was complete, I was asked to locate Jeff from Malaysia and David from the Netherlands in class. I knew the instructors personally, so it was easy for me to get specific system questions answered for my colleagues. The kink in the plan was the multitude of May bank holidays, allowing me a five-day jaunt to Barcelona. Who wanted to babysit coworkers when I had a trip to get ready for?

Reluctantly, I noted the contact details of my visiting coworkers and took down their questions. Scanning the classroom, no one matched the descriptions of my colleagues and class was about to start. I sat down, deciding to look for them later. Training began and I dutifully took notes. I noticed a guy in the front with a guttural accent I thought might be Dutch. Maybe he was one of my lost colleagues. People from my organization are usually easy to spot, but in this case, I wasn't sure. When he stood to ask a question, I saw the bright red pants he was wearing and I was even less sure. Truthfully, I desperately hoped that this was not the Dutch David I'd been asked to locate.

At mid-morning, we broke for coffee. I was flipping through the course material when a finger tapped me on the shoulder. I turned around to see a seriously good-looking face smiling down at me. This guy, who was not wearing fire engine red trousers, extended his hand and introduced himself as David.

It happened in slow motion—a halo of white light surrounded his face and his slate blue eyes matched his button down shirt. Trying not to appear dazed, I stood up to shake his hand and suggested we get coffee. He stood over six feet tall. Babysitting coworkers in a foreign country might not be such an inconvenience after all.

"Follow me," I said, leading the way to VDS' cavernous welcome center. My heels clacked down the spotless black marble floors and I pointed out the obvious coffee cups and sugar. Pushing the cappuccino button, I stole another side glance and felt my pulse quicken. Though it was only May, I pointed to the doors of the outdoor courtyard. "Let's get some air."

"How was your flight?" I said, reaching for an innocuous question.

"Good. I drove down. Utrecht is only a few hours from here." David answered.

"Oh, right." I tried to cover, not having a clue how big Holland actually was or in what direction. "How long are you staying?"

"I'm here until the end of the week. Jeff has to leave on Wednesday. I have some questions I need answers to about the CRM system for Utilities."

"Me, too," echoed Jeff.

"I can help you with that. If I don't have the answers, Hanna will know," I answered, with more confidence than I felt as the system was still under development. Having an excuse to keep in contact with

David was just fine by me. "We'd better head back, but maybe we can all get together later tonight in Heidelberg."

"Sounds good," came the Dutch and Malaysian accents in unison.

Class droned on, but I didn't hear much of what was said. I was too busy working on our social agenda for the evening. David and Jeff would meet the rest of the team at a favorite spot for dinner. After that, the evening was wide open. Excitement showed up for the first time in months.

Brauhaus Vetter is a Heidelberg institution. The Vetter is an old brewery with the atmosphere of a Shakespearean tavern. It's dark and crowded with heavy wooden tables and benches. Each table is topped with thick, white candles in brass candleholders and the menu recommends the specialty of the house: pig stomach. Germany is dominated by meat and potatoes. If you are a vegetarian in Germany, very dull cuisine lies in your future. I hope you like lettuce, potatoes, and corn—a lot.

If you aren't vegetarian, but don't fancy pig stomach, the German menu is has many delicious dishes. My favorite discoveries were *flammkuchen* and *spätzle*. Flammkuchen is flaky rectangular crust pizza. I love the regional version from Alsace, heavy with bacon, onion, and cheese. Spätzle is a homemade German dumpling, often served with beef in thick peppery brown gravy.

Do not come to Germany and ask for things like fat-free salad dressing. You're better off going back where you came from and being spared the Deutscher stare. In summer and autumn, there's nothing better than the random beer and bratwurst festivals that pop up in every German village. The big daddy of them all is the Munich Oktoberfest, which takes place in late September.

We got some good laughs from the menu, but there were much more interesting things afoot at this crowded table of coworkers. I lived the closest to the restaurant, but, trying for perfect hair and makeup, was last to arrive. Rushed, I slid into the only open spot with Dora on my right. As a Vetter virgin, I was slightly taken aback by the pig stomach. I stalled for time by cracking jokes while I looked for something safer.

From the corner of my eye, I saw David get up from where he was sitting and move Jeff over so he could sit on my left. This was highly unusual in a group of American coworkers—attraction or no attraction, it was way too obvious. Dora and I stole a glance at each other, but I didn't dare speak. The temperature of the room skyrocketed, but I was determined to play it cool. My heart had taken a beating and it wasn't excited about getting back into the ring.

Heidelberg is a special place. Any one of us would have said it's "small enough to get around and big enough to get into trouble." There are as many great restaurants as there are bars. It even has the requisite strange after-hours bar that you only go to when you've already been drinking and therefore never end up with a clear memory of it.

Pushing back the Cave's heavy black velvet curtains, you immediately descend a tiny spiral staircase to land in the near-total darkness of a stone cellar. The cellar is complemented by two cavernous rooms and a small dance floor. I say *small* dance floor because I fell off it more than once, but others might remember it as normal size. No matter what you ask for to drink, they don't have it and you don't care. We once drank maraschino cherry juice and vodka, because cranberry juice was unheard of in Germany. It didn't matter because it was all about the experience. It was cool to be at The Cave.

Nancy and I took David and Jeff to The Cave after dinner, hoping for a little bit of craziness in a place that rarely disappoints. This particular evening, however, was a letdown. David didn't make any further moves despite his initial boldness. For as much as I've heard about legendary Dutch courage, David didn't appear to be much of a drinker. I was surprised he didn't push it, but I was also relieved. For the moment, I was happy feeling the chemistry between us.

At class the day after, our discussion centered on our plans for the long weekend: his brother's wedding, and my trip to Barcelona. When class was dismissed, we were greeted by an absolute downpour. David impressed me by asking to borrow my umbrella to walk my colleague to her car. They then brought the car back to collect us, so everyone could stay dry. Chivalry is not dead.

CHAPTER 8
PROVING GROUND

The day after the course, I stopped by Dora's place for a chat and to borrow her scarlet-red nail polish before continuing on to Frankfurt Airport. Part of the discussion was David. She agreed that he was friendly and very funny. Quickly, we proceeded to more pressing topics on the agenda. How would he figure into our upcoming trip? In three weeks, our annual company utility conference was taking place in Amsterdam. Who else but a local would be the perfect guide when we hit the city in June? Dora and I would get a double room, but not necessarily in the same hotel as the rest of the team. That would enable us to roam the city without an entourage.

Plans decided and nails dry, I drove off to the airport, very excited to see Barcelona. Finally, a country where I spoke the language! Six months understanding only scraps of the local language contributed to the sense of isolation I often felt when Dora was away. I was picking up German fairly well, but being able to use my seven years of Spanish was a relief.

I had always wanted to see Spain, any part of Spain. My high school Spanish teacher was amazing. My fellow students thought he was a lunatic, but I respected how hard he worked to show the radical difference of Latin American culture from what we, small-town white folk, understood. He ran around the classroom grunting, one finger pointed up above each of his ears, pretending to be a bull, as each student took a turn as a matador.

It was both weird and hilarious, but it was a great diversion from an otherwise tough academic program that claimed many victims. He was a disciplined instructor who loved life, especially life in Spain and

Latin America. Unfortunately, those cultural differences he imitated were less obvious than a grown man pacing through a school classroom snorting like a bull.

The landing gear struck the ground as the sun was setting, so I saw only glittering lights splashed across a sprawling city and the white coastline. I knew Spaniards eat dinner late in the evening, so I looked for a place to people watch. The Swede had once mentioned Maremagnum, a large tourist complex on Barcelona's waterfront. My trusty guidebook said it was crammed with shops and an equal amount of bars and clubs. It sounded like a safe place to venture out on my own. I found a restaurant with a table under the stars and dined on tender calamari washed down with sparkling *cava*. It should have been perfect, but, surrounded by big laughing groups, I felt awkward being solo. I called my friend Karla in Ohio to stave off loneliness, but it was the middle of her work day and she couldn't chat for long. Both of us wishing she was with me, she cheered me on to make the most of it. Who knew if I would ever come back again? I knew she was right.

If you take Spanish dinner hour as an example, ten or eleven, you can imagine how late it is before anyone shows up at a bar or club. I felt so conspicuous, everywhere alone. I pretended to be a savvy nonchalant traveler, but I was a fraud. I wanted the bars to fill up a bit before I chose one, so I could see what the crowd was like. Eventually, after eleven, I found a place performing group dances like the Macarena, but with actual style. That had to be a safe bet. Before now, I had gone into a bar alone only once and it was one I knew well in college. My nerve was breaking, but Barcelona's nightlife is legendary. How could I leave without a glimpse?

Taking a deep breath, I bee-lined to an empty bar stool in this well-lit bar and ordered a drink. It was tricky to make polite chitchat as it wasn't an old dingy bar filled with grizzled regulars who have no one to talk to at home. It was filled with young people in groups or in pairs. Eventually, I was greeted by the couple next to me from Columbia.

I chatted with them for the next hour. They introduced me to their friends and asked me what brought me to Barcelona. They smiled and nodded, which I took for understanding. Watching the crowd work the dance floor was sufficient entertainment. I was content on the sidelines. More than once I was approached and asked to dance, but I politely declined. A few minutes after midnight, just after I'd ordered a third *cuba libre*, the scene began to deteriorate rapidly. The lights were lowered dramatically for one, and two, a strange hand appeared out of nowhere to caress my bare leg. *Check please!* I was out the door in a flash. I didn't stop to say goodbye to my new Columbian friends. No explanation necessary. *¡Adios, amigos!*

The fun continued when I returned to my hotel and the snooty concierge regarded the single blonde female, returning at 1 a.m., like a leper. I didn't realize then that in a predominantly Catholic country such as Spain, certain things would not go under the radar. Honestly, I didn't care, beyond the slight irritation of being judged by someone else's rules.

After the wobbly start, my adventures in Barcelona were outstanding. Early the next morning, I found the Picasso Museum in a very old part of town, surrounded by tasteful boutiques and fashionable galleries. Waiting in a long queue on the cobblestone alleyway outside the museum, a violinist began to play exquisite music. It echoed, enveloping me and my impatience to enter the museum dissolved. To end a perfect day, I stopped for a drink at a café near the Santa Maria Del Mar. My timing was perfect, a wedding ceremony had just finished. Groups of sharply-dressed *amigos y familia* gathered outside to wait for the bride and groom to exit. Their smiles were visible for miles.

Barcelona seduced me completely. I could have stayed forever watching the fire-eaters and musicians on the Rambla and relaxing at Olympic Harbor, with its explosion of seafood restaurants. The stupefying Sagrada Familia cathedral rendered me speechless, and I waved to the albino gorilla named Snowflake at the Barcelona Zoo. I even tried out the topless beaches, and attempted (in vain) to leave my insecurity behind.

I was getting used to the highs and lows of these trips. I wasn't expecting the heavily chauvinistic culture of southern Europe and the intense, okay, I'll admit it—creepy, stares that followed me everywhere I went. While walking the Rambla, the tourist-crammed promenade of the city, a teenage pickpocket grabbed for my bag. I whipped around to face him, tight grip on my bag, shouting "Thief! Police!" as loud as I could. His olive face and dark brown eyes registered shock, before he vanished from sight. I could still feel his glare from behind the bushes and allowed myself a chuckle for foiling his crime.

I left Barcelona knowing I would return. Strength came from managing another new place on my own, and I wondered what bounty other Spanish cities had to offer.

* * *

When I got back to the office in Walldorf, the buzz was the upcoming Amsterdam conference. I was asked to speak about the new software I was supporting and agreed without thinking. Our projects around the world were sending speakers to the conference. This was my first time attending and I had never given a professional presentation. I was excited to return to Amsterdam with Dora and to see David again, but the business end I dreaded. To suppress my anxiety, I researched my material like a madwoman. I spent many hours working on the presentation slides, and circulated it to my boss and Dora to get their feedback. Taking their advice, I made changes and practiced my speech numerous times in hopes of reducing my anxiety. I was fairly comfortable with the subject matter, but many of the attendees of the conference were experts—consultants who had spent their entire careers thus far working on similar software. I was no expert.

My second arrival in Amsterdam was smoother than the first. The Dutch were out in full force enjoying the unusually dry summer weather. We were a big group this time. Matt was lurking in the shadows somewhere. He was the executive sponsor of this event, so he had VIPs from all over the world to hang out with this time. I didn't expect to see him except at the formal conference activities, which was fine by me. When we checked into the hotel, it was a Friday, and everyone was ready for a drink. Having agreed to his nomination as tour guide, David was on his way to meet us.

Despite getting lost on the way to our hotel, David proved to be an excellent tour guide. He reserved a table for dinner at a seafood restaurant near the Rembrandtplein, which everyone raved about.

The Devil Wears Clogs

Holland is an odd duck from the cuisine perspective. There are Dutch specialties, but there is really no such a thing as cooking "Dutch." Items considered to be culinary delicacies are, in my opinion, revolting. You may have seen drawings of the blonde Little Dutch Boy, probably the same one who put his finger in the dyke, holding up a herring by the tail above his open mouth? This is real. People consume herring by the boatload this way and are excited by the yearly new-herring season. Red-and-white carts are positioned at strategic locations around every large city, selling herring with the heads lopped off smothered in onions.

The location will be given away by squawking flock of seagulls plotting to steal their food back. Another insider tip, expect to take some time mulling over the cart menu because you might want to indulge in another national favorite: *paling*. If you like the jelly-like consistency of old tofu, smoked eel is the snack for you.

Another secret of the Dutch cookbook is *erwtensoep*, a soup made of peas. It's often called split pea soup, because no one can figure out what else to call it. To equate them is to miss the most interesting aspect of the famous green soup, its thickness. I was told that the way Dutch people evaluate the quality of erwtensoep is by whether a spoon will stand straight up in it. A *spoon!*

I ordered the sole, the buttery goodness melting in my mouth. The others raved similarly over their choices. I later discovered later that it was *sole meunière*, a classic French dish. At the time I gave credit to the Dutch, thus setting expectations in the very wrong direction for Holland's culinary scene.

Back at the table, I was less interested in the food and much more interested in David. Strangely, David didn't repeat his signature move. We sat at opposite ends of the table. I convinced myself that this was fine because it was a group outing, not a "date." I ignored the fact that the last time we saw each other we were also surrounded by colleagues.

After dinner, David led us through the best neighborhood pubs and we hit the dance floor at one called the Three Sisters. It was a red-velvet and mahogany kind of place, nothing at all like the dives I had experienced in the red-light district. We drank too much, stayed too late and had a great time. David and I talked, but to my disappointment, nothing happened. Instinct tells you when attraction exists and when it doesn't. I was confused.

Rather than being consumed with David's interest in me, or lack of it, I had bigger fish to fry. My presentation loomed large in two days. Already, I was nervous. Plotting the undercover investigation of Amsterdam with my good friend was a handy avoidance tactic.

The weekend flew as Dora and I experienced Amsterdam exactly as planned, well, almost exactly. We shopped, lunched, and uncovered the city's seedy underbelly. I was less awestruck about being there this time, so I began to see some of what lurked below the city's "tolerant" exterior. Dora and I were intrigued by this bizarre, legal soft-drugs culture, but we weren't going to get involved. We just wanted to dip our toes beneath the surface, to swim lightly across the sea of temptation. There was zero intention of diving in headfirst.

Crossing Dam Square at two in the morning, a bedraggled man approached. "Want some Coke?" he wanted to know.

"Ecstasy, man?" another demanded in a harsh whisper.

We shifted up a gear and kept moving. Under the dark of night with no one else around, we didn't know whether or not we were in real danger.

Relieved, we flew through the hotel lobby. Arriving at our room, I quickly shut the door and we slammed our backs against it, looking at each other wide-eyed. My heart rate was off the charts. It was an unwelcome surprise that the daytime tourist playground, complete with performers and pigeons, became a shark-infested feeding frenzy at night. I shouldn't have been surprised with the number of salivating, drunken men we saw stumbling through the Red Light earlier in the evening that there would be as big of an appetite here for illegal drugs as for the legal ones, but I was. You can take the girl out of Ohio, but apparently you cannot take Ohio out of the girl.

The morning after our reconnaissance mission, I woke after only four hours of sleep. It was Sunday and Dora snored on in the other bed. Not wanting to disturb her, I quietly showered and dressed. It was a pleasant discovery that most Amsterdam stores are open for business.

The Devil Wears Clogs

Losing myself in a new place is my favorite pastime, so despite my hangover, I busied myself with the goings on about town. I bought a baguette at Deli France and parked myself on a sunny bench in front of the old Royal Palace where I had watched the Dutch royal wedding with the Swede.

There were more people than I expected on the street. I looked each one over and decided that most didn't appear to be the "clueless tourist" type nor the "Sunday church" type. More often than not, they were the "desperate lost soul" type, characterized by black, vacant eyes, bed head, and soiled clothing. My name for the species is *drugginus Amsterdamicus*.

I didn't feel threatened by the shabby figures struggling to walk at nearly noon on Sunday. It was nothing like the feeling that I'd experienced hot-footing it back to my hotel in the dark of night. The feeling was sadness. Souls like these come to Amsterdam to dive headfirst into that sea and allow it to pull them under. It's one of Amsterdam's classic but unfortunate traits, the many individuals who come for its anonymity end up drowned in it.

From my seat on the cold stone bench in Dam Square, I thought about it. While Heidelberg had its drunks, it doesn't have a blanket of criminality like this. I remembered conversations with Dutch cab drivers and smiling waiters about how tolerant the Netherlands is as a nation. That's the word they always use: tolerant. It didn't look all that tolerant to me on that Sunday morning with locals scurrying away from these men, straining not to make eye contact. It looked apathetic.

After my gloomy morning observations, the city shopping experience felt less joyful. I did much looking and little buying before returning to my hotel to see if Dora was alive and well. She was, so we rejoined the entourage and enjoyed the sights and sounds of tourist Amsterdam.

The conference opening was nine o'clock Monday. Until late afternoon, we listened to presentations on projects all over the world. While two or three were interesting, the rest were torture by geek speak. It was a long afternoon of listening and struggling to pay attention. At first, I was relieved that my presentation was on the second day.

Later, when my nerves took over the entire day before I had to speak, I realized that it would have been far better to have gotten it out of the way immediately. No matter what I was doing on Monday, the thirty minutes I had to stand in front of everyone on Tuesday never left my mind.

That evening an elegant cherrywood canal boat collected the thirty conference participants at the dock outside the office. I had been on a similar tour through the Amsterdam canals with the Swede, but that one didn't involve a crew of colleagues and copious amounts of wine. A boisterous tone began to rumble throughout the crowd. An hour of cruising the city's central waterways flew by before the boat dropped us at a waterside restaurant for dinner.

I think the evening was pleasant; there were no suspect foods like paling or erwtensoep. Monotonous thank you speeches were read and highlights of the past year flashed across the screen during dinner. Mere minutes seemed to pass before the majority of the attendees filed out of the restaurant in search of the nearest pub. Multiple taxis sped off in a convoy and the party volume increased significantly over Heineken and what David claimed was popular Dutch music. For the record, I am not a fan. The fun for everyone else was in full swing, but I could think of nothing but my presentation. I tried to push it to the back of my mind, but it was impossible. Alone, I left the bar by midnight. David's surprised, disappointed face when I waved good-bye across the crowd stayed with me.

I went through my bedtime routine and reviewed the presentation until I could barely see. Finally, I lay down and closed my eyes, only to find my heart pounding and my throat as dry as the Sahara. Sleep wasn't going to make an appearance and I'd been a fool to think she would. The more desperate I became to control my anxiety, the more it dominated my entire being. It felt as though my mask was about to be ripped off in public to expose me as a fraud.

Dora wandered in happily a few hours later, asking why I was still awake. I couldn't explain. If you aren't the type to experience this avalanche of fear and anxiety, you wouldn't understand those of us who do. She told me I'd be fine and was out cold within minutes. I was so jealous. I continued staring at the ceiling and trying to breathe deep until the clock said 5 a.m. By then I couldn't be bothered to try anymore, so I got up and walked though my presentation again in the bathroom, silently praying to be convincing.

With few exceptions, the meeting attendees looked pretty rough after the previous night's boozy carnival. Dora said that once they closed the bar down, the survivors went looking for kebabs. Those things alone would give you the green tint I saw on faces that morning, not to mention all the beer. I was relieved that some had already returned to their project locations and the number of people in the room was about half of what it was on day one. David was around, but he was in and out of the meeting room, attending to other business.

After what felt like an eternity, I walked on weak knees to the podium. That's the last thing I remember. Blinded by anxiety, I completely blanked on all the material I had so thoroughly prepared. I stuttered and flipped through slides. People asked questions and I suppose I tried to answer. I failed miserably to demonstrate my knowledge to the audience. My rock, Dora, said it wasn't the disaster of epic proportions that I made it out to be, but I didn't believe her.

The only consolation was that David had been out of the room when I spoke. At least I hadn't embarrassed myself in front of him too.

CHAPTER 9
LAYING THE GROUNDWORK

I would have preferred to crawl under a rock when I got home to Germany after my ill-fated presentation, but instead I analyzed what went wrong. A new cardinal rule about presentations was born: never, under any circumstances, use slides created by others. My presentation had incorporated several slides, created for sales and training by the Germans to illustrate certain points. It was a disaster when I got nervous, and my thoughts became a runaway train.

Desperately, I wished I'd presented the content in line with my own logic. Had I done that, I wouldn't have found myself mute when asked a question. Regardless of the "shoulds" and "coulds," I picked myself up, dusted myself off, and got back to the business at hand.

The end of June delivered day after day of beautiful weather. I worked with the cool morning breeze drifting in through the open office windows. My strategy document, the assignment I was developing throughout the year, was to be completed by the time I left in October. It was a detailed description of how to effectively integrate two types of software.

Along with this, I was invited back to Amsterdam to contribute to a software training class in July. Addicted to life in Europe, I had zero intention of returning to the United States in October. Time was of the essence. I had to I find my next project. If it hadn't been for this, I'm not sure I could have shown my face in Amsterdam again so soon.

During the summer, I relished how independent Germans are at work. When meetings became less frequent at the end of June and then by mid-July when they stopped all together, I still had plenty to do. This was my first experience with European holidays.

Please note that it is not referred to as "vacation," not ever. "Vacation" has some sort of déclassé connotation in European society, and is a dead giveaway that you are American. While I do not claim to understand why, I've adapted my vocabulary. By now, I was used to imitating the behavior of the Germans as closely as possible when it didn't make me look ridiculous. This way I didn't stand out more than necessary. Obviously, opening my mouth was still a problem, but you get the drift. I stopped asking why, hoping to pick it up on my own later.

Since there wasn't much need for my presence in the office in July, making my third trip to Amsterdam to participate in the course was easy. It was also a convenient cover story to see David again. I booked a room at a hotel next to the office to save time commuting. I had meetings with two of Dutch executives and a general manger in the office, in addition to contributing content course. Despite appearances, my mission was twofold: find an assignment in Holland and have dinner with David alone. Every time I spoke to him, he insisted on referring to me as a "colleague." I needed to see how he reacted one on one. I love people watching, but it is nice to have a friendly face at dinner.

U.S. business travels had broken me in to dining alone, but from what I'd seen, this was not at all common for European women.

For the first time in Amsterdam, I was blessed with sun-drenched days and warm canal breezes. The city wore her best attire. I scheduled my trip with a weekend for exploration, so I finally had time to take in the more highbrow Amsterdam attractions. Strolling across the Museumplein and lingering in the Van Gogh Museum were food for my soul. Meandering through the colorful petals at the *bloemenmarkt* and purchasing a gorgeous black-leather handbag at Claudio Ferrici had me grinning from ear to ear. At the end of the day, I stumbled upon the vast cheerful Vondelpark. Students vied for every inch of grass, and the outdoor cafés overflowed with tables full of laughing patrons.

Amsterdam was a stark contrast to the tiny altstadt that was my Heidelberg world. It was bigger and more intoxicating. As much as I'd enjoyed my German team members, time alone outside the office was horribly isolating. Germans were not outwardly friendly or inviting, but the Dutch came across differently. Despite my previous experiences that made clear what lay on the surface was not the whole picture, I wanted to believe that I would be happy living here. I *needed* to believe it because only in Amsterdam was there potential for me to remain in Europe post-October.

Around this time I noticed that seeing so many incredible places was increasing my desire to continue roaming, not the opposite. I began to feel like I had a sense of self for the first time. I thought I'd figured out what made me so different from my friends and schoolmates in America. Many people say they want to move abroad, but when push comes to shove, very few people will actually do it. Of the few that take the ride, fewer still will enjoy it.

I certainly didn't gain "enlightenment" by living in Germany, but I felt closer to what I was searching for in Europe than anywhere else. There were so many different types of people here and so many unlikely couples. No one paid any attention if the couple were mixed-race or nationality, or both. People led their own lives and didn't seem to conform to the singular way of living that is subconsciously promoted in the United States. You must own *this* type house and *this* fancy car and shop at *these* stores, which can be found anywhere in the nation but carry exactly the same clothes. That's the message: Be one of us. Conform. So far, on this adventure, I'd been able to both be myself and live under the radar.

Germany had shown me that social rules exist in Europe. In fact, there are far too many to mention and you only find them out by accident. There is no manual to study. What is clear is that I am much happier being forced to use five separate bins for my trash and being loudly reprimanded by my German neighbors when I get it wrong than I am being told what to wear or where to live. I can handle the trash, but please stay out of my business.

I had no master plan on where this was heading, bit I refused allow my grand adventure to be terminated by someone else's decision. Friends and colleagues both wondered why I wanted to stay in Europe. The only way to explain it was that after living in a place where even a trip to the corner market for milk is an adventure, going back home would be incredibly boring. I simply wasn't done yet.

* * *

I had a packed agenda for my third Amsterdam trip, but I reserved one evening for dinner with David. He wasn't familiar with the city because he'd grown up near Rotterdam and attended university in Groningen, so it took some wandering to find a restaurant. No small feat considering the speed at which a six-foot-five hungry man can move. Ultimately, we landed in a tourist restaurant on one of the city's main arteries that advertised Argentinian steaks. I couldn't have cared less where we went. My mission was to learn more about this mystery man.

Dinner conversation was tame and consisted of me asking a lot of questions about Holland. One thing I did find amusing and David found infuriating was that the waiter would only address me. He acted, rather rudely, as though David wasn't even there. At least it gave us something to laugh about when I ran out of questions. The food was mediocre at best and we had no reason to linger. And yes, if you must know, we went Dutch.

During dinner, David dropped a bombshell. He casually told me that he lived with his girlfriend of seven years. *What girlfriend?* Though I tried not to show it, the barely-healed scar on my broken heart was straining not to break open again. Now I understood why he'd kept a professional distance on my visits to Amsterdam. I asked him what he told her when we were out having dinner, and he told me that was easy, "just dinner with a colleague." I stared at my empty plate, saying nothing.

After another drink at an Irish bar, he drove me to my hotel. Before getting out, I hesitated a few minutes. Not knowing what else to say or do based on his recent revelation, I thanked him for a nice evening, and got out of the car seriously confused. Walking back to my hotel room, I convinced my disappointed self that I must have read him all wrong.

Before I flew back to Heidelberg, I gave him a quick call to thank him for showing me around. He started to say that he'd enjoyed it, but before he could finish, I heard a female voice in the background and the phone disconnected. If I were just a colleague, as he so casually put it, why would he be worried about what his girlfriend thought? I was still processing this when my phone rang a few minutes later. David was apologizing like mad, but didn't explain. I shrugged it off and went back to Germany.

* * *

On the July business calendar was the global annual sales meeting for the Germans. As one of the organizers, Hanna made sure I was invited. Knowing it would be a major coup for Matt to get a speaking slot, I lobbied to get him invited too. One afternoon over lunch in the canteen, I pitched the idea to Hanna and Adrian. Interested in the idea of combining forces, they agreed to get back to me.

In the summer of 2002, recession was hitting the United States. The consulting industry was not faring well. Layoffs had begun prior to my departure for Germany and as many as two hundred of the company's top executives quietly left the company. Major restructuring was underway. This wasn't long after the Enron scandal broke, also leaving a trail of consulting bodies in its wake, and people were nervous. Matt was one of those nervous people. The Golden Rule of the consulting biz is that every team and every job must be chargeable to a client. If it isn't, its value will be immediately questioned by executive management. Our Walldorf team was not chargeable and Matt was responsible for it. Its value was realized in the mutual cooperation between our two companies on many major projects worldwide, but that's difficult to measure in billable hours.

With all of this going on in the background, Hanna answered my question by saying that her management also liked the idea of Matt's participation, and I thought I'd pulled off a win. This annual sales event had always been internal employees only. Outside speakers weren't permitted. Mine would be the only firm making a presentation to senior sales staff worldwide, which had great potential to boost our bottom line. The main reason this was being permitted was due to my efforts for genuine communication and relationship building with my German colleagues. I'd heard from Hanna and Dora both that before I joined the team, much of the work was done dividedly. As much as possible, I crossed company boundaries. Truth be told, I had started to appreciate the way the Germans conducted business more than my own firm's processes and rules.

I rushed to call Matt and tell him what I'd negotiated. He sounded thrilled. His presentation for a restricted sales-focused audience would gain him much-needed publicity at a critical time, although I knew he would never admit it. My hope was that he would return the favor and use his professional weight to help me secure my next project in Europe. We had spoken many times about my career path and he knew exactly where I stood on returning to the States.

At the conference, I sat grinning in the audience watching my German colleagues and Matt give their perspectives on the world with regard to software integration and development. I enjoyed being a participant, but I was extremely disappointed that I never received a simple thank you from Matt for making it happen. We were all busy, so I didn't obsess over it. I just looked forward to the event dinner at a winery in the nearby countryside. Matt showed off by picking me up in a BMW, complete with a navigation system. Such gadgets were very new then, so I admit to being impressed. Wildflower breezes poured in the open sunroof, good music flowed from the speakers, and I had high hopes for the night. Apparently, Matt did too, but for different reasons.

At the restaurant, we were given a tour of the wine cellar and invited to taste their vintages. I learned how many variables have the potential to impact the contents of a wine bottle and what my favorite grapes were called. Later, amid the confusion that accompanies seating a hundred people for dinner, Hanna and Adrian motioned for me to join their table and I happily sat down in the one available seat. Outside under a clear starry sky, dinner was served, white wine flowed, and the laughs were plenty. Hanna and I were becoming good friends and her friends accepted me in turn.

The others had been provided with company transport, but Matt had driven us and by now he was pacing, obviously ready to leave. I would have preferred to stick around listening to the Germans a bit longer, but I didn't want to cause an awkward situation by letting Matt drive back alone. I said my good-byes and like a child being told it's time to go home, I reluctantly walked with him to the BMW waiting in the gravel parking lot.

The drive back to Heidelberg was a treat as I rarely left the city limits in the evenings. Far from the city lights, stars lit the sky for miles. We kept the sunroof open and the music playing, and inside I smiled with contentment at the perfect evening. That is, perfect until Matt said, "Why don't we stop and admire the stars?"

Was he serious? We were in the middle of nowhere. Okay, I admit I flirted with him a little at the beginning, but that was before I discovered that he had girlfriends in multiple countries and was (consequently?) recently divorced. Granted, that was a step up from the married Swede, and Dutch David with the live-in girlfriend, but it wasn't good enough for me. Claiming I was "*so* tired," we drove without stopping.

A week later, Matt was back in the United States. Lucky me, I had the good fortune to be copied on an email he sent to all of the senior executives in my business unit. In this email, he raved about his great triumph at the sales conference for several paragraphs, not once mentioning that it was I who gave him the opportunity. Nor did he thank me privately or help me in any way to achieve my objective of staying in Europe.

In fact, I was told by my manager at review time that he had given me the highest possible rating for the previous period, but somehow it had gotten knocked down a level at the executive level. I wonder how that might have happened...

CHAPTER 10
WHAT LIES BENEATH

As we entered August, Germany began to boil. Maybe I am embarrassing myself by admitting to having no idea that much of Europe lacks air-conditioning, but I'll take my chances. Looking back, it shouldn't have been a newsflash that the older architecture of European buildings made no accommodation for a modern luxury like central air, but it is equally true that there is normally little need for it. My personal opinion is that the spectre of global warming began rearing its ugly head in Europe that summer.

According to both Hanna and the German weather bureau's web site, summer temperatures in Northern Europe normally don't exceed 90º Fahrenheit. Now it's clear why Europeans jam the motorways in August. The simple truth is that it's so stifling in most offices that it's impossible to concentrate. What I find most amusing is the name for this migratory phenomenon: "Black Friday." Black Friday is the one August day when thousands of families clog Switzerland's San Gittardo tunnel, the main gateway from north to south Europe. Woe unto you if you hit the tunnel on this day. Pack a lunch and a pillow because you won't be moving anytime soon.

Walldorf's hallways and offices were eerily quiet. There wasn't much point in suffering heat stroke in my office, so I often worked at home. When it became too stifling there, I moved to outdoor cafés and watched the tourists while working on my year-end writing assignment. It wasn't the optimal environment for concentration, however. When August empties Europe of Europeans, North Americans and Asians arrive en masse to fill the void. When planning a European holiday, August is best avoided. There are no interesting attractions without queues three times their normal length, and peace and quiet make themselves very scarce.

One muggy afternoon, I sat in Heidelberg's Market Square watching yet another troupe of American senior citizens do their best to keep pace with their young and overly-cheerful tour guide. The ubiquitous red umbrella revealed her status as their leader. Several pairs of wide eyes took in Heidelberg's legendary architecture and I read their excited expressions. From my vantage point, it looked like many of them had waited a very long time for this. Requisite grumpy old men were mixed in with the ranks, but they were the exception.

Every time this scene played out, I thanked my lucky stars to be seeing so much of Europe at the age of thirty-one. Not only was I spared the agony of having to climb hundreds of steps at an age when walking to the second floor of your house is an event, but I was getting paid for it. In these rare moments, when I could escape my own head and immediate worries, I felt with my whole being how fortunate I was. I'm not forgetting the many times I was beyond frustration with the obstinate Germans and the days I longed for the sheer convenience of America, but largely everything else was cast aside by my real-life adventure. True perspective of another culture's way of life is difficult to come by.

There were times, however, that I would have liked to have been less privileged with this unique insight. Times when that inside knowledge takes a dark turn. It might be something ordinary, but unsettling, like the day I learned that European overcrowding even extends to cemeteries, and the dearly departed aren't entitled to remain in their final real estate forever. The solution is to rent graves for a finite period of time, like twenty-five years, before they are given to someone else.

Or maybe it's something less obvious, like the time I bought a Nazi military medal for my dad, the collector, at a London street market, and I discovered that Nazi symbols are illegal on the European continent. To avoid further law-breaking and embarrassment, I quietly asked Hanna what was appropriate to discuss on the subject of Nazi Germany. Patiently, she explained that Germans have no sense of national pride. Even though the current generation of Germans had nothing to do with the atrocities committed during World War II, they are no less deeply ashamed of the legacy left behind by Adolph Hitler.

Hailing from a country where patriotism is displayed on every street corner and pledged in every grade school classroom, I felt sad for the innocents who were tainted with the irreparable damage of their ancestors.

The day that this "privileged" insight rattled me most was the day I visited Dachau–the former German concentration camp on the outskirts of Munich. It was one of the first such camps and was referred to as a "training center" for SS camp guards. My only frame of reference for the Holocaust before this visit was when my eighth-grade English teacher required us to read memoirs from camp survivors, and we watched a scratchy black-and-white Auschwitz documentary. When reading about and watching the horror played out on a television screen is shocking, you can imagine what it feels like to walk in those footsteps.

Outside of school, my experience with the Holocaust was limited to a visit to my college roommate's Jewish family in New York. Her *oma* still had the ID number tattooed on her hand. Her father had been born in the same camp that had tattooed her grandmother. None of these things prepared me for the overwhelming sorrow that crushes your spirit the minute you place a foot on the grounds of this collective misery.

Researchers say that the Dachau crematorium and gas chambers mechanisms were never used. Münchner, the people of Münich, were told the weak and sick were transported to Austria for "extermination." This knowledge did not make the experience easier to bear. I declined to enter the crematorium, and when I saw the thick black cast- iron gate inscription *Arbeit macht frei* or "Work makes one free," the tears refused to be held back any longer.

School kids in the United States are taught about World War II. We learn that American troops were Europe's saviors–it's common to joke that if it weren't for us, Europeans would be speaking German. I understood that, in this story, my team was the hero and Germans were the villains. What you can't get from a history book is the tangible reality of war and the horrific consequences suffered by millions on this continent. Face to face with that cold hard reality, I was forced for the first time to acknowledge the existence of true evil.

My knowledge, prior to arriving on European soil, was factual detachment. It had no emotion. Visiting Dachau and Vienna, entirely rebuilt after German leveling, showed me the magnitude of suffering. I don't claim to know how Holocaust survivors feel, or that I can relate to their experiences, but I did get an understanding of the depth of terror and deep-rooted fear that I'd never even had a glimpse of before. With new eyes, I read the plaque placed thoughtfully at Dachau's exit written in English, French, German, and Russian. It says simply, "never again." If only that were true.

* * *

My company's German-based team was always changing. People moved in and moved out all the time. I continued searching for a path to my next assignment in Europe before my number was up.

Dora was considering a new project in Belgium and was due to leave before me. I dreaded saying goodbye. We were more like sisters than friends. I wasn't sure how I'd keep my sanity intact without her to confide in. The experiences we shared living and working abroad didn't translate with friends at home. I didn't tell my U.S. friends everything anymore. It was too hard for them to relate, and their eyes glazed over when I told stories of Europe. Dora was the only one who understood.

Before she left for Brussels, we made one last voyage. This time, her friend from Ohio was coming over and the destination was Rome. Rome, a classic European "must see" city. We rented an apartment for three days in the Campo dei Fiori, a main square close to Piazza Navona.

Our arrival at the apartment was a case study in miscommunication. Dora was told when booking that minor construction was underway near the apartment, but was assured this wouldn't interfere with our holiday. We struggled with oversized, heavy suitcases up the steep, narrow staircase in ninety-degree heat. As the massive wooden door to the apartment swung open, a collective, audible gasp was warranted as we saw for the first time what kind of work was going on. Not only were we in an apartment in southern Europe in August *sans* AC, but every window was covered with plastic. Thick, industrial-grade, zero-ventilation plastic!

Aside from the complete lack of air, fresh or otherwise, the place was cool, not literally cool, of course, but the layout. It had two bedrooms and a ton of space, so it was much roomier than the average European hotel room.

"It's just a few days and that square is fantastic," said Dora, remaining optimistic despite having the heaviest suitcase.

"I can't imagine trying to find another place with zero notice," I said, daunted by the possibility of having to start over in this enormous city.

We looked to Leah, Dora's friend who had traveled the furthest for this experience. "Let's not waste any time. The location is perfect."

It was a relief to flee from claustrophobia, even if the afternoon sun was blinding. The minute my sandaled toes hit the street, I felt good. Seeing the stone pathways, which passed for roads and feeling the city's beating heart, made me come alive. Following our stomachs, we went in the direction of Piazza Navona. We darted between deranged drivers, narrowly managing to avoid the loss of limbs by speeding Vespas. Finally, we landed in the square, which was a marketplace and public gathering spot as early as the first century. Towering statues by Bernini dominate the open air of the piazza while red-and-white-checkered tablecloths line the square.

Walking from one café to the next, we carefully perused the various menus before settling in and ordering our first bottle of *vino bianco* and *pizza margherita*. As we waited, we mulled over the mysterious ingredient that makes everything *better* in Italy. Food is mouth-watering, the wine is exceptional, the language is musical, and the men are a feast for the eyes. There is a beauty to Italy, which manifests itself in every aspect of life, yet remains impossible to define. Far be it from me to attempt to solve the mystery so many philosophers and intellectuals have pondered for decades. All I wanted was to be a part of it, if only for a little while. My travel partners clearly agreed. Content to sip homemade *limoncello* and chat with the locals over *antipasti*, we had all the understanding we required.

The following day, we came, we saw, and we conquered Rome's attractions. We ate gelato with a view of the Colosseum, and took a tour led by a knowledgeable Kiwi art student named Kim. Her stories, which shed light on centuries of history, silenced us. She told us that construction began in A.D. 72 and the building held up to fifty thousand people. It is, in a word, magnificent. From the upper level, we could see the remains of the pit area and I imagined the terrified Christians running for their lives.

Kim continued, explaining in graphic detail the various exhibitions and games held in the ancient Colosseum. I admit to being shocked by the blood thirst of the Romans. You don't learn world history without tales of the French guillotine or English public hangings as entertainment for the masses, but aside from native tribes in Central and South America, this was my first vision of death as spectator sport. If I'd been forced to witness such games in the flesh, someone would have had to collect me from the *vomitorium*, housed in the lower level of the building.

Leaving the Colosseum, I was lost in thought while walking. With the ominous landmark at our backs, a variety of sidewalk artists displayed their colorful works on the sidewalk. I was looking at a pretty pastel watercolor when I noticed a smiling, sculpted Gladiator walking straight toward me. I have no idea how I missed this, but there were many. They hunted for tourists who wanted their photo taken outside the Colosseum with a real-life gladiator. While the idea was abhorrent, the looks on this guy and his bronzed biceps were enough to make me think twice. Retreating from him, I slowly caught up with the others and heard Kim talking about the Forum.

When we got there, I wondered what all the fuss was about. In contrast to the Colosseum, it's a couple of crumbling stone walls. That was before I heard the story of its discovery. The Forum was the center of political and commercial life in Ancient Rome, and the very stones we walked on were once the regular route of Julius Caesar. Eventually, the growing city populace demanded a newer and grander Forum be built to replace the original one in 46 B.C. Over time, the previous grounds were abandoned and eventually became a grazing field for cattle. It was not until the nineteenth century that archaeologists discovered the ruins of the old Forum, completely by accident, and began excavation. The poor farmer must have gotten quite a shock!

Sight-seeing behind us, we sat philosophizing over plates of ravioli and linguine seated at an outside table in the Campo dei Fiori. We were reeling with the discoveries of the day and allowing time for history to sink in. The tales of Rome are worthy of far more than a quick read of a museum panels or a few hours' tour. Rome grabs hold and refuses to let go. You are a different person and your previous perspective ceases exist.

This was especially true later that evening when I dragged Dora to a nearby café where I could call David from my mobile phone. I didn't want to sit alone at night, nor did I want to have a private conversation in the apartment. I wanted her opinion on whether I should do it or not—typical female over-analysis. My partner in crime came through again with her support, even creeping away when I reached him so that I could talk in private. David sounded pleased—and surprised—to hear from me. During our long conversation that night, he told me that his live-in girlfriend was now looking for a new home. I couldn't wipe the smile off my face for days.

Dora and her friend left the following morning to fly further south, but I needed one more Roman day. I still hadn't decided what to do after Germany and my European days were numbered. Every day counted. For my last night, I moved out of the suffocating apartment and into a modern hotel close to the Forum. The chic exterior looked perfect, complete with a rooftop bar-restaurant overlooking the Forum grounds. After checking in, I went for a walk about town to look at the sites I'd missed in the days prior.

Lost in my own world, I happily strolled along and took a few million photos. I didn't think much about it when a local approached me and attempted to strike up a conversation. When it happened twice more in quick succession, I couldn't ignore it. *What the hell?* This never happened when I was with the other girls. Why was I suddenly being pestered this way? The third time around, the scowl on my face should have been a clue that I was a woman to be avoided, but that didn't deter these guys. I need to learn Italian for "persistent." Escaping through the sliding glass doors of the hotel to change clothes for dinner was a relief, and not because of the air-conditioning.

Unable to bear the thought of wasting my last night in Rome in a claustrophobic hotel room, I took a cab to the Piazza Navona instead of walking. Our initial stop there had been perfect and I knew it would be the same again, loaded with tourists. It never occurred to me that I wouldn't be able to eat a simple dinner, people watch, and enjoy the evening undisturbed.

When I arrived, the scene was as expected, teeming with red faced, tennis shoe clad tourists and a carnival-like atmosphere, complete with artists and street performers. I chose an upscale restaurant for my Last Supper and piled my tour books on the table. At first, everything was fine. Sipping my pinot grigio, I was engrossed in a description of the Vatican, where we hadn't spent enough time, and marking what I wanted to see on my next visit. I was sure that there would be a next visit.

As usual, I was friendly to the waiters and I practiced my *per piacere*s and *grazie*s. I always wore a smile because I was in Italy after all, but that was the extent of my flirtatiousness. I would proudly admit it if I'd been flirting with anyone interesting, but that was not to be on this particular evening. After I'd been served and continued to sit and read, I felt the penetrating stares of the male wait staff, who all seemed to be looking at me and not in a nice way. Unnerved, I racked my brain for anything inappropriate I could have done or said, but there was nothing. I especially didn't like the looks of the greasy older one who appeared to be the Top Dog waiter.

Finally, Signore Top Dog couldn't stand it anymore. He approached my table and stood next to it, looking at me but saying nothing, as if I owed him an explanation for something.

"Can I help you?" I said, irritated.

"*Why?*" he demanded.

"Why *what*?"

Eyes widening, full of indignation, he practically spit at me saying, "Why are you *alone*?" as if it were a criminal tendency.

The Devil Wears Clogs

It was madness. Here I was, a modestly-dressed American tourist with a mammoth *Fodor's Italy* guide on the table, and he was accusing me of sinister motives? Where was the TV camera? This had to be a joke.

Anger flew from my mouth, "Because I *choose* to be." Well, you should have seen him then. Apparently I'd already treaded on thin ice by enjoying a pleasant evening unaccompanied, and he wasn't about to let it pass. He said nothing but his demeanor said it all as he stormed off. In the background, there was a waiter conference going on with a great deal of hand gesturing in my general direction. I signaled for the bill—no *per piacere* and no *grazie* this time.

Catching a taxi back to the hotel was easy, but I was pissed. The evening was still young and I didn't understand why I was expected to follow the local code of conduct when a) I didn't know what it was and b) I was not a local! The only thing I could imagine is that they thought I was a prostitute, a woman on the hunt for paid company.

The next morning, I packed my bag and went to the rooftop restaurant for breakfast. Under the fluttering navy-blue umbrella in the bright morning light, the events of the previous night seemed like a distant dream. Frankly, it's impossible to be unhappy while looking out over the immensity of Rome. The trials and tribulations of centuries of human experience lurk at every turn, and it's absurd to feel that yours are anything but insignificant. Rather than hold onto the unkind behavior of people I'd never set eyes upon again, I savored the creamy froth of my cappuccino and counted myself lucky to be made anew by the Roman experience.

CHAPTER 11
FIRST DATE

When I got back from Rome, it was difficult to focus. Those four days had strengthened my resolve not to return to the United States. At work, I had to give 100% because my illusions of career support from Matt had evaporated. The next step was up to me. I searched for ways to continue working in Germany in a different capacity, and kept my ear to the ground for any staffing needs at international projects. My final assignment on the software implementation strategy was evolving into work I was proud of, and my confidence that I could stand on my own professional merit increased.

With the coast clear of his now *ex*-girlfriend, David and I spoke frequently. We had a lot to learn about one another. For hours, we laughed and joked over the phone while I lay on my bed in the shoebox. We explored each other's likes and dislikes. I learned that he wasn't an avid traveler and that he was four years my junior. We made plans to see each other again since his home was only a four-hour drive from Heidelberg. He was so open and funny that I felt the door of hope open a crack. I respected the fact that while he was involved with someone else, he made no moves in my direction. Despite confusing the hell out of me in the process, he had done the honorable thing by someone who was once very important to him and that counted. After my Swedish nightmare, that counted a great deal.

The only obstacle to our next rendezvous was time off. My frequent gallivanting didn't leave me much vacation time. He, on the other hand, seemed to have been stockpiling his for decades.

"Why don't we go to Venice?" he blurted out one night.

"I can't. I don't have enough time off," was my brilliant knee-jerk reaction.

I was about to learn one more thing about David—he rarely took no for an answer. For him, being un-coupled meant he was also unstoppable. My second excuse also went down in flames. When I claimed I didn't have the money for the plane ticket, his reply was, "No problem. I'll come to Heidelberg and pick you up. We can drive." *Drive?* To *Italy?* Eight hours in the car with a near total stranger? My head was spinning and I remained non-committal. I had to be out of my mind to even consider it, and the discussion of one hotel room or two hadn't even come up yet!

Despite my complete shock at the bold suggestion, my gut said, "*GO!*" I had always retreated from intimacy, hiding behind the excuse of ambitious career goals. Things had changed. I was exactly where I wanted to be. Telling myself that a relationship would throw a wrench into my professional plans would turn hiding into lying. Of course I was apprehensive about protecting my heart from taking another beating, but I had to admit that I was actually living. The feeling of joy and even the soul-crushing lows were a hell of a lot more exciting than playing it safe.

Knowing it was well past time for a different approach, I said yes. I also said we could share a room. Hey, hotel rooms in Europe are expensive! It goes without saying that we were both feeling the same mix of nervous excitement. Being the one with more free time, David took on the planning. He found a hotel in a perfect location and plotted the quickest route. All I did was try to get a reasonable amount of work done before he arrived in Heidelberg on September 11, 2002. Regardless of my distance from Ground Zero, I found it ironic to be on the cusp of such happiness exactly one year from the event that pushed me into making the decision to go abroad.

David came to Heidelberg the night before we left for Italy. We were definitely going *out* for dinner. Cooking and entertaining at my tiny apartment was not an option, but I did ask if he wanted to stay that night to save the cost of a hotel room. If we were going to be spending five nights in one Venetian hotel room, what was the point of throwing up boundaries the first night? It seemed old-fashioned. I told David I'd be glad to have him over as long as he didn't snore. Without missing a beat, he assured me that he didn't.

Despite hours spent on the phone and several meetings in recent months, his imminent arrival frazzled my nerves. Pulse racing, I changed clothes at least four times before David called to say he'd left the autobahn and would be in parking garage next to my place within fifteen minutes. I hastily explained where to meet me and continued running around my place tidying up things that didn't need to be tidied. Already late, I ran around the corner to the square to find David sitting patiently on the designated park bench. Breathless, I welcomed him to Germany. After saying hello, the first thing he did was point out the small hole in the neck of my brand new black top. I was wearing the shirt for the first time and never saw it. *Great.*

My nerves quieted in parallel with my wine intake as the evening progressed. Oddly, the conversation was more strained than during our many late night phone calls. I guess I should have expected a little awkwardness due to the unorthodox way we were getting to know each other.

The more time I spent with David, the more I was struck by just how *nice* he was. I know that no man wants to be described as "nice," but that's exactly what he was. He went out of his way to make things easier, and, for me, that was new. He wasn't big on feelings, not from the very beginning. Instead, you would call him a man of action. David was the personification of the expression "actions speak louder than words." I smiled to myself the next day at work when I grabbed my phone to call him and his name had been changed to Mr. Nice Guy in the directory.

As the German countryside flew by the next day, we talked about European life. I learned a lot from David. We discussed the difference between Dutch people and Germans and I touched a nerve when I uncovered the intense dislike of Germans by the Dutch. At first, I wrote it off as similar to Americans making Canadians the butt of many jokes before I realized there was more to it. Many Dutch go out of their way to avoid Germans, because of the terrible treatment Dutch citizens received at their hands during the occupation of Holland in World War II. Again, I was flabbergasted that something I only understood through history books was still daily reality for Europeans. I knew about the German invasion, but I'd never read about their brutal retaliation for Dutch resistance. Embarrassed by my ignorance, I remembered to keep quiet and listen.

After more conversation in a similar vein, I decided it was my duty to lighten the mood. I told David that, for me, two things were clear about Germans. First, their sense of humor was non-existent. The things that made them laugh out loud were a total mystery to me. Sarcasm was a way of life for as long as I could remember. Not cracking a joke in the office for the past year had nearly killed me. Well-versed in the smart-ass approach to life, David could relate.

Secondly, German men seemed extremely sexually repressed, or at the very least, painfully shy about admiring women. While I didn't think I was Marilyn Monroe, I was used to a few glances in my direction. Germany had turned me into the Invisible Woman. David laughed. The only reason I'd even mentioned it is because I was so relieved when in the Netherlands or Italy, I actually attracted attention. Granted, it wasn't always the type of attention I wanted, but I was noticed.

I told David a story I'd read online about my German workplace. It is a massive organization, with eighty thousand employees, the majority of whom are men. An American female software developer who had worked at the German headquarters had written on a web page about the potential for finding relationships there. Her exact words were, "The odds are good, but the goods are odd." He found that very funny. Software developers are not known for their social prowess.

* * *

Despite the distance, the ride to Italy passed quickly. We drove into the city at dusk, just after 8 p.m. The sidewalks thrummed with people as we turned into the long-term parking garage. Silently, I marveled at David's maneuvering abilities in the extremely tight Italian parking spot. The city's medieval center is a pedestrian zone, so we unloaded our bags and rolled them over to the dock. We found the boat marked "82," which carried us on the ten minute ride across the Venice's Grand

The Devil Wears Clogs

Canal.

Arriving on the opposite side of the canal, I was immediately grateful that David was commandeering this journey. Streetlights must be pricey in Italy because they were few and far between. The winding pathways were a cryptic code I could not decipher, but Captain David fearlessly led the way to our hotel in record time. He even had the wherewithal to help out fellow stragglers along the way, while I felt like I'd been walking in circles.

The animated concierge at Hotel Scandinavia greeted us cheerfully, as I noticed several colorful bright Murano chandeliers hanging from the ceiling. He checked us in and told us how pleased he was to have us as guests. He then whispered in a conspiratorial tone that he had something *special* to offer: two available seats on the next day's cruise to Murano Island. Our new friend just knew we would be interested in this free opportunity to see the glass factory and was thrilled to offer it. We looked at each other, knowing it was imperative to think fast. David acted apologetic and told the concierge we had too little time in Venice due to our short visit. Just like that, we were free of the net about to fall from above to seize the tourists. The concierge smiled patiently through pursed lips, as if to say that we didn't know what we were missing and reluctantly handed over our room key.

We were not exactly shocked to discover another "beautiful" Murano chandelier hanging from our room's ceiling. It didn't take a rocket scientist to figure out that the glass factory tour would be more like a hostage situation, unless you coughed up enough cash in the form of glassware to buy yourself a trip back to the main island. I unpacked my pj's and went into the bathroom to change and brush my teeth. He did the same. We kissed goodnight and fell asleep side-by-side, still giggling over our narrow escape downstairs.

The next morning, I received my first lesson on cultural difference. Waking up, I would have been perfectly happy to put on the clothes closest at hand, brush my teeth and my hair into a ponytail to go down to breakfast, leaving my shower until after we had eaten. David was having nothing to do with that. Europeans *must* shower, shave, and put on the proper appearance. Later I learned this was true regardless of whether it's the office, the gym, or the corner store. Americans have different rules for different destinations. In my townhouse, I remember passing entire weekends watching movies back to back and never seeing the inside of my shower. Quick trips to the grocery store only required that you were indeed wearing clothes.

I've never been known as a morning person and this cultural enlightenment didn't help to convert me. There wasn't much time for debate before the breakfast hour ended, so grudgingly, I showered and dressed. Being the one with the least amount of available information on such matters, I gave in. Having my normal behavior put on trial and "guilty" verdict rendered, did not endear David to me that morning.

Breakfast ordeal over, we went directly to Piazza San Marco. On my previous visit to St. Mark's Square, a giant scaffold covered part of the Palazzo Ducale, and the gold-domed *basilica*. I remembered how disappointing it was not to be able to see the whole structure at fourteen. Seventeen years later, the golden dome sparkled in the bright Italian sun and nothing obscured our magnificent view. David grabbed my hand and we crossed the square. My irritation was forgotten.

It was mid-September and there were long queues to enter these unbelievable examples of Byzantine architecture. To be fair, I don't think a calendar month exists when Venice isn't throbbing with tourists. It is one of the European treasures that everyone wants a piece of.

Even the Japanese tourist whom I watched from my place in line for the Palace could not contain his enthusiasm. He stood in the center of the piazza, arms outstretched, covered with pigeons. By "covered," I mean that every available inch of both arms and the top of his head had a bird on it.

I would have been mortified because I find pigeons disgusting, but the Japanese guy was having the time of his life. He found it hilarious, laughing the whole time, as his fumbling companion tried to take a photo. I watched him, thinking about how many kinds of people it takes to make the world to go 'round. Even though I searched my surroundings for any lurking pigeons with similar ideas, I maintain the mantra "to each his own."

David and I slowly climbed the narrow stone staircases to get a view of the sparkling Adriatic. We took a ridiculous amount of photos of the Bridge of Sighs, and read stories of prisoners who passed this way after being sentenced in the Doge's Palace court. We wandered further to the Rialto Bridge and its cluster of merchants. After hours of fighting the crowds, it was time for a breather.

In need of cold drinks and comfortable seats, we snaked our way through the maze back to Piazza San Marco. There, in the center of the square, was a sophisticated café complete with an outdoor grand piano player. It was perfect for wine drinking and people watching. We drank glasses of crisp, fruity pinot grigio and devoured plump green olives while listening to the romantic notes drift across the square. It couldn't have been more picturesque. Then, the bill arrived.

The food and wine were not expensive, we were in the land of wine and olives. The last item appeared on the bill was the kicker. We were expected to pay twelve euro for the music we heard in the ninety minutes we sat at the café. I was appalled. While I had the money, it was the principle of the matter that disturbed me. David didn't appear shocked and didn't make much noise about it. I didn't either, until we left. I was thoroughly annoyed by this "tourist tax," and the gall of these Italians. I was still ranting when we saw the Bridge of Sighs again for the seventh or eighth time and realized we were lost. David used his rant-stopping tactic on me for the first time that day. He grabbed me tightly and kissed me hard. When I still tried to talk, he kissed harder and kept my mouth covered. It worked.

That evening, we searched high and low for an intimate candlelit Italian restaurant to have dinner in. It was weird. Every restaurant we passed was extremely well-lit. Wasn't this the capital of Romance? The search went on for nearly an hour until hunger won. We gave up and entered a restaurant that looked charming, despite the glaring searchlights on the ceiling. Picking up his camera, David took embarrassingly extreme close-ups of me in that restaurant and soon we forgot all about the lights. We devoured our *primi* and *segundi piatti* and walked home to a good night's sleep.

Showering the next morning (yes, *before* breakfast), I realized I'd gotten very used to doing everything solo. The more unpleasant part of that realization was that having someone constantly by my side was irritating. After making the adjustment to independent traveling, the constant companionship consumed a great deal of energy, especially after a few days. We were leaving Venice the following day, and I wanted to do a little shopping before leaving.

For me, shopping is a solo sport. I plan and execute strategic missions to get what I want and usually I'm not looking for a second opinion. I mentioned to David that I wanted to spend some time in the shops around Piazza San Marco to look for a new backpack, and asked if we could meet up in a few hours. He seemed annoyed by the idea, but didn't say why. Puzzled, I asked what the problem was and again got no reply. He insisted on joining me. I was not pleased. No one was going to tell me what I could or couldn't do. Still, I relented. We had to spend eight hours together in the car the next day and I was no mood for arguing.

We had a good time on the trip, but differences of opinion and preference caught me off guard. After initially getting along so well, I expected this to be a piece of *torta*. Reality proved different. I brought up shopping alone because I'd already had enough of his opinions on everything I had admired in shop windows. "You *like* that?" he'd said more than once when I stopped to look at something that caught my eye in a boutique window.

I don't know why I didn't say, "Yes I do, and what's it to you?" I just shrugged and said nothing.

In my scarce moments alone, I recalled a conversation between Dora and I in Rome. Walking along a city street, the Italians in front of us were walking so impossibly slow that I couldn't help but remark that they were "Sunday walkers." Only it wasn't Sunday and we had a tour to catch.

Thinking about cultural differences in general, I asked Dora if she thought people of different nationalities could have a great relationship. By then, I had begun to see that cultural roots run deep and often seemed set in stone. Differences between two cultures cannot be easily be challenged or changed. The conversation stuck in my mind during the days with David in Venice. Dora and I both thought that yes, it could work, but it would be much harder than having a partner from your own country. There is much more immediate common ground when you date someone from the same nation. It seemed to me that an awful lot of explaining, not to mention patience, was necessary in a dual-nationality relationship. I have never been long on patience.

These thoughts were tucked securely in the back of my mind, when David and I set out on my mission of finding a backpack. Fine Italian leather is considerably less expensive at the source. My beaten-up backpack had taken a lot of abuse and wasn't pickpocket-proof. It was time to upgrade.

Entering a small leather boutique that I'd been eyeing for days, I inquired about prices. David stood in the background turning up his nose at my selections. Finally, I had reached the end of my rope and threw an angry glare in his direction. His eyes widened, but he said nothing.

"Unless you are planning to carry the bag yourself, your opinion isn't necessary!" I whispered harshly, frustrated by the crowd and the heat. Satisfied that my message was received, I went back to business and purchased a soft black-leather bag. David sulked.

We left the store in silence. I didn't care to analyze what happened and we both wanted to ignore it. There were "must see" items left on our Venetian tourist list, so David suggested that we take a *vaporetto* to San Giorgio Maggiore. The tiny island, visible from the main island and St. Mark's Square, is home to a church dating back to 1566 where Tintoretto's *The Last Supper* resides. The bell tower looms high above the island like a sentry on duty, and we'd both been itching to climb it since we first spotted it.

My tension began to melt the moment I stepped off the boat. San Giorgio is the polar opposite of teeming St. Mark's Square. Only twenty or thirty people were visible compared to the hundreds in the central piazza. I filled my lungs with sea air and we headed for the bell tower. At the viewing platform, we stepped into the best view Venice had delivered so far. Mercifully, we were alone on the top level of the tower, so we lingered to watch the boat traffic on the Grand Canal and the sparkling dome of St. Mark's under a cloudless blue sky. Gentle sea breezes cooled us through the openings on the small tower landing, and it felt remarkably better than being trapped in endless crowds and queues. I must have taken fifty photos of that view, to remember it forever. David had been smart enough to read the posted times for the ringing of the tower's enormous brass bell. He grabbed my hand to make a mad dash and escape the noise, which would surely be deafening. I didn't want to leave the peace and tranquility of the small island once the bell's vibration diminished.

We sat at the water's edge for a short rest before moving on. My emotions were in turmoil. Here was this man, a.k.a. Mr. Nice Guy, who now appeared to be judging my every move and clinging to my side. I sat thinking about the parts of myself that I'd kept hidden, and wondered whether I'd ever be able to be completely honest with another person. I wanted to. I wanted so much to have the experience of a loving relationship, but I didn't know how I didn't trust my instincts anymore. Every one of my previous relationships had either been superficial or too controlling for my liking. I had to leave those things in the past, no matter what happened next.

David read the troubled thoughts in my eyes and asked what I was thinking. I was evasive. I felt like, the "real me" wasn't worth showing. I watched speedboats cut swaths in the aqua sea and held onto my silence. A few minutes later, I signaled I was ready to go by standing up.

The last night in Venice, we managed (finally!) to find the quintessential romantic restaurant. It was perched at the side of a canal, further from the tourist madhouse we'd spent most of our time in. Here, we feasted on mouth-watering *antipasti* and tangy lemon *scallopini* with capers. We drank Chianti by candlelight and watched the locals come and go. A stylish gent arrived via private gondola, extending his hand to assist a tall beautiful brunette step up from the boat. As they glided into the restaurant arm in arm, the gondola sped off to await its call to return. Admiring the Bond-like entrance, I envisioned romantic evening walks from their villa under starry skies and waiting jets that carried them swiftly across the globe.

The last item on our To Do list was our own gondola ride. Friends and colleagues had offered advice on how to get the best deal and we tried to bargain with the gondoliers until the moon lit the sky. It wasn't very romantic after such a lovely dinner and I was ready to walk away from the idea. As usual, David thought differently. Finally, sensing that I was about ready to bolt like skittish colt, he made a deal. We clumsily boarded the sleek black Venetian gondola trimmed with gold and sat on plush scarlet seats. To me, riding under the cover of darkness is far more appealing than in the glaring light of day. Mornings and afternoons, the Grand Canal is a super-highway of activity. We'd even spotted a speedboat full of fire fighters careening through dangerous blind turns to get to its emergency.

The dark nighttime waterways take on an air of mystery with few streetlights to destroy the illusion. Swiftly and silently, our gondola glided beneath the Rialto Bridge and the Bridge of Sighs, amongst several others. We paid the gondolier *not* to sing but David, was overcome with romance. He kissed me and held on to me as we watched the dramatic scenery float by. The feeling wasn't mutual. It just wasn't there. Back at the dock, I was halfway off the boat when David and the gondolier called me back for a photo in the boat. The awkward result is a great reminder of my impatience to get away.

Back at the hotel, we could no longer avoid a discussion about "feelings." David said that he'd expected us to fall madly in love on this trip and was confused that it hadn't happened. His words were blunt, but his handsome face revealed genuine concern. I said I had the feeling things weren't going to work out between us, but didn't elaborate, in hopes of ending the conversation. David pressed me to explain me why I looked so sad sitting at the waterfront at San Giorgio.

All the possible reasons I could give went through my mind, but I couldn't get any words out. I said it was nothing, but he refused to let it go, so I got up and left. I went into the bathroom and closed the door. Finally alone, I started to cry. A tidal wave of emotion overwhelmed me and soon I was sitting on the cold marble floor bawling like a two-year-old. I made so much noise that I never heard the door open. When I felt David's arms wrap around me, I was shocked. Never in my life had I broken down like this, let alone in front of someone. I was mortified to be seen like this. He didn't say a word. He just lifted me up and led me back into the bedroom where he continued to hold me for as long as I let him. It was the kindest thing any man had ever done. I was so physically exhausted that I fell asleep in his arms–only after apologizing several times for being a mess.

Confusion was king the next day. We'd rationally discussed that we were not a match, but my emotional outburst was impossible without a feeling of safety and security about what was going on between us. True to my usual *modus operandi*, I remained tight-lipped. We were both determined to keep the mood light on the long drive home. Silently, I made up fairytales based on the picturesque scenery of Italy and Switzerland. Each one had a happy ending.

David didn't stay in Heidelberg. He opted to continue to Holland after dropping me off. We said our farewells without much emotion and I walked up the Donkey Path to my four silent walls. Inside, I was deflated. My hopes for this relationship had been so high, but the trip had left me feeling broken. I declared myself too damaged for David.

Who wants to be around someone who can't stop weeping in one of the world's most beautiful cities? I didn't know exactly what made me break down, but I suspected it was the realization that David was, once again, not the man for me.

How much further would I have to go to find him?

CHAPTER 12
TICK TOCK

After Venice, I had to face how little time I had left in Europe. It was the middle of September, which gave me three weeks at most. Having made networking in the global software community a priority along with several trips to the Netherlands, I had earned a credible reputation in our Amsterdam office. I kept in constant contact with two Dutch executives interested in hiring me onto their projects. While September rolled mercilessly on, I put the polishing touches on my masterpiece of technical documentation and followed up with everyone I could think of that was in a position to help.

My unique position in Germany allowed me access to a great deal more information about current deals than the majority of my colleagues. In my eagerness to help one of the Dutch executives, who promised me a role on his project in return, I spilled too much confidential information without realizing it, and infuriated Hanna. It was a dangerous game to be playing. My firm and a competitor were in a bidding war for a multi-million dollar software project, and any indication of impropriety or bias towards one of the bidding parties would result in a smear to the Germans' reputation and possible legal action.

It was not easy showing my face in our shared office in the days following my indiscretion, but thankfully Hanna knew the person I was dealing with, and she also knew I was desperate to stay in Europe. Hanna, though some team members called her a "diva" because she was beautiful and had office romances, was nobody's fool. She deduced, well before I did, that I was being manipulated. To my great relief, it didn't permanently damage our relationship. Strangely, it served to strengthen the bond as two women looking out for one another. What I had revealed wasn't serious enough to impact the ongoing negotiations, so no harm was done. I would have been devastated to cause problems for someone I liked and admired.

Not long after this drama played out, I received a call from a Dutch female manager named Dafne. She was leading a large software implementation at a waste management company in Holland and was looking for staff on a sub-project with one of their subordinate companies. She called to ask if I wanted to be part of the project team for three months in Amsterdam. *Interested?* My bags were mentally packed in an instant. Despite my dubious dealings with two of her male colleagues, I liked the Dutch team and already knew several people there. After one more phone call to discuss the role itself, I happily accepted the new assignment.

Hanna did not hide her feelings upon hearing I was moving to Holland. In her less than subtle way, she told me what the Dutch were like. Her impression was that the Dutch enjoyed preaching about their tolerance as a nation, but the truth was that they preferred to remain ignorant when it came to controversial topics. Having no real experience with the cultures outside of Germany, I didn't get the message. She didn't criticize the entire Dutch population, but she did tell me to watch my back.

As a farewell present, Hanna gave me a book with stories about Dutch character and history. After learning so much from watching her deftly handle international crowds with grace and intelligence, I was sad to be leaving my office-mate and cultural mentor. Hanna had traveled more and had a different way of looking at things than most Germans. I would miss her frank sense of humor. I knew we would stay friends, but it would never be the same as sharing our Walldorf office. Along with Dora, she was one of the few people I had come to trust in the past year.

I agreed with Dafne that I would start in the beginning of October, so there was time left to enjoy Germany. When I'd arrived, my new U.S. colleagues couldn't stop talking about Munich's Oktoberfest. Since the event, one of the world's largest parties, begins in the end of September,

The Devil Wears Clogs

I'd just missed it in 2001. That made me determined to get there in 2002. I convinced my friend from back home, Allison, to come over and join me. Her arm didn't need twisting. Allison ranks in first place on my list of travel buddies. She is easygoing and will go almost anywhere. She was the perfect partner for this escapade.

Allison arrived in Heidelberg two days before we left for Munich. This was her third trip to Germany, so she was familiar with the people, customs, and dearth of service. I was always grateful for a visit from Allison. With her around, I not only had the company of a good friend, but I had a visitor savvy enough to find her own way. I didn't have to explain every little thing or create itineraries while she was visiting because she usually knew exactly what she wanted to do before she landed.

The wintry blast that greeted us on the train platform was a newsflash that Munich was much colder than expected. Survival required a trip to a nearby department store: scarves and gloves weren't optional. Regardless of how many German photos I've seen, I simply didn't expect to see people walking through the city streets in *lederhosen*. Nor did I expect to see people paying hundreds of euro for these traditional costumes, no matter how elaborate they are. I wasn't about to show off my legs or my cleavage in this weather, and I didn't think Allison was either. I bought a blanket-sized black-wool scarf the size of a small country to keep the chill to a minimum while Allison found the gloves she was looking for.

Munich during Oktoberfest is like New Orleans at Mardi Gras. It's a carnival atmosphere far bigger than any I've seen. Enormous beer tents for the largest German breweries are set up on the Theresienwiese, which covers 420,000 square meters of open space. Six million beer enthusiasts invade the city for these two weeks every year.

The tents reach maximum capacity well before noon and visitors must brave the outdoor elements, fingers crossed, for a rare chance to enter without a table reservation. Tables are often booked out a year in advance. In 2002, it hardly ever stopped raining for more than an hour during our three days in Munich. We arrived at the festival on a Thursday afternoon, not knowing how lucky we were to find open tables at the Paulaner tent, known as *the* party tent.

Entering just after noon, the first thing that struck me was the number of older Germans, people who could be your *oma* or *opa*, knocking back huge beers inside the tent. I don't know why I was surprised, I just didn't picture it that way. Then again, I hadn't pictured anything like this.

We quickly found two open seats in the middle of a large table and ordered two overflowing steins of beer. The alcohol content in most German beer is between 6 and 8%, twice the average of American beer. To someone who doesn't drink much beer, these tiny numbers probably don't seem significant. If you are one of those people, trust me, the numbers are *very* significant.

It wasn't long before Allison started chatting up our German tablemates using her high school German and, after a few more beers, we were all swearing to be friends for life. The toasting mantra was "*Ein, zwei, drei, zupaaaaaaaah!*" which loosely translates into "One, two, three super!" Simple, yet profound. It can't be a long toast because those thick glass steins weigh over a pound each. Only a body-builder or a German opa could keep his arm held high while a drunken buddy pontificates.

Add to the picture the *oompah* band on a giant raised center stage playing *Take Me Home, Country Road* by John Denver, and you have a slight glimpse of the surreal situation. It got even better when a tiny lederhosen-clad German put the moves on Allison. His appearance alone had us in tears, never mind that by this point we couldn't understand a word of what he was saying. All I could think of was an old movie comedy I'd once seen where the dashing main character rushes in to save the damsel in distress in Germany, and says, "Wait! I know a little German! He's standing right over there!" and then points to a dwarf in lederhosen who does a little bow and tips his felt feathered cap to the lady. It's a good thing the man in pursuit of my height-challenged friend was also very drunk, because he just laughed right along with us.

No question, our Oktoberfest experience was awesome. We laughed until we cried and made new friends from every corner of the world. Everyone should try out this circus as least once. In fact, David had originally planned to come with us, but got stuck working the weekend instead. He and I had remained friendly after our not-very-romantic trip to Venice, and I was disappointed he wasn't there. I felt robbed of the opportunity to find out if any spark was left. Regardless, we bravely carried on having the time of our lives and wondered why we hadn't made this trip sooner.

When we returned to the beer tents on Friday, the pandemonium level had gone up several notches. The crowd had grown exponentially with the advent of the weekend and that led to a much more frenzied atmosphere. We were relieved to get back into the Paulaner tent because all ten others were packed to the rafters. We managed to squeeze into the standing area in front of the band. Squished as we were, it was still fun to be part of it all. We managed to put down several more steins and lasted a few more hours.

One good thing about this crowd was that it was friendly. In the United States, with the combination of this much alcohol and this many people, someone always gets aggressive and starts a fight. I never saw that at Oktoberfest, not once. The crowd was very friendly, but the down side was that, as the day wore on, men became way too friendly. We had to push through the crowd to get to the restrooms. It became so bad that Allison and I took one of the guys every time we went because of all the inappropriate grabbing we experienced. We still had fun, but I was relieved leave the tent behind once we'd had our fill. I later read that there had been eleven reports of rape that year at the festival. That's the side of Oktoberfest that no one ever talks about.

All things considered, it was quite an experience. We spent the rest of our time trying to see the sights of Munich, but the bone-chilling rain didn't add much appeal. When Saturday afternoon arrived, Allison and I were happy to re-board the train to Heidelberg. By then, all we wanted was to get warm, dry, and catch up on some much needed sleep.

* * *

The shrill ring of my phone rudely pulled us from dreamland the next morning. Who the hell was calling me so early on a Sunday? Finally, after turning over the contents of my entire apartment to stop the infernal ringing, I found it. The voice on the other end was none other than Mr. Nice Guy himself. I thought I must be dreaming when he said he was on his way to Heidelberg. *What the*? I made David repeat himself to be sure that he was in fact speaking English, and I'd heard what I thought I heard. It defied reason that my not-quite-but-maybe-boyfriend was on his way to my house after I'd spent the last three days swimming in beer. I grabbed a mirror and was properly horrified at the face that looked back. Bed-head and streaked mascara do not make for a good look upon the imminent arrival of your White Knight.

Breathe. I told myself. *Just breathe.* "Oka-ay," I heard myself say, "How long will it be before you reach Heidelberg?" (Read: "How long do I have to make myself look presentable?")

"I'll be there in about an hour. Is that all right with you?" he wanted to know.

Maybe I'm mistaken, but isn't it a little *late* to be asking? "Umm. Yeah. I mean, umm fine. What do you want to do? Allison is here too, and we're kind of tired after the crazy weekend." How do you tell someone, who has already driven three hours specifically to see you, to *turn the hell around*?

"We can have lunch somewhere?"

"All right, sure, I'll figure something out. Let me know when you're here."

"See you soon." "Right, bye."

"Ho-ly shhhhhiiiiiiiiiiiiiiiiiit!! Allison, get up! We have to move fast!" I yelled at my poor tired friend, pushing her into the bathroom.

So that's how my next "date" with David began. He must have left Holland by 8 a.m. Later, I asked him what he'd been thinking, and he confessed that he'd called me only when he was fairly close because he knew I would not tell him not to come. That's when I realized this guy was too smart for his own good.

Allison already knew the David story, the Swedish tale before him, and the extravaganzas of fun known as my "past." Given the state we were in, she was surprisingly enthusiastic about the last-minute lunch date. If he was being that pushy and she was that interested in having lunch with a guy she never met, I realized that I must be showing symptoms of ... well, *like* where David was concerned.

Around the corner from my shoebox was a lovely little Italian restaurant with an outdoor terrace. I was fretting over about how the three of us would get along, but it was pointless. After hearing only one or two comments from David, Allison remarked, "I like him! I didn't know he was fluent in sarcasm!" And that was that. Pasta was served and laughs came easily. My new friend and my old friend were on their best behavior. That alone should have tipped me off that there would be more to this story.

David stayed all afternoon and even offered to transport my fragile possessions to Holland. The movers were coming within a week and he had room at his place for the things I didn't want them to handle. We said our good-byes and agreed to talk later in the week about meeting in Holland. I felt something I hadn't felt the other times we parted. My heart stirred in a way that was new. Allison grinned like the cat that ate the canary.

The last week in Germany was a blur of good-byes and to-dos. I've always been much better at the latter than the former. I hate saying goodbye. I always feel like I'm leaving things unsaid. Every time, something prevents me from uttering the important words. I was relieved to be leaving the rigid German ways behind and the adventure that lay before me was exciting, but I couldn't shake the feeling that I was leaving something behind in Heidelberg. It could easily have been bit of my heart or a sliver of my soul.

I was a different person after living in that city with those friends, in my tiny shoebox underneath the schloss. I knew I'd never be the same again.

CHAPTER 13
GOEIEMORGEN ALLEMAAL

Even as I write these words, I wonder how I didn't know better. As planned, I spoke to David before my arrival, and he pointed me in the direction of a convenient hotel, twenty minutes from his place. He also said that the distance between the Amsterdam airport and Utrecht was only thirty minutes by car. Having a friend nearby made Utrecht an attractive home base, but I should have known what to expect when arriving in a place where people don't speak English, and they speak Greek for all you can understand. Yes, I should have known that the Netherlands might as well have been a different planet.

Dafne had denied my request of a rental car in Amsterdam, claiming it was unnecessary, because Holland has such wonderful public transport. I didn't question this, I just assumed that was what all the other consultants did. So, arriving at Schiphol Airport with two huge bags, I had to find a taxi to take me to Utrecht.

Finding a taxi wasn't the issue. There were plenty. The amount on the meter when I arrived at my hotel was. For a thirty-minute ride, I was to pay the driver over one hundred euro! I couldn't believe I was paying U.S. $125 for a ride that would cost me less than half of that in New York City. Knowing the driver wouldn't have understood me had I complained, I paid the man and got out.

My next challenge was the grumpy hotel desk clerk. He spoke no English, unlike most hotel staff in Amsterdam, nor was he inclined to be accommodating. Had I not been part of a large international company, he would have kicked me to the curb. At least, that was the impression he gave me. I wasn't even asking for anything besides a room that I planned on paying for. Note to self: if you want to keep a roof over your head, no special requests.

When he finally handed me a key, I found my way to the proper room and shoved my ridiculously-fat suitcases inside. God forbid I ask for any assistance. Without unpacking, I connected to the analog internet to send my final assignment to Hanna, and called David to announce my arrival. It was still early afternoon, so we agreed to meet later at the hotel for dinner. Not knowing what else to do, I decided to shop. Privately, I'd always referred to Germany as The Land of No Style. The opportunity to buy new clothes in another country was a thrilling moment. I had only American tailored suits in my wardrobe and very little casual clothing. The Park Plaza Hotel in Utrecht was perfect for shopping and situated next to the train station. My commute to work would be a breeze.

After wandering in and out of several stores, I was still empty handed. It was impossible to find anything in a style that I could see myself wearing. Every piece of clothing was covered with some annoying trend and my style was anything but "trendy." I prefer to think of myself as "classic" and I like to add flair to quality basics with jewelry or a well-cut jacket. I flipped through one rack after another. *Corduroy? Are you kidding me?* Finally, in an act of desperation, I purchased two pairs of corduroy pants in a decade that was *not* the 1970's, and walked home defeated.

Coming straight from work, he was handsome in his smart gray suit and blue button-down shirt. He was even wearing a tie. I wore jeans and a sweater because I couldn't bear to put on the corduroys. He suggested a nearby pizza place and that was fine with me. I am always excited about pizza, no matter what form it arrives in, because there are no mysteries of etiquette associated with eating it.

As we left the hotel and walked toward the city, I noticed he was acting strangely. He was furtively glancing around, as if afraid to be spotted. Thinking that maybe his ex-girlfriend lived in the city, I didn't question him. I wasn't anxious to meet her either. The "restaurant" turned out to be a gloomy basement pizzeria. As I said, I have no issues with pizza, but it was a letdown that our first meal together in his territory would be a rundown eatery with no windows. I said nothing and tried to seem upbeat, even though Dutch Day One hadn't been my idea of fun.

We both had to work the next day, so it was an early night. I asked for advice on using the trains and he glossed over the question, saying everyone spoke English. He described the machines where I could buy tickets, instead of wasting time in line, and claimed it was self-explanatory. What a relief. Arrival in Holland was a flashback to the frustrations of landing in Germany. I was hoping that things would be different this time around.

Before my first day of work, I reviewed the location details sent by Dafne. Initially, she told me that the project site was in Haarlem, just outside Amsterdam. Once I'd accepted the assignment, she called the town "Velserbroek." It was unfortunate that I didn't catch the distinction. Haarlem is a medium-size city with a fairly large train station and multiple connections to Amsterdam and Utrecht every hour. Velserbroek, on the other hand, is a village.

Standing in Utrecht's madhouse of a central station, I was unnerved when none of the ticket machines had English options, and every sign showing the proper *spoor* listed information only in Dutch. I expected the destinations to be in Dutch, but seriously, a little help with the words, meaning "delay" or "no service," wasn't too much to ask, was it? Even the conductors in the station spoke only in Dutch. I thought I might faint.

By the time I figured out which train went to Haarlem, I had little patience left to find the bus to Velserbroek and its departure time. I flagged a taxi to take me the last fifteen minutes to the project office. At least, I had remembered my favorite taxi communication protocol: piece of paper with written address in local language. Otherwise, I sensed my irritated driver would have made my life difficult. Or perhaps I should say, more difficult?

At the office, I was greeted by the receptionist, who did not (*surprise!*) speak English. She was smiling, at least, which was an improvement over the others who'd crossed my path this morning. She had me sign the register and when she saw Dafne as the person I was meeting, she knew why I was there. Ten minutes later, Dafne appeared to show me the way to the project office. I had met her briefly in person a few times by then. She was a little shorter than me with mid-length mousy-brown hair and a typically large Dutch mouth. I had to admire the way she exuded confidence, even if she had been the one to tell me about Holland's "wonderful public transport."

We went into the empty cafeteria and sat at a long table. She talked about the project and her team structure. The surprise came when she added that she wasn't the one I'd be working for, but another project manager who led the sub-team of Dafne's larger project. Her name was Hazel and she was South African. If we ignore the fact that I'd agreed to this assignment because I knew Dafne from numerous phone conversations and because I expected to be working in Haarlem, then things would be going great right now. That wasn't the case. I was already wondering what the hell I'd agreed to when Hazel strolled in.

My first impression of Hazel didn't tip the scale of doubt in the opposite direction. Her matronly bun and old-fashioned clothes seemed out of step in a high-tech firm. I listened to her ramble for too long before she got to the point, which was that she had a she had not yet determined the responsibilities for each member on her team of five. This was not reassuring given the short project duration, which had already been explained to me, but clearly I was not one to judge how things worked in Holland. I put on my best fake smile and asked where my desk was. She led me to the desk she reserved for me, right next to her. I'm sure the joy was written all over my face.

I started digging into the project documentation, only to discover that it was written only in Dutch. In Germany, all documentation was written in English and German, so this was another unpleasant surprise. The German client was an international software development company, and where I sat now was a Dutch waste management plant. They had no reason to duplicate documentation in two languages because there were no subsidiaries or system users outside of the Netherlands. The fact that the official language of my company is English didn't seem to have any bearing on the situation.

That afternoon, Hazel called a team meeting to introduce me to my coworkers for next three months. Somewhere in the Dutch I listened to for five minutes, I heard my name and the team turned to stare, as though I hadn't been noticed before.

"I'm sorry, but I don't speak Dutch. Could we please do this in English?" Her slightly ill expression said it all. Apparently, neither of us was expecting me to be the lone English-speaking team member. Despite the fact that every person in the room was capable of speaking English, and was required in order to work for my company, Hazel put it to a vote.

"Would it be all right with everyone to speak English?"

Groans, slumped shoulders, and the shaking of heads all around indicated that the answer was no. And so, the light at the end of the tunnel, my saving grace from having to return to the United States, turned out to be an oncoming train.

* * *

At the end of the day, I asked where the bus stopped that would take me to Haarlem station, and someone walked outside with me to show me the way. While my new teammates drove off in their own cars, I walked ten minutes behind the building and through the fields to the empty bus stop. I tried reading the schedule to make sure I was in the right place, but even that was confusing. I crossed my fingers and the bus rolled up within minutes. Thankfully, the way I pronounced the words "Haarlem" and "station" was recognizable to the driver, and was grateful to take a seat.

Reaching the Park Plaza, I was in a state of shock. Already, several things that I'd been told about my new assignment had turned out to be false. What recourse did I have since I'd already packed up my apartment and committed myself? How could I possibly succeed in an environment where people on my own team weren't willing to speak my language? My head pounded. I stifled a panic attack by reminding myself that I succeeded on difficult projects before.

I wanted to stay in Europe so badly that I knew I couldn't live without giving it my best shot. Besides, what would happen with David if I simply got up and left? Nothing, most likely. I'd never find out if we could work as a couple. No, I couldn't let that happen. I blamed my frustration on the logistics and hoped that once I learned the ropes, life would get easier.

David and I spoke briefly, but skipped getting together since the next day was a work day. We made plans for the weekend instead. I kept the harrowing details of my day largely to myself because I didn't want to be a downer on Dutch Day Two. In need of some comfort, I invited him to stay Friday night after dinner and sightseeing in Utrecht.

My second trip to work did not go more smoothly. I took the bus from Haarlem station only to discover after fifteen minutes that it was the wrong one. The driver was very kind however, and he dropped me off at the place to catch the right bus, even though he was not allowed to stop there. He must've taken pity on the harried woman, lost in a place where she couldn't communicate. Whatever his reason, I was grateful.

Holland is very strange from the language perspective. Most Dutch people have studied the English language in school and can speak it. They just don't choose to, especially outside of Amsterdam, tourist capital of the Netherlands. As far as I understood, the "Holland" versus "The Netherlands" thing, the Kingdom of Netherlands is the proper name for this country and has been since the mid-nineteenth century. The terms *Noord* and *Zuid Holland* refer to the provinces of North and South Holland, which are two of the twelve Dutch provinces. The locals refer to the country as Holland. No matter how technically incorrect it is to use it to refer to the whole country, I followed suit. I was in no position to aggravate the natives.

With every bit of cheer I could muster, I smiled at my new receptionist friend and gave her as good a *"goiemorgen"* as I could muster without mastery of the guttural "g" that always makes the Dutch sound like they're hacking up a fur ball. She waved kindly and I walked past to my new favorite spot next to Hazel, who wasn't in yet. I powered up my laptop and searched for caffeine.

Recognizing me as potentially harmless and obviously clueless, a blonde-haired blue-eyed angel approached. "The coffee is over here," she told me with a giggle, pointing to a cupboard. "Oh thank you. I'm new around here. My name is Jennifer." I extended my hand, trying to read her accent.

"Marlena," she said, smiling and grabbing my hand. My savior told me that like Hazel, she was South African. "Welcome to the team," she added.

I thanked her and asked about her job, grateful for someone

to chat with. What a relief it was to see her smiling face across from my workstation, especially now that I'd discovered that she was well acquainted with the English language.

An hour after I arrived, Hazel breezed in. I had already downed two cups of coffee and dealt with my email, so I was anxious for details on what exactly I was doing for the next three months.

Hazel paid me no notice until she was ready to, at nearly 10 a.m. She asked me if I'd join her in the "conference room."

We settled in again at a cafeteria table and she proceeded to give me her vision of the team and its mission. Apparently, one of the team members, the most experienced one, had tendered his resignation the week before, forcing Hazel to shuffle the responsibilities of the players. She had decided that I would take his role leading the conversion and migration of data from the old system to the new system. I'd never done it before, but it was well known that data conversion the most tedious, but critical, task in software implementation. If the data from your existing system either doesn't appear, or doesn't appear correctly, in your new system, you are, shall we say, *screwed*.

Immediately, I raised my concerns, starting with the fact that the system documentation was in another language, and ending with my total lack of experience. Hazel waved off my hesitation, adding that she had no conversion knowledge either, but Dafne's project team had a resident expert who would gladly help. I saw no way out. My firm had a long history of putting pressure on employees to take the roles they are asked to do, experience or not. I honestly believed that, with some coaching, I'd be fine.

The crucial fact that escaped me before agreeing to take on the responsibility was that this was brand-new software, which was rarely free from "bugs." Depending on the size of the bug and your system, this little pest can turn into a swarm of doomsday locusts.

Hazel claimed to have given me this distinguished role because of its importance, so I extrapolated that to mean that success would raise my professional profile locally and agreed to take it on. That settled, she blithely mentioned that the "go live" date (read "go live" date as "the day before which you must have every conceivable problem solved") was January 1, 2003. Translated by an experienced software consultant, this means Christmas and New Year's Eve are annihilated by work. Obviously this was not great news for my new Dutch life or budding romance.

Since I wasn't experienced in the realm of data migration, I didn't know I was being tasked with the impossible. That is, not until I started picking the brains of the more experienced consultants in my circle, David and the resident "expert," Florence, who was running a larger migration for the same client. I spent the first few days learning how our system was integrated with the larger system from the members of my so-called "team," people–including Hazel–who weren't inclined to contribute to a group effort. No one cared if I sank or swam.

David's advice was, due to the newness of the software, I'd better stay close to my German contacts. Florence said that when planning the migration of data, working backwards from the "go live" date, was the way to go. She forwarded me her own file that she used for planning and, looking at twelve pages of detail, I thought my brain would explode. It made no difference that it wasn't in English. Some things require no translation.

For a change of pace, David took me on my first tour of the Dutch countryside over the weekend. I hoped the fresh air would do me good and I was right. The windmills and canals were enchanting, not to mention the cows and sheep on every inch of green grass. He took me to Gouda, where I was pleased to find a beautiful old city, not just cheese. Presiding over Gouda's center square is the breathtaking city hall, dating back to the fifteenth century. My small camera lens was terribly insufficient at capturing the stately *Stadhuis*, so I walked slowly around to take in every tiny detail.

Afterward, we went to a small café for lunch where I was offered the famous green erwtensoep. After David's description about the soup his grandmother made, so thick that a spoon would actually remain upright in the bowl, I passed in favor of smoked salmon on toast. Seated on the top floor of the café next to the windows, we looked out onto the square and the city hall. It was the kind of building that demands attention, with its sharp Gothic spires and grinning gargoyles. It was

The Devil Wears Clogs

like an evil Disney castle, but more detailed. I had to see more of a country that could produce a masterpiece like this.

There was a quick trip through the town where his grandmother lived and where David grew up. Afterwards, we took the car across the river Lek on a ferry to Schoonhoven. I'd never been on a ferry that carried only a few cars at once, and I found it charmingly old-world. Exiting the ferry and parking the car, we walked through the medieval entrance gate of the Veerport into the walled city of Schoonhoven.

Patiently, David translated a plaque for me stating that Schoonoven first became a settlement in 1247. One hundred years later, impenetrable stone defense walls were built around the commerce and residential center. Again, history came alive. Text describing walled cities never seemed real to a girl whose country was a mere two hundred years old. Now that I could picture the silversmiths and clock makers renowned in the Zilverstad, I could see the human side of the story. The tragedy of thousands lost to the Black Death made it even more vivid. History was no longer only found in books.

David was full of knowledge on the area, which turned Mr. Nice Guy into Mr. Smart Guy, and I loved that too. I filled my camera's memory card that day and smiled at him as we walked along the river's edge. A small pier jutted out across the water and I wanted ferry pictures, so we walked to the end. After the numerous unpleasant revelations of the past few days, I finally felt a stab of happiness, warmed by the sun and new discoveries. I grabbed David's hand. A few minutes later, I went for a kiss, but he pulled away. Shocked and embarrassed, I resumed my photo-taking and walked back to the car.

Crossing the Lek again, I asked David what was bothering him, but it was his turn to be silent. We were both tired from the long day and the previous week at work, so I didn't push. He asked me if I wanted to see where he lived, and I eagerly said yes. Over the course of our marathon phone calls, I'd developed a mental image of what his apartment looked like, and I was curious if reality coincided at all with my imagination.

For the longest time, I couldn't pronounce the name of the place where David lived. It's called Ijsselstein. Now, can you blame me? I challenge anyone who isn't Dutch to get it right without hearing it pronounced several times first. Ijsselstein is the stuff of fairytales. In medieval times it was also a walled city, and the city gates still stand. A canal surrounds the old center, giving the appearance of a moat. I'd stepped out of a time machine into the Middle Ages.

As we made our way slowly through the cobblestone streets, we took a sharp right turn onto something that reminded me of Heidelberg's Donkey Path. It was David's street, where he expertly parked in the available tiny spot. At the end of the path stood an enormous windmill, fully restored and simply beautiful. David's home was less than 150 feet from this magical structure. Walking inside, I understood what he'd been trying to tell me, it was a large canal house divided into apartments. David's place, on the top level, had a tiny balcony overlooking the muddy water. His total living space was quite small, but the location of the apartment made up for the inconvenience. It was a peaceful setting, minus a little loud quacking outside that gave life to the canal. He described his neighbors and how long he'd been living there, giving me the feeling that he was proud of his castle. He had moved a few years ago from neighboring Nieuwegein, which is equally difficult to pronounce but far less charming.

David offered me a glass of wine and some of the tangy yellow Gouda cheese we'd bought. Sitting in his miniature living room, we talked about the day's travels. Our arrival in Ijsselstein had obliterated my concern over the incident on the pier. I was so full of questions about Holland that we didn't immediately get around to discussing that. When I remembered it, I wasn't sure how to bring it up. I beat around the bush until I realized that since English was not David's first language, subtlety would get me nowhere. With a deep breath, I got straight to the point. "Why did you pull away from me?" I said.

"What do you mean?" he asked, even though I was quite sure he knew what I was talking about.

"I was holding your hand, which you seemed to not want to do, and then when I went to kiss you, you backed away!"

"Um. I don't know. I just didn't feel like it. I don't like to do that stuff in front of other people."

"Other people? There were like three teenagers and an old lady down there. Why do you care about what they think?" I demanded. No response at my raised voice. "Are you embarrassed of me? Is that what the problem is? This started in Utrecht the day I got here. You've been acting weird ever since I came to Holland."

"It's your clothes," he said, refusing to meet my eyes. "My clothes? What the hell are you talking about?"

"You don't dress like the people here. It's too casual."

"So, you are calling me a SLOB? Is that what I understand here, David?" I shouted.

"I think you are taking this too strongly," David stammered nervously.

"Oh, I think I've finally got the story straight for once. I think you don't want to be with me because you don't approve of my choice in clothing! I don't believe this. Did it ever occur to you that perhaps people in other countries dress differently than the Dutch?" I was on a roll now, unstoppable. Even if David had wanted to get a word in to clarify what he meant, he wouldn't have been able to.

I went on. "Well, I certainly don't want to be the cause of your embarrassment, my friend. Please give me a ride back to my hotel. I'm done trying to figure this out." My wounded ego took control. Adding this juvenile attitude to all that I faced at work, I had had enough.

Granted, I realized the weakness of my position, not being able to make an exit by slamming the door and angrily driving off, but I had to *go*. Unbeknownst to me, he'd been walking around judging me, and I simply wouldn't allow it for one more second. David dutifully put on his coat and did what I asked him. He didn't say anything else. I know now that he didn't have the words to express what he was trying to tell me, so he said nothing rather than make the situation worse. That certainly didn't help at the time, however. I got out of his car without a word and did not look back.

* * *

Sunday was bleak. True to my female nature, I continued over-analyzing the situation. After less than a week in the country, it was obvious that Dutch women were very different from American women. They wore trendy little outfits and zero makeup. They didn't bother with a hairdo beyond maybe getting a comb through it. American women are all about hair and the make-up, but women my age rarely wear skirts and dresses on the weekends. We wear jeans, and jeans go almost everywhere.

Of course there are weekend skirt and dress occasions, but they usually involve a party or a wedding. When we are going to visit or have an outing with friends, it's safe to say that nine out of ten people will be wearing denim. I had been trying to find a more "European" look for the past year, but had been unsuccessful in the Land of No Style, and in Holland the shopping was so depressing that I had been forced to purchase corduroys! Too bad I hadn't put them on.

As much as I couldn't fathom that our romance was over because of something as stupid as my choice of weekend wear, I wasn't about to apologize for it. When he called later that day, David didn't seem to expect me to, either. He admitted that, yes, people probably were used to wearing other clothing outside of the Netherlands and that he had not considered that. I told him I knew that I was different here, and I was trying to find a way to fit in, but I would always be different. He agreed to be more understanding after I told him that I had even asked Dafne about proper dress at the office and she'd waved me off as if it were a ridiculous question.

Once we talked through the situation and I got over my wounded pride, I realized that "slob" was my word, not his. So much for people being accepted in Europe even when they're different. That idealism went out the window. The real deal is if they assume you are a tourist, Europeans expect you to look different. They expect you to be poorly-dressed. When you live in their country, Europeans expect you to assimilate and this applies especially to the Dutch. It is frowned upon in the Netherlands to stand out in any way. Conformity is the name of the game. The Dutch want things as they want them—period.

Because I didn't grasp the full extent of Dutch culture, I thought he was just being a snob. I was damned sure I'd never look like a Dutch girl, but I decided to keep trying to navigate the cultural minefield. There were so many things I loved about David. He was good-looking and kind. He was smart and funny. He loved his grandparents and he

The Devil Wears Clogs

was more than fascinated with yours truly. If he wasn't, why would he drive eight hours for a lunch date in Heidelberg, or take a too casually-dressed American girl to Italy?

CHAPTER 14
THE DUTCH DAILY GRIND

Privacy and a place to cook my own meals were the priorities the following week. Cheaper than hotels, apartments are commonly used by project staff for implementations longer than a few weeks. The Dutch office provided the name and number of a leasing agent who assured me that he could help me find suitable accommodation. I looked at over thirty photos of spacious airy Amsterdam apartments on their web site, but each one had the same problem. Dafne dictated my housing allowance. It didn't take long to figure out that, for the amount I had, I'd be living in a rat hole across from Station Centraal. I rang Dafne who sighed audibly before telling me to find the best deal and she would raise my monthly housing allowance. Satisfied, I made an appointment in Amsterdam with the agent.

On the appointed day, I couldn't wait for a glimpse of Amsterdam apartment living. I sat patiently, dreaming about my new home, on an ice cold bench in Dam Square. My mobile phone vibrated in my coat packet. The agent, already twenty minutes late, was now calling to cancel. The excuse? A "traffic problem" prevented him from getting to Amsterdam. Was this guy serious? Who cancels an appointment because of traffic?

Incensed, I asked when he thought he might be able to follow through on his commitment, irritated at losing half a day's work for nothing. Sadly, my living space wasn't at the top of his priority list. He rescheduled for a week later without further explanation. I was disappointed to say the least, but I needed his help or I'd be living in a Utrecht hotel forever. I wasn't dressed for the office, and God forbid

I show up dressed inappropriately, or I would simply have taken the train to the office. Instead, I decided to work remotely from the hotel.

After the initial shock of public transport, the length of my commute, and the degree of difficulty of my work responsibilities, the cast of characters involved began to come into focus. The number of consultants working at this client was over a hundred at its peak. At this late phase, there were roughly thirty working in the project room. Being a latecomer, after most of the team had been working together for nearly a year, was not conducive to bonding with my coworkers. I was also the lone American. Even Hazel and Marlena had a language advantage as South Africans. Their dialect, *Afrikaans*, is derived from the Dutch colonial days of their home country.

My heightened sensitivity to the iron fist of Holland's language and culture prompted me to ask Dafne for permission to charge Dutch lessons to the project budget. Her curt reply was that it wasn't necessary for my position, and that the project could not afford it. How could it not be necessary when my team members refused to speak English? In an attempt to convince her, I said I was looking at the instruction as a long-term investment, because I was interested in transferring from the Cleveland to Amsterdam. When she continued staring at me blankly, I offered to pay half of the cost as long as I could use company time for my lessons. Finally, Dafne agreed. The exchange taught me that everything in Dutch culture is a negotiation. This was just the tip of the iceberg. The invisible tome titled *The Social Rules of the Netherlands* is long and curiously complex.

* * *

In reality, the "decision" to allow my Dutch language lessons took weeks during an already short-term assignment. Dafne worked four days a week and, on the one or two she was present in the office, you had to take a number to get an audience with the Queen. This, combined with Hazel's four-day work week and banker's hours, showed me that Dutch women look at career and ambition very differently from American women.

Hazel spent hours discussing the horseback riding lessons she took with her daughter and delivered numerous long-winded tales of South

The Devil Wears Clogs

African life, but if you pressed her for a project-related decision, you could be waiting a very long time.

Even with a sixty to ninety-minute commute, I was always in the office before 8:30 a.m. and most days before eight. Never did either of these two women arrive before me. Given that the female project leadership made the briefest appearances of anyone, I should have figured out that Dutch women were a different breed entirely. Quickly adding to the pile of information in the "con" column, sexual discrimination laws didn't seem to have been widely read or distributed in this country, where more than 70% of Dutch part-time workers are female. Yes, I was different in more ways than I'd ever imagined. A mere costume change wasn't going to make a difference on this battlefield, no matter what David thought.

To collect information on this curious new species, I read several articles in English newspapers about women in business. It was shocking to read the unflattering portrait painted of American businesswomen. One in the *London Telegraph* screamed "Over Done, Over Coiffed, and Over *Here*!" and lamented that American women held the majority of female power positions in British companies and worse, this horrifying trend was on the increase. According to the author, something had to be done about this pronto. From where I sat, the tip of the scale in favor of American women was likely justified.

With regard to Dutch women, Michael Bliss of *Radio Netherlands* had some interesting remarks. "Whether they have children or not, Dutch women don't want to work full time. This is the conclusion of a report published by the Social and Cultural Planning Office today. Only seven percent of women who work part time would prefer to work a thirty-five-hour week if they could." 7%?

Armed with a slightly better understanding of the Dutch corporate game, I worked long days. I worked weekends and holidays because I had to be exceptional to achieve my goal of transferring to Amsterdam. When she refused to issue a general rule that team meetings take place in English, I understood that Hazel wasn't inclined to make unpopular decisions. With all of this happening on the work front, I could have been committed to an institution for my decision to stick with it, but there is, as there always is, another side to the story.

When I did finally connect with the housing agent, we looked at four well-appointed comfortable apartments in the center of Amsterdam. I chose a *heerenhuis,* on the elegant Vossiusstraat, bordering the beautiful Vondelpark. My new tree-lined boulevard was considered prestigious, lying just one block from the P.C. Hoofstraat, *the* upscale shopping street of Amsterdam. On the corner was the famous French jeweler, Cartier, and walking further down the street were Gucci and Chanel.

My apartment, the penthouse, was a fourth floor walk-up in a gorgeous turn of the century building. It was a private home with suites of rooms on each of the four floors. The high ceilings were beautifully molded, and the penthouse came with a private roof terrace overlooking the city. Living here felt like winning the lottery. Me? Move from the shoebox on a donkey path to the penthouse suite in the snootiest district of Amsterdam? *Me!* I couldn't have been more excited. Looking out from the roof terrace, Amsterdam sparkled before me like buried treasure.

The inside of my new living space couldn't have been a bigger contrast from the Heidelberg shoebox. The enormous living room had a sunken leather couch and a fireplace to ward off the chill of winter nights. The bed was above the living area on a small wooden loft, which also contained the closet and stairs to the roof terrace. All of the paneling and molding was a rich creamy white, including the deep bookshelves, which stretched from floor to ceiling, stuffed with titles from travel to gardening. The black-and-white-checkered kitchen held two mini refrigerators, which would be more than enough for supplies for one person (and hopefully a guest), and the appliances were modern. Standing in that kitchen, I felt utterly sophisticated and terribly spoiled. I felt like I had actually made it. Living in a glamorous European capital with a successful career and a new love was more than I ever thought possible.

* * * **

David and I explored Amsterdam nearly every weekend. He knew as little as I did about it, but we loved getting lost together. During our expeditions, we nicknamed "Tourist Hell" everything from my apartment toward the Amsterdam Central Station. The "real part of town" was my street and further into the *Oud Zuid* district. Oud Zuid means Old South, and in this area lies the majority of the Vondelpark, as well as many historic homes and architectural gems. The real part of town is mainly tourist free, so the prices in bars and restaurants aren't ridiculously inflated.

Thinking I lived on The Right Side of the Tracks, some characteristics of the neighborhood were a surprise. The cost of street parking on the Vossiusstraat was outrageous. It cost six euro an hour, the equivalent of ten to twelve U.S. dollars at the time. When David stayed all night, he had to pay fifty U.S. dollars for the privilege.

As glamorous as it was, I discovered that petty theft is rampant in Amsterdam. One night when he stayed, he found his Audi's passenger window smashed the following morning. As I began to watch more local news with my personal interpreter, I learned that theft was a nuisance in the Netherlands as a whole, not just an unfortunate fact of life in Amsterdam. David was smart enough not to leave anything of value in his car. Thieves did manage to get two things that really pissed him off, however: his Ray Bans and his candy stash.

After living in Heidelberg's safe little altstadt, I'd never worried about theft when looking at apartments. I did tell the leasing agent that I wanted a place that allowed permits for parking. While the number of break-ins didn't occur to me, a bigger worry was the revelation that residents sometimes wait three to four *years* for parking permits after buying or renting an apartment. *Years.* The wait was longest for homes next to city canals because those streets have the scarcest parking. Finally, I could see why it was so expensive.

Since I had no car—Dafne still denied me the privilege afforded even to entry-level employees of the Dutch office—it was irrelevant for me personally, but I hated watching David go through the hassle of car repairs and the expense of overnight parking. Luckily, he didn't seem fazed at the inconvenience and never complained about staying.

If we had been working on the same project or even projects in the same region, David would have offered me a ride to work. Unfortunately, my project with Dafne and Hazel was in the opposite direction, so I didn't get to escape the funhouse of public transport.

Usually, I left the house at 5:50 a.m. to catch the tram in the main square closest to me, the Leidseplein. From here, three tram lines went directly to the Central Station. The first leg of my journey took fifteen minutes, but invariably I would dash to the Leidseplein only to see the tram pulling away.

One hard and fast rule of Amsterdam that no one lets you in on, is that no matter how fast you run, or how close you are to the doors, once they slam shut, they are slammed for good. I am convinced that the tram driver Code of Conduct states "Show no mercy!" Missing this tram, and waiting five to ten minutes for the next, ultimately meant a deviance of at least thirty minutes in the chain of tram-train-bus-walk to get to the office. More than once, I wished desperately that I knew how to swear in Dutch.

The week after I moved into my apartment, a team new member was brought on board. Coincidentally, Martin lived in Amsterdam. We were into a frosty November by the time he appeared and I was truly grateful that he agreed to pick me up at my apartment a few days a week, so that I didn't have to stand on the freezing train platform every day. Martin was in his twenties and had just joined my firm. Even he was deigned valuable enough to be given a car to drive to work! But I didn't complain. I was thankful I wasn't at the mercy of the Evil Tram Driver day in and day out.

* * *

Over time, working at the project became a more complex game. While it was annoying that Hazel's horseback riding lessons and "client meetings" took up the majority of her week, it was worse when she wavered back and forth on difficult decisions that had to be made regarding the client's existing data and the new system. Piecing her story together, I eventually figured out that the new system was much more advanced than what the users required. The naked truth was this: We were implementing a large, complex system that was used by massive, often multinational firms, at a client had less than ten employees and a database containing a few hundred thousand records. These requirements could have been handled by any off-the-shelf software system, all of which were less expensive, more user-friendly, and considerably more flexible than what we were designing. To me, it was outrageous.

My team was the sub-project of Dafne's larger implementation team. The waste management company and the subsidiary I was working with were linked. The new design, with both companies on one system, was sold as *the* way to share data, but I knew it was possible for them to share data regardless of the type of software they used. For this project, Dafne was being hailed as a hero for selling the small subsidiary on the need for the same software system as the waste company.

I knew no one was interested in my opinions. For obvious reasons, Hazel and Dafne would not take kindly to me asking pointed questions. Much to the dismay of my conscience, I kept my mouth shut.

Instead, I continued working ridiculous hours and commiserating with Marlena, my new friend, at our situation as foreigners on this bizarre planet. To add to the fun, we discovered a charming new side of our co-workers. Dutch women liked to hang out in cliques. This was especially fun when maligning any foreigners in their midst. Dafne and Hazel weren't around enough to be part of it, but the others on the team began acting like spoiled teenage brats. They made rude comments about how we dressed and Marlena's accented Dutch.

When we knew each other better, Marlena confessed that this had been the case the entire year she worked at the project. These women, one definitely wouldn't call them "ladies," smelled blood in Marlena's gentle nature, and she was on the receiving end of far harsher treatment than I. It was so common that four of the six South African colleagues who had come over to the Netherlands with her had already left the country.

Sharing a love of travel and adventure, we quickly became close friends in this nerve-wracking environment. She knew she could trust me. If you had heard the stories about how my soft-spoken friend was treated, you too would see that she was much stronger than any of them imagined. Had they known how tough she really was, I doubt that they would have played such childish games. It wouldn't be pretty when she was finally pushed to her limit.

Our so-called team members eventually found a weakness to

exploit as they obviously couldn't fault my English. Finally, they figured out that I was American. It should have been obvious from day one, but it took this mob time to work up the courage to approach. When they did, it wasn't with the usual pleasantries of "Where are you from?" or "What brought you to Holland?" but went straight to "Why did George Bush invade Iraq?"

I have no idea what gave my new colleagues the impression that I had a direct line to the President, making me privy to his personal thoughts, but that didn't seem to matter. Nor were these questions asked politely. Any normal person might inquire, "We'd like to hear your opinion on the matter, so that's why we're asking." Nope. They launched their comments like missiles, as if I'd personally made the choice.

It could have been their basic level of English, which made beating around the bush and basic politeness difficult, but I didn't appreciate being provoked. I was even less tolerant after hearing Marlena's stories. Just like everyone else, I was here to work. The number of times my male Dutch coworkers raised this topic, as if I had secret knowledge, was ridiculous. The women didn't know enough about politics to even attempt the discussion.

After numerous similar encounters, I made it clear that I hadn't voted for President Bush, but that didn't give them the right to pass judgment. Down the line, I recognized that passing judgment is a Dutch talent. It is especially fierce when you do not follow their implied social rules. Never mind that you have no idea what those are. Simply by your presence, you are obligated to follow their script.

CHAPTER 15
SILVER LINING

At work, an already tricky assignment looked impossible. Increasingly, I relied on weekends spent with David to keep my spirits up. We continued exploring Amsterdam hot spots, and former colleagues from Germany still scattered about Europe came for visits. David got to enjoy a traditional American Thanksgiving in Brussels.

In November, we drove to Bruges for my first visit to "The Venice of the North." Completely unknown to me before making the two-hour drive south of Amsterdam, it was love at first sight. Before seeing Bruges, I couldn't have imagined a place where time had stopped so completely.

The city lies in northwest Belgium, and according to the tour book Bible, it was one of the most important commercial trading centers of Europe during medieval times. Today, it's a frozen portrait, because the channel that breathed life into the city in the 1100's also took it away four hundred years later. This was a natural phenomenon of the river silt building too high for ships to pass. The incredible irony is that the tragedy for the Bruges' medieval villagers is also what makes this city a tourism goldmine today. Trade and commercial development came to a halt when the river silted up.

Entering the city center, I found horse-drawn carriages rumbling along the cobblestone streets, and graceful swans floating on glassy lakes. Granted, a flotilla of narrow boats glide through the canals so laden with tourists that they seem likely to capsize, but incredibly, that does little to destroy the magic. While Heidelberg's old city has similar historic beauty, it is no equal. Despite its charm, Amsterdam has been overridden by commerce and tourism. Bruges is quite possibly the most romantic city on Earth.

Spotting a rare short queue for the canal boat, we hopped on board. Camera held steady by the wooden rail, I snapped one beautiful crisp autumn view after another. The clear blue sky allowed the sun's golden fingers to grasp the red and orange leaves, making them glow like embers. The still water reflected leaning brick canal houses with sunlit halos. I tried to listen to the guide tell the city history, but using my eyes to full capacity seemed to override the ability of my ears. The photo finish was the 360-degree view of the city from the serene Lake of Love at the end of the canal. My camera was woefully inadequate at capturing such beauty.

The ride lasted an hour, leaving plenty of time to see the city on foot. Bruges isn't that big, so it is best covered that way. On the way back to the city center, we passed silver-haired Flemish ladies, making intricate lace, seated in doorways. Reluctantly, we side-stepped several chocolate shops where I feared gaining twenty pounds from the mouth-watering smell alone. I found that Belgians have an intense affection for "tea rooms," as there seemed to be hundreds in this tiny town. Finally, we came upon a restaurant, which we simply couldn't pass up. The crackling fire greeted our arrival in the entryway, and the menu made a simple choice impossible.

As we stepped through the doorway, the maître d' immediately took my coat and led us to a table for two by the fire. He pulled out my chair, and I was relieved to find that a fireside table did not mean close enough to get third-degree burns. We had been walking for hours and I was happy to give my feet a rest and my full attention to the Belgian culinary scene.

For the first time, I heard Dutch spoken with a Belgian accent. It was so different that I barely recognized the basic words I'd learned. Fortunately for me, Belgians also speak French, in which I can get along very well. Even more fortunate, Belgian cuisine is prepared with a decidedly French flair. Since I've made my feelings on food in the Netherlands clear, I was pleased to discover that what is available in Belgium is at least one step up on the culinary ladder. I savored a

The Devil Wears Clogs

steaming pot of *moules-frites*, mussels prepared in a white wine sauce with French fries. Ever the carnivore, David was equally happy with his *steak frites*.

Wanting to see the rest of the city before it was hidden by darkness, we strolled along the waterways admiring the architecture. I could do this for days without noticing the passage of time. Every insignia or face carved into these historic façades provides a clue of the first residents. It might be the owner's name or family shield. If the building was owned by a sea captain, there might be a sailing ship carved into the front door. If they had a beloved family dog, it might guard the entrance forever in stone. I couldn't help stopping to decipher this new code in the symbols that decorate these impressive homes.

This time, I wasn't completely in my own world. I didn't think David was interested in the architecture as I was, but he was clearly enjoying himself. In one courtyard, ivy dominated every wall of the building, burned red by the autumn sun. I carefully crafted the perfect photo. While I did this, I caught David admiring me and ignoring the building. I would turn around to find him grinning, which made me smile like an idiot too. When butterflies made an appearance in my stomach, it dawned on me that there was more to this than simply liking him. I realized I was approaching the point of no return. Standing on this precipice gripped me with fear and elation simultaneously.

We continued to walk, stopping occasionally for photos, until I found the perfect spot for my photo to be taken. I was always looking for interesting photos to show my grandmother. She had been a great traveler in her day, and she reveled in my tales as I had in hers when I was young. I handed David my camera and asked him to take a photo since no one was near enough to take one of us together. As I was posing, feeling silly and self-conscious, a man walked by and said something to David. He spoke in heavily accented Dutch and I couldn't catch the exchange. I asked him afterward what was said.

"He said it was going to be a great photo of a beautiful girl, and I told him I knew it," David shyly confessed.

"Oh." Never having thought of myself as beautiful, I was at a loss for words. It made me feel very special, but I didn't have a single clue how to let him know.

The rest of the afternoon was a blur. I was falling hard for David, and everything—even this wonderful, magical, jewel of a city—faded into the background. Finally, our willpower failed and we stopped to indulge in rich, whipped-cream-covered coffee and insanely good handmade pralines. When the sun had almost disappeared, we walked back towards the parking lot.

Arriving at David's car, it took no time to decide to use the overnight bags we'd brought "just in case." Smiling and holding hands, we got a list of vacancies from the tourism desk. The height of the tourist season had passed and rooms were plentiful. The perfect one was waiting in the center of town, so we walked back to check in and leave our belongings. I made a call to a colleague from my German days who lived nearby, and asked if he and his wife wanted to join us for dinner. You might wonder why I would want company that evening after this afternoon of romance, but I was still standing on that precipice. I wasn't convinced I had the guts to dive headfirst over it after my experience with the Swede.

Another Belgian secret: their beer is out of this world. Super potent and tasty, you can sample over three hundred varieties, each with its own glass designed to maximize the flavor. Our friends took us to a favorite restaurant of theirs where we laughed and drank and told tales of Germany. Mr. Nice Guy didn't pressure me, and I certainly didn't put any on him. We had no map for where we were headed, but I, for one, was determined to enjoy the ride.

* * *

Throughout November, my project crept along at a snail's pace. True to my prediction, the new software was proving a more difficult than expected to fit into the customer's environment. This means a great deal of additional work. In the IT project world, this is called "customizing." Once you've done one of these projects, you learn that customizing is expensive and time-consuming, and ultimately causes other code in the software to fail. I'd heard many such tales of woe, but I was new at this game and not yet savvy enough to avoid getting myself into a similar mess. Being barred from direct communication with the client by Hazel, who cited my poor Dutch language skills as the excuse, did not improve the situation.

The Devil Wears Clogs

With the end of November came my thirty-second birthday. Some people like to downplay their birthdays, but I am not one of those people. I love an excuse for a party, but can't stand being the center of attention. The result is usually a road trip with close friends. Being within shouting distance of so many interesting places, I analyzed where my accumulated air miles could take me for minimal cash and came up with Edinburgh. Scotland was appealing, and a prior attempt to get there had fallen through, so I asked David if he wanted to come. He said yes without any hesitation, and I booked the tickets.

With the promise of another weekend away in a new European city tucked safely in my back pocket, I could handle the barrage of work problems and opinionated colleagues. I plodded onward with numerous phone calls and heavy support from my German developer connections. David had been right, not having this lifeline would have meant failure. If not failure, then certainly delay. In either case, the result would have jeopardized my plans to transfer to Amsterdam. The pressure was immense.

* * *

A Thursday night in late November, David and I were en route to Schiphol Airport. We had taken Friday off to allow three full days of Edinburgh exploration. As we were in dark ages of air travel, the American airline told me that I had to collect the tickets in person at the airport. For tickets purchased using air miles, the company did not allow e-ticketing. I expected this to take an extra thirty minutes at the airport. I thought wrong.

Walking directly to the counter, the sight of a placard on the desk, and no people, alerted me that something was amiss. After September 11th, American airlines took deadlines for check-in very seriously, adding extra stress to every trip. "The Union Airlines Service Desk will reopen at 7 a.m." the small black and white sign announced. Reopen? 7 a.m.?

My heart raced. I looked around in desperation for someone to help us and spotted the unlucky man at the neighboring counter.

"The desk closes every day at 1 p.m.," he said quietly. My watch said 5 p.m. and our flight left at 7.

"They demanded that I pick up the tickets in person. How could they FORGET to mention this?" I barked, fury blinding me until I remembered he didn't work for Union. He was an innocent bystander. Anger stepped down and disappointment took its place. How could I spend my birthday in this place? The glue that held me together during my first Dutch months was my time away with David. When I realized there was nothing I could do, I plummeted straight to rock bottom.

Reading my face, David took over. "Do you have any flights to Edinburgh tonight?" he asked at the next counter, one of Union's partner airlines.

"Yes, sir. I can see the reservations for Mrs. Burge," the suited man replied, his face taking on the green glow of his computer screen. "But I cannot print the tickets. Only Union can do that."

"How much for a new ticket on that flight?" "Seven hundred euros."

We looked at each other and laughed. I had paid less than a quarter of that. There was no more anger in my body. I went numb and sat down with my bag. David didn't waste a minute. As I waited, he strode confidently from desk to desk, asking about the evening's flight schedule. The last counter was McGreg Air, a well-known U.K. budget airline.

Knowing this was our last chance, I watched his every move. A slight smile begin to emerge on his face as he nodded to the agent's reply. The smile broadened and he waved me over. I practically ran.

"They have a flight tonight at 10 p.m. for one hundred and seventy-five euros?" There was optimism in his voice.

Unable to speak, I nodded and grabbed his hand. The price was barely over what I'd paid for the Union tickets. The only return was at dawn on Monday morning, but the weekend was salvaged. I couldn't believe it. No one had ever taken charge and done something like this just to make me happy. At that moment, I dove off the cliff and fell completely in love.

* * *

Plane tickets in hand, we went from gloom and doom to giddiness. The fact that David made it happen—just because he knew how important

The Devil Wears Clogs

it was to me—sent me over the moon. I don't think he cared one way or the other whether he saw Scotland. He was only interested in spending time with me, away from the place that was crushing my spirit. He was in it for me alone. From my point of view, this was an unbelievable concept. It pulled at my heartstrings and made me nervous at the same time. I now understood what falling in love is: allowing yourself to fly emotionally, knowing all the while about the dark bottomless pit that is your possible alternate destination.

Arriving in Scotland at midnight was not ideal, but we managed to get a little sleep in our first hours in Edinburgh. The following day, Friday, the 29th of November, was my big day. I was determined to celebrate in style. We decided the first stops should be Edinburgh Castle and the Royal Mile. These attracted the most tourists on the weekends, so we thought we might have a slightly less-crowded experience by visiting the castle early on Friday.

Mastering the usual maze of one-way streets between our hotel and the castle, it was only a short walk to the ticket booth at the top of the hill. The ticket agent told me my tickets were discounted because some of the rooms were closed to visitors. I was about to be disappointed when he explained why. "The Queen is visiting," he said in a bored tone. Wide-eyed and breathless, I ran over to give David the news. I had only seen the Queen of England on television. For a small-town Ohioan, the concept of monarchy was larger than life.

The words were barely out of my mouth when the booming voice of the guard cut through the noise of the crowd, "Please clear the way! The Royal Car is coming!" I fumbled for my camera. We had just crossed a massive stone bridge and stepped through the high walls forming the castle's main entrance. There was nowhere for the car to go but right past us! We waited only a minute before the gleaming black Bentley came. I tried both to peek in the back window and get a photo at the same time, which wasn't the best approach. The resulting prized photo is a velvet-gloved hand in the air and a wide-brimmed hat in the back seat of an extremely expensive car.

What I didn't expect was the figure in the bright pink hat and purple suit to look back at me with the same surprised expression that

I undoubtedly had on my own face. After fifty years of being Queen, how can she possibly be surprised at crowds gathering to greet her? What an incredible start to the weekend! I joked to David, "See how important I am? Even Queen Elizabeth has arrived for my birthday!" He laughed and pulled me to him. Happy doesn't begin to describe that moment. If I could give just one story to explain why I sought to continue my European travels, this would be it. How could I live the same monotonous day to day life in Cleveland when every corner of Europe delivered magic like this?

Grinning from ear to ear, David and I walked into the castle. My curiosity forced me to approach one of the guards to ask a few questions. We learned that the Queen had been present to officially open an exhibition of new artwork. Her presence led to the attendance of an entourage of Scottish dandies. There were black morning suits and bowlers, and there were bagpipes and leopard skins over kilts. The women wore smart suits and gigantic hats. It was much more fascinating than the castle itself. This was a level of society I'd only read about. I even asked the man with the bagpipes and the leopard skin if he would take a photo with me. Normally, I don't play tourist quite so obviously, but I couldn't help myself.

Buoyed by a lovely day at the castle and warming glasses of peaty Scotch whisky afterward, I called my parents when it was finally morning in Ohio. My mother wasn't home, so it was my dad who got the full force of my enthusiasm about our surprise visitor. He sounded underwhelmed. When I made my joke about the Queen visiting for my birthday, he said, "Oh is your birthday today? Out of sight, out of mind, I guess."

Did he really just say that? Talk about taking the wind out of one's sails! That put an abrupt end to the call. Why did he feel the need to kick me when I was so happy? I tried not to let it bother me.

David and I snoozed under heavy Tartan wool blankets to recharge our batteries in preparation for the continuance of my birthday festivities and I forgot all about Ohio.

Old Town was our next target. I had read that the Grassmarket area was wall-to-wall pubs. Scottish pubs intrigued me. It was a new experience to sit down with a pint or a glass of whisky and soak up the atmosphere of a place that's been around for decades, possibly over a century. The concept of the pub as the town's beating heart doesn't exist in the United States. U.K. pubs, with their rich red-velvet décor and gold-lettered leaded glass windows, are so inviting. Since the U.K. weather is famously awful, it's no surprise that the indoor ambience is considerably more pleasant.

Grabbing some "pub grub" at the only Grassmarket venue serving food, we found out that England and Scotland had something else in common: bland food. I'm talking about bar food, not haute cuisine, but shouldn't there be *some* taste? We drank cold pints with our steaming fish and chips while watching the locals come and go. I can never get enough of watching people; how they interact, how they dress, what they find funny, and how friendly they are to outsiders will keep my attention rapt.

In David-world, knowing that I was having a good time seemed to be enough. He finally confessed that the thick Scottish brogue was extremely difficult to understand. That was the reason he let me take over communication with the locals. The biggest kick I got that night was in the ladies room: a wall mounted vending machine selling whisky-flavored "McCondoms." Pumping pound after British pound into the machine, I grinned when I thought about my single friends discovering these in their Christmas stockings.

Well after we should have been tucked in for the night, David and I stopped for one last whisky. By this point, I had observed the locals enough to see that the grinning, quick-witted bartenders were usually happy to banter with the patrons. We sat down at the bar, blindly guessing which whiskies to try and then I could contain myself no longer. After we exchanged names and where we were from, I blurted out, "We saw the Queen today at Edinburgh Castle! I could not believe it!" to Mick the bartender. I don't know whether I expected him to be equally impressed or to know her personally, but I did not expect the silent scowl I received in reply.

Edinburgh is divided, with the castle standing guard over the medieval Old Town. The New Town was built in the late eighteenth and early nineteenth centuries. From nearly any angle, there are sweeping views of the stunning architecture surrounded by iridescent green landscape. As painful as it is to admit, on my first visit to Scotland, I did not realize that it was part of the United Kingdom and ruled by the British monarchy. My pre-trip reading about Edinburgh was focused on the city attractions and this crucial fact had escaped me.

David visibly cringed, knowing much more than I about European history. The bartender didn't say anything negative about Queen Elizabeth, but he made his feelings clear with a single expression before his abrupt departure. Determining that I was quickly in need of education, David told me about the many bloody wars between England and Scotland and, crucially, the fact that Scotland is no longer an independent nation. Had I been that bartender, I would have glared too.

The next evening, we found a restaurant above a quiet, upscale pub in the Old Town. Knowing we had to elevate our culinary game from the previous night's pub food, we felt lucky to find such an inviting inn. This evening's "first" was being presented with the whisky menu—complete with recommendations for the best accompanying foods—along with the dinner menu. I love fish, so my main dish was an easy choice: applewood smoked salmon with potatoes and vegetables. The whisky decision was considerably more difficult, so thank goodness for the waiter/ whisky sommelier! He brought over samples to help with the difficult choices, given our inexperience with the infinite number of Scottish whisky varieties.

Warmed by hot hearty cuisine and smoky Scotch, we had a great night. Aside from my faux pas the night before, I found the Scots funny and welcoming. They are quick with a joke and proud of their heritage. It is easy to be happy in Scotland–provided you know a little of their history.

After covering the tourist hotspots, I zeroed in on Christmas shopping. I didn't expect my friends to fall in love with the heavy wool knit sweaters, but the wool blankets would definitely keep the chill out of the northeastern U.S. winters. Clearly, it wouldn't do to leave without taking along some of the whiskies we'd enjoyed. Despite the cold, the sun shined bright in the clear blue sky. Ruddy-faced, red-haired people everywhere smiled and the air was thick with booming laughter. The holiday hustle and bustle and good cheer on the streets were intoxicating—with or without the whisky. I couldn't bear to leave.

While taking our last photos of Edinburgh dressed in her Christmas finest, we happened on a random parade through the city. Out of nowhere came bagpipes, bands, and fireworks galore. Simultaneously, we pulled out cameras and started snapping. The colorful explosion of fireworks lighting up the sky also lit the shining tears streaming down my rosy cheeks. After all of this how could I go back to a place where I felt dead inside?

I tried to keep the tears hidden, but he harder I tried, the more they came. "What's wrong?" David was clearly at a loss.

How do you tell someone that their country drives you to this kind of despair? "I don't want to go back to Holland," I whispered. He didn't take it personally, just squeezed my hand tight.

We spent the last night quietly in the hotel as we had to be up before dawn for the 6 a.m. flight. Few words were spoken. At Edinburgh airport, another "first," the sight of U.K. soldiers patrolling the airport with machine guns shocked us both.

In the big picture, there were more important things were afoot than my career problems.

CHAPTER 16
HOLIDAY CHEERLESS

The 5th of December arrived. Unbeknownst to me, this is a significant date on the Dutch calendar. It's the day when all good Dutch children put their shoes next to the chimney for *Sinterklaas*—remarkably similar in appearance to Santa Claus—to fill with treats. The shoes are an interesting twist, but they are far from the most interesting part of the Dutch holiday spectacle.

Sinter Klaas doesn't do anything so flashy as to arrive on rooftops carried in a sleigh led by eight reindeer. No, Sinter Klaas is more down to Earth. He arrives on the Dutch coast by boat from his home in Spain. His arrival in the Netherlands is televised so the kids all know when he's on his way. The Sint, always arrives accompanied by an entourage. His helpers are not elves, but Spanish Moors. Picture it—Sinter Klaas chugs up to the dock on a tug-style boat with a crew of men wearing blackface makeup and curly black wigs. The Moors are called *"zwaart piet,"* literally, "Black Pete." I am not making this up.

David loves showing off the traditions of his country, and tried to explain all this Christmas Dutchness. He tried so hard to make the picture clear, but sometimes only seeing is believing.

The fire was blazing in my living room on a rainy Saturday afternoon when David found the live television broadcast of the Sint's arrival. As the boat's curious crew came into view, I gaped open-mouthed at the TV. To me, it looked very much like Santa had slaves, well-dressed slaves in jewel-colored silks, but slaves nonetheless. The topic of slavery and any blackface makeup are taboo to Americans. I could hardly believe my eyes. The Sint's booming voice greeted hundreds of screaming kids and the piets danced merrily through the massive crowd, tossing candy into the air. It was like a comedy *noir*, pardon the pun. I could do nothing but laugh. Was there no end to the surprises that Europe had up her sleeve?

The *kerst dagen* or "Christmas days" are a superficial celebration in Dutch homes. Families gather for dinner, but more often the two-day holiday finds people shopping for furniture. Yes, furniture. Two public holidays are dedicated to Christmas, the 25th and 26th of December, known as "first" and "second" Christmas days. Everyone knows the second Christmas day is known to be one of the busiest times of the year at the *woon mall*. I suppose this is good old-fashioned Dutch practicality. You don't want to use your personal time to look for furniture, so hey, it's the day after Christmas; let's go get a dining room set! I get a kick out of the fact that the Dutch are out shopping when you couldn't drag most Americans into a mall after the Christmas shopping marathon was finally finished.

Realizations fall like dominos, one bringing the next on its heels. This willingness to enter a mall immediately after Christmas illustrates something else about the Dutch: their notorious frugality. There is no competition of extravagant gift giving. Admittedly, this Dutch characteristic isn't flattering, but I found the lack of emphasis on presents a welcome relief. No matter how long I searched to find the perfect gifts for my family, they always seemed disappointed. Why? It's a gift. Someone took the time to go out, look for, and purchase something they thought you would enjoy. If you can't appreciate the end result, certainly you can show appreciation at the effort.

* * *

My project end date loomed large and, with it, unexpected delays. Deadlines became tighter. Going to the United States for the holidays was out of the question, and I was glad to have an excuse. Flying, which I love, was much more stressful in the months and years following September 11, 2001. Every time I was about to board a plane, the "Terror Alert" colors went haywire. The system put in place by the Bush administration made no sense. The color escalated from anxious amber to overwrought orange to risky red without accomplishing anything but scaring the hell out of the general public. Usually, there was little or no public information accompanying the change.

The Devil Wears Clogs

It would have been nice not to be working myself to the bone and commuting for three hours a day over Christmas, but in the years immediately after the attacks on the World Trade Center and the Pentagon, even that was preferable to flying through the east coast cities. The "Go Live" date for our new system was January 2, 2003, and I was determined to win this game. My successful data conversion was crucial. Projects in boring Midwest locations like Indiana or Kansas haunted me, providing all the motivation I needed to find a way to stay in Europe.

Before the 2nd of January, I was at the office every day except for the first and second Christmas days. David's parents lived two hours north of Amsterdam in a town called Lellens. He couldn't wait to introduce me to his parents, so we agreed to drive up the afternoon of December 25th. Winter in Holland was colder than usual according to the locals. On the way, I saw several frozen canals overrun with ice skaters. Pride filled David's voice when he told me that skating is one of the Olympic sports in which the Dutch are often medal contenders. A lot of practice takes place on those frozen canals.

Normally, I loved hearing Dutch trivia, but I was anxious about my first meeting with David's family. I loved being with David and was secretly worried that they might not like me. After all, I was just a weird foreigner who didn't even speak their language. How would we even understand one another?

David said his parents bred English bulldogs and Labradors. I had never known a breeder before, so it was a surprise to find dogs everywhere. Most of them were penned up in a kennel built by David's father adjacent to the house, but there were several favorite "house dogs" always under foot. Had I been less nervous about making a good impression, I would have sat on the floor and played with them. In a house full of activity, worrying about scrutiny was a waste of time.

Meeting new people has never been my forte, especially when their impression matters. The bonus in this unusual situation was that I couldn't say more than a few polite words in Dutch. It was the same for David's parents with English. There would be no lengthy discussion on any topic, which should have made me relax, but it didn't. David's lovely mother could not have been more kind. She was all smiles, "*Koffie?*" she asked.

"Yes, please." I smiled back, grateful for that word.

It was immediate family only, David's mother, father, brother, and sister-in-law, that day. Had it been a big family gathering, I'm not sure my nerves would have held out. The only unsettling thing about this visit was David's father. David stands six feet five inches tall. His father is even taller with a deep voice which booms throughout every room he enters. At first, he thought that if he spoke to me loudly in Dutch, that I would understand. Consequently, I had a six-foot-something giant yelling at me in a language I barely understood. Luckily he also had a great smile and a glint in his eye, so I knew he didn't mean any harm. Everyone, including me, got a good laugh out of it.

We passed the hours sitting in the cozy living room next to the wood-burning stove, talking and eating my favorite Dutch cheese and *worst*. They were curious about me, and we did our best to understand one another. David was forced to do a lot of translating, which is exhausting, but he seemed happy to do it. After coffee, glasses of wine were poured and I was more at ease and a little bolder about trying out my Dutch. Soon, I was actually enjoying myself. I should have known that the people who raised a kind and intelligent son like David would be easygoing, but I had learned to assume nothing in this country.

Feeling relieved at passing the parent test, we drove home to Amsterdam to spend our brief holiday at my place. David put wood on the fire and I called my U.S. friends to wish them Merry Christmas. I chatted and David busied himself in the kitchen. He enjoys cooking, something that I personally have never excelled at. It impressed me that he knew what he was doing with food. Clearly his mother had taught him well. I nearly fell asleep on the couch, thinking how lucky I was.

Out of nowhere, darkness crept in. My "perfect life" was so tenuous. What if it came crashing down and I had to return to Ohio? Why did I think I deserved all this? Refusing to allow the beautiful evening to go up in flames, I pushed away the shadows. David motioned me into the dining room by pulling out a chair. We took our seats at the table, adorned with burgundy flowers and elegant white candles. It was just what the doctor ordered, quiet and romantic. We toasted our good fortune, dove into David's delicious pasta, and then dozed, wrapped up in each other in front of the fire.

CHAPTER 17
REALITY BITES

The 27th of December was a cold dark Saturday. David wasn't working, so I didn't ask him to drop me off at the station. At least one of us should be enjoying the weekend. I found it nearly impossible to remain in a good mood during this long trip every day. When I was lucky, Martin picked me up. Between Christmas and the arrival of 2003, I was rarely lucky.

By the time I arrived at the office, it was a crisp and bright. Only one teammate and I were working to perform tests for the final data conversion on the second of January. I am not, nor will I ever be, a hands-on system techie. Fortunately, my wizard of a teammate, Jan, was a programming genius. He was a laid back character with enough experience and determination to know the tricks to the best software performance. Despite it being Saturday, I didn't mind working. My job was to make judgment calls, test the run times, and report our progress in the trial conversion run. Armed with that information, I would be able fine tune my plans for the Big Day.

It was a very quiet afternoon waiting for the system to finish running. By late afternoon, we were able to leave. We'd made some progress, but not as much as the perfectionist in me would have liked. I still had the best possible connections in Germany to solve any issues that Jan couldn't, so I was feeling positive overall.

The Dutch winter was in full swing, which meant by evening it was cold and drizzling. Not wanting to walk to a restaurant in the shitty weather, we opted for another quiet night at home.

"They broke into my car again." David declared.

I must have looked shocked because he went on to explain. "Never leave anything in the car, especially in plain sight." The tone that started in frustration quickly escalated to fury. "It isn't just Amsterdam, it's the same in Den Haag or Utrecht. There are gangs, which go around on motorbikes so that the police can't catch them in all the traffic. It's the Moroccans."

I had no idea what to say.

"One of the most common scams is to break a back car window when the driver stops at a light. They grab a laptop or a briefcase and just disappear."

Now I was alarmed. Nothing so dramatic happens in small-town America, so I found this revelation about my newly-adopted city shocking. Germans have earned their reputation for honesty. I saw it first-hand when Dora's wallet was returned after she left it in a cab, which is unheard of in the States. I never expected gangs to be at work just outside the front door of my affluent apartment building. If I had given it a moment's thought, it should have been a given. This was a legal soft-drugs capital of the world. Even though it isn't common for the Dutch to be hanging out in coffee shops, there are people arriving hourly via planes, trains, and automobiles to dive into the drug-and-prostitution cesspool. I started to feel like I knew nothing about the world after all.

* * *

The end of 2002 consisted of work punctuated with train rides and very little sleep. In 2000, I had taken up running in the mornings and I continued this during my year in Germany. In the Netherlands, my commutes were so extreme that I would have had to leave the house at 4:30 a.m. to get any running in. I was rarely making it home before 11 p.m. on most nights. Getting up after so little sleep was an ugly proposition. Zero regular exercise and non-stop work were taking a toll on my attitude–and not for the better. I just wanted to make it through each day until this project was over.

As my data conversion tests went forward, Marlena was a gift from God. She was responsible for putting the necessary changes into the system, and allowed me to bend the rules slightly when it came to deadlines for submitting my changes. Our cooperation was covert, to keep the wolves at bay. They delighted in critiquing everything from Marlena's Afrikaans accent to my American wardrobe. In the office, we ignored their antics. Privately, we marveled at their gross immaturity.

New Year's Eve came quickly. My test plans were on schedule and aside from one nasty bug, which I could not solve without German help, my successful conversion seemed imminent. I was living in Amsterdam. I had a good-looking, intelligent boyfriend. Against all odds, it seemed I would pass my first career test in Holland with flying colors. As David and I readied the champagne and prepared for the night's festivities, I was filled with gratitude. I was eager to transfer to the Amsterdam office to remain in Europe and I was optimistic I would accomplish that too.

Early in the evening, David started giving me the lowdown on Dutch New Year's traditions. On my way home, I'd heard the crackle and pop of fireworks whizzing by already from every direction. According to my Dutchman, on this one night, fireworks were legal in the Netherlands. Compared to what I was used to, a fireworks display put on by professional firemen and a city safety crew, it seemed crazy. Any old Jan, Dirk, or Willem could light them on *Oud en Nieuw*. I thought that I had gotten the picture, but I wasn't at all prepared for what happened at the stroke of midnight. That morning, David had been stressing about having his car parked on the street. It wasn't because of the vandals, but of damage from stray fireworks. I didn't say it, but I wished he would get a grip and stop acting like an old man.

At 11:30 p.m., we donned our winter woolies and grabbed the chilled Moët et Chandon before climbing up to the roof terrace. As I opened the hatch, the wind screamed and immediately bit my fingers. Grateful for the layer of protection that came from the wine we'd already drunk, we crawled outside. My entire body trembled. David had to take over Operation Champagne as I hugged myself for warmth. Jumping up and down to random flashes and booms to keep the blood flowing, we tried to capture the moment on film. It's hard to take photos when you can't stand still, so mostly we guzzled champagne and huddled until the clock struck midnight.

Then I forgot that I was freezing. The city lights below glittered like diamonds and the stars echoed the effect. Everything I despised about Amsterdam faded into the background when she appeared in her holiday finest.

The display of Oud en Nieuw blew my mind. I knew everyone was allowed to set off fireworks if they wanted to. Reality was that every single person in this cramped, overpopulated city lit them, and lit them at once! The multitude of shimmering gems in the sky was magnificent. *KABOOM* was seen and felt every five seconds. Rockets whistled past my ears. It seemed to go on forever.

With shaking hands, I dialed Allison in Nebraska and shouted into the phone, "You've got to hear this!" I held the phone up into the sky. I couldn't hear a damn thing, but thought I heard her laugh before I promised to call back later and hung up.

Like a lightning bolt, David's concern about the car made sense. All the debris would have ruined the paint. I grinned from ear to ear at the spectacle and gave David huge sloppy kisses, as we stood shivering but happy on the roof. For once, I didn't worry about what could go wrong.

CHAPTER 18
BREAKTHROUGH

On January 2, 2003, the final system conversion began on schedule. Once it was complete and the data verified by a third party, I would be finished. This project, Hazel, and my freezing three-hour public transport nightmare would be history. I was counting the hours. My only problem was a stubborn software bug we'd uncovered that refused to budge. After several discussions with the Germans and numerous email exchanges, a solution was found that allowed the program to run. Just to spite me, it ran excruciatingly slow and took over a day to complete. This was my final step before the third-party audit was checking the original client data against the data appearing in the new system. If it wasn't registered correctly or appeared in the wrong place, the conversion would be a failure and I'd be forced back to the drawing board: a fate worse than death.

During the entire process, I sent regular detailed progress updates to Dafne and Hazel. I covered all the bases and my project plans were meticulous. My programming guru, Jan, and I analyzed each data stream several times and high-fived each other when we were sure it was right.

The rest of the team ignored our positive results and not one supportive word was uttered by Hazel, until after the auditor begrudgingly signed off on the completed system documentation. When she was sure no one could contradict her and someone else had given approval, she told us how certain she'd been of our success the whole time. From day one I'd had support from Jan and Marlena, and no one else. I couldn't have cared less what she thought. Someone who spent more working hours outside the office than supporting her team wasn't entitled my respect. Dafne was the one whose approval mattered because she had influence over my request to transfer.

It felt good. Never had I accomplished anything so technically difficult with a less cooperative team. Dafne confirmed it when she delivered my performance review with an above average score. In person, she said I'd proven capable of "outstanding performance." The only reason my score wasn't higher, she explained, was that my results were compared with those of the full project team of over a hundred consultants, many of whom had been working on the project more than a year.

Just to make sure I didn't get too comfortable, she had one more thing to say, "You were a bit too slow in the beginning, but in the end you brought everything together."

I was surprised, but I let the last words be the important ones. How did she think I might have moved faster without English system documentation and her initial refusal to grant my request for Dutch lessons? Since hers were the words that either would allow me to stay in the Netherlands or force me to return to the United States, I smiled graciously and thanked her for the opportunity to play an important role on her team. My next question was if I could change my allotted round-trip ticket home to another destination of equal cost. Ohio in January was not the rest I needed. "Yes, of course," she answered. Inside, I patted myself on the back for learning to play the game.

After the tedium of a data conversion, I needed a mental break. I thought visiting old friends in Arizona, or any place the sun would show its face in January, but the most appealing thought was sitting on a beach alone with my thoughts. I had no idea where I could go from Amsterdam that would be affordable. David said that the Dutch Antilles were a popular destination from Holland, so he expected I would find reasonable airfare, even in mid-winter. As usual, he was right. Without a second thought, I booked a ticket to spend ten days in Curaçao. I needed to escape both the gray rainy weather and the demanding Dutch.

David was surprised at the speed with which my suitcase flew open. He hadn't known me long enough to know that I don't linger

The Devil Wears Clogs

over decisions. I see an open door, window, rabbit hole—whatever—and I run straight for it. This is especially true in times of great stress. With a couple of kisses and the reassurance that I was indeed coming back, I vanished into the great blue yonder of the Caribbean Sea.

During the project, I'd remarked to an American friend how surprising it was that the Dutch were so rigid. Everything had to be done one way–theirs–and new ideas had no place. My friend, ten years older than me, nearly deafened me with his laughter. "The Dutch are responsible for apartheid! Of course they are rigid!"

There are few times when my ignorance has been brought to my attention more emphatically than that moment.

* * *

The flight to Curaçao was uneventful. Nine hours is a long time to sit in a cramped economy class seat, even when dreaming of aqua seas and sun-drenched beaches. Reading the island information I'd brought along didn't help. First sentence: The capital city is Willemstad. Second: The national language is Dutch! I knew that the islands of Aruba, Bonaire, and Curaçao were previous Dutch possessions, but I'd been to former island colonies and never noticed that the former culture still had a stranglehold. I flipped through the pages, looking at tourist sites and activities on the island, and my depression deepened. The iron fist of Dutch domination extended five thousand miles from the Motherland.

I considered hiring a boat to take me to another island, but thought better of it when I arrived. Jetlagged and sleep-deprived, but still moving at corporate speed, I went directly to the concierge desk with my list of preferences and questions for my nine day stay. "Does the room have a sea view? Am I close to the beach? Do you have newspapers in English?"

The gregarious man with the toothy white grin behind the desk just laughed. "Welcome to Curaçao!" he boomed.

His generous greeting forced me to check myself. Where were my manners? I should have started with a big "Hello! I am so happy to be here!" but I hadn't.

"Thank you. I'm so sorry. It's been a very long trip." I stammered, making a mental note to slow down effective immediately, and stretching to shake off the stress that should have been left behind at Schiphol Airport.

"No worries, m'am. You will love our island. Let us show you to your room," he said, motioning to the bellman.

Clearly used to the daily arrival of harried tourists, he did me a favor by holding up a giant mirror. I appreciated the reminder that I was here of my own free will and about to have the relaxing vacation that I so desperately needed. The bellman quietly appeared and gathered my belongings. It was early evening when I looked out at the tranquil sea from my balcony and inhaled the salty warm air. The swaying palms and spicy tropical flowers were a sedative. I didn't move from the bed for the next twelve hours.

* * *

On my first day in the Antilles, I decided to do absolutely nothing. Not yet adjusted to the six-hour time difference, I woke before dawn. A quick peek out my window confirmed that the beach was deserted. Even the sun was taking her time rising over the sea. Pulling on shorts and a t-shirt, all I wanted to do was feel my toes in the water. No matter where I am, I am instantly relaxed by that sensation. Carrying my sandals, I took a look around the resort buildings. Spotting the dark blue waves, I headed straight for it. The water was perfect, somewhere between an Arizona swimming pool and frigid Lake Erie.

I splashed along toward a boathouse where a few earlybirds were organizing gear for a morning dive. My hotel was known for its dive instruction and proximity to pristine sites. Having no interest in scuba, I wandered down the beach to see what else going on. As I strolled, the sky turned from midnight blue to reddish purple as the sun prepared the sky for her grand entrance.

A seasoned beachcomber, I noted the various pinks and browns of seashells resting on the white sand and the prime position of several beach chairs. The breeze picked up swiftly and the sun finally began her climb from sea to sky. I did not question my choice of destination again. As the clouds dispersed and changed their hues, my heart filled with gratitude. It didn't matter that I was alone; in fact it made me

The Devil Wears Clogs

appreciate it more. I dropped to the sand to give my full attention to the majestic performance in the sky.

When the final pink hues evaporated, I stood up and dusted the sand off. I noticed someone else had been silently watching nearby. "Good morning," I said, smiling and more relaxed than my last encounter.

"Good morning to you." He waved.

"You're lucky to see this every day. It's so beautiful," I gushed.

"The rising sun is my favorite," he said nodding. With his deep coconut skin, he looked like he'd been around long enough to do considerable comparison. I wished for that existence, to sit still and compare sunrises and sunsets. Everyone I knew was constantly rushing from place to place, oblivious to things like the sun's daily activities. At least today, I was luckier than most.

As for the rest of my island days, I wanted to see the sights, but that idea was in constant conflict with my desire to look inward and decide what to do with my life next. When I did make my way into Willemstad, I was charmed. The capital was bursting with color while remaining true to its Dutch heritage. In a weird juxtaposition, there was Heineken everywhere and clogs in the tourist shops. Restaurant menus were full of European fare, but there was enough succulent seafood and fresh tropical fruit to ignore it. I admired wooden carvings and handmade clothing in the massive central market. I crossed the celebrated Queen Wilhelmina footbridge, to admire the primary-colored storefronts and bars lining the waterfront. Strong salty winds had their way with the multicolored restaurant umbrellas, and I sat down with a Corona to people watch.

One Corona became two while I lapped up the friendly atmosphere. Here I sat, on a picture-perfect Caribbean island, on vacation from my job in Europe. It's probably not even polite to mention the fact that the company paid my airfare. It just didn't make sense. What had I done in my previous life to gain such perfect karma in this one?

I spent a considerable amount of time thinking about my issues with the Germans and Dutch, and for that matter the Americans who sent me to Europe to begin with, but what was better? The opportunity to see every far-flung location while being paid handsomely for my hard work, or being content with an equally well-paid job in an American city which presented little or no challenge and zero degree of the exotic? Yes, it was hard. Yes, I missed everyone in the States. Yes, it made my heart pound every time I had to take on another location, bus route, highway, or language, but the alternative was going backwards after I'd already started on the road less traveled. From the outside, I must have appeared insane, or at the very least an adventure junkie. Had I lived within driving distance, my friends would have staged an intervention.

I spent a week on the beach with my books. I tried sorting out my conflicted head and heart by starting a journal. Ever since arriving in Holland, I had questioned what I was doing. Everything seemed so ridiculously hard, and the gloomy Dutch winter climate only intensified my doubt. Caressed by gentle island breezes, looking out over the shining sea, life felt different. Hope returned that maybe this project was the hardest because it was my first in the Netherlands. Surely life would get easier as I better understood the people and the language, right?

David was the tie-breaker. At thirty-two, a relationship had never come before career. Perhaps, for once, it should. If I didn't keep fighting to stay a part of the Dutch office, our relationship would not survive. Having been guilty of this so many times in the past, I finally had to admit that this course of action wasn't working. I decided to keep going, convincing myself that the worst was behind me. Working with a new team and project in Holland would be a fresh start. Besides, I had succeeded, hadn't I? With all odds stacked against me, I still won.

No, I wasn't about to give up what was most important to me because a few people wanted to make my life difficult. They wouldn't get rid of me that easily.

CHAPTER 19
OUT OF THE FRYING PAN

What waited for me when I returned to Amsterdam should have been an indication that, no, the worst was not behind me. A stopover in Aruba was scheduled before the flight continued to Schiphol Airport. Looking at my itinerary, this alone stretched the flight time to eleven hours. Having made peace with my decision to remain in the Netherlands, I was anxious to get home and find out what I would be working on next. I hadn't spoken to anyone in the office to find out if there was another project, but Dafne had given me the impression that she was satisfied and I would be able to stay longer.

I watched passengers walk through a type of scanner I'd never seen before at the Curaçao airport. A black-and-white body photo flashed over the screen to be read by the security guard rather what I normally saw produced by an x-ray machine. I was curious about the new machine, but my interest was 99% vested in getting on that plane and home to David. I noticed that several people were pulled aside by the security guards after they walked through.

Impatiently, I waited for takeoff. The concept of "island time" hadn't stuck despite my stint on Curaçao's beaches. I was fuming to be stuck in Aruba so long, but as a post 9/11 traveler, I knew I was in captivity for however long the airline deemed necessary.

The captain's voice eventually reported that our delay was caused by twenty-five people who didn't board after checking in. Seriously? Twenty-five people who had fully intended to board and checked their luggage didn't make it through security? That number seemed unusually high.

Finally, the plane took off and I assumed whatever drama had happened in Aruba had been left behind. In Amsterdam, I'd be able to quickly get through luggage claim and find the train. At least I hoped so.

Touching down in Amsterdam brought the familiar sight of the black runway slick with rain. I had arrived back in the Land of Perpetual Precipitation. One by one, we were freed from our seats to gather belongings and head for the door. Barely moving, I started to suspect that something was definitely up. I followed the crowd creeping onto the jet way where all movement halted. A German shepherd tethered to a Dutch police officer then stopped for a sniff of every person in line, and we were rudely directed to line up single-file. This was a new one. It wasn't enough that we'd been on that plane for over thirteen hours, now we were treated like kindergarteners. I was not amused.

After standing in that line for forty-five minutes and spending every ounce of my energy not losing it on whoever was responsible for this ridiculous routine, I finally saw what was happening. The three hundred exiting passengers were each being questioned by a *single* interviewer. Before we could exit and collect our bags, this man wanted to know our reasons for being in Curaçao. *Are you fucking kidding me?*

How could the police have zero consideration for the non-criminals among us who just wanted to get home from our holiday? I had no idea what the background was for this intense scrutiny and frankly, I didn't care. I inched along toward the plain-clothed enemy whose only sign of authority was the clipboard he held and tersely gave him one-word answers to his questions. When I said I'd gone to Curaçao alone, he raised his eyebrows and pointed me toward the longer, less-desirable second queue. It was longer because an agent was opening every carry-on, searching them one at a time.

The bed-headed customs agent demanded to know what I was doing in the Dutch Antilles by myself. Every fiber of my being wanted to inform her that it was none of her damn business, but I managed to refrain from making my situation worse. I said I'd gone to relax and didn't elaborate. She then opened my bag and saw the three bottles of Caribbean rum I'd brought back. Never asking why I had them, she

The Devil Wears Clogs

cracked each one open and sniffed. Since two were gifts, I was mightily pissed off, and finally I couldn't keep quiet any longer. "What are you looking for in a bottle of rum that is *sealed*?"

The ill-tempered woman regarded me with disdain, not considering it her responsibility to educate the ignorant foreigner. "Drugs," she replied. "Next time, be aware you are only allowed to bring two bottles of spirits into this country. NEXT!"

What the hell kind of drug goes into a bottle of clear liquor? I wondered. Apparently, Europeans were innovative when it came to illegal substances. Behind me, the German shepherd from the jet way released a deafening bark at a scruffy young man. Immediately, he was led away with force to a waiting area where several others sat surrounded by cops.

Along with my growing confusion, the battle continued. At baggage claim, the carousel assigned to our flight was cordoned off from the others, the last one of twenty. Next to the carousel were makeshift tables for searching the bags. Of course, the final degradation for the day was suitcase contents analysis. You might have guessed by now that my poor attitude made me an unlikely candidate to escape the final screening, and you would be right.

In the fourteenth hour of this travel ordeal, I had the pleasure of watching a rumpled angry Dutch customs agent remove every item from my suitcase including dirty underwear, and then say, "Go ahead." I did not hear, "Sorry that I've made a complete mess of your contents" or, "Apologies for the inconvenience, ma'am, clearly you have done nothing wrong." Nope, his words told me I could go. His body language told me I could go to hell. He seemed pissed off not to have found anything.

Obviously I've had a lot of time to rethink my decision to stick it out in Holland during all this. On other Caribbean trips, I'd experienced intense customs routines, but I'd never seen a setup that assumes that you are guilty, and you must prove your innocence. I felt guilty and, aside from one bottle of rum too many, I hadn't done anything. I decided to let it go until I spoke to my favorite Dutchman. Finally free, I sent him a text that I was on my way back to my apartment by taxi. I had no stamina left for the train-and-tram adventure.

When I opened the door to a smiling David, I immediately felt better. Shocked by my dark tan, he said I looked like a native. His huge grin said he was just as happy to see me. When I started talking about what happened at the airport, he interrupted, saying he'd already seen it on the news. I didn't have time to figure out why such a thing was newsworthy before he was in full explanation mode about the major drug running problem between the Antilles and Amsterdam airport. I described the machines I'd seen that took pictures rather than x-rays, and he said they were looking for *bolletjesslikkers*.

"They were looking for *what*?" I stared at him. By this point, I had figured out many Dutch words, but either the exhaustion or the jetlag prevented me from being able to put these ridiculous syllables into a context where they made sense.

"A bolletjesslikker is a person who swallows condoms filled with drugs, like cocaine. If they survive the flight, they stay with someone on this side who collects the drugs and pays them off. There is a special jail at Schiphol where they keep the ones they've caught, because it is too dangerous to transport them."

The picture was suddenly clear. It became clearer when we flipped on the evening news, which reported that thirty people had been arrested as smugglers. A further twenty-five people carrying contraband had been caught in Aruba before the flight took off. The specialized scanners showed photos of the drugs in their bodies as they attempted to board the flight. It was insane. Nearly sixty people were arrested from a total of three hundred passengers.

The poverty level of the Curaçao' islanders wasn't lost on me during my island wanderings, but I couldn't imagine risking death for a payoff of a few thousand dollars. I found the number of people willing to risk these odds staggering, but I've never felt such desperation. These thoughts were the last through my brain before it went into shut down. Safe in David's arms on my comfy couch at the Penthouse, I was out like a light.

David quietly showered the next morning and left for work. Hearing the door close, I adjusted my pillow and threw another blanket over myself before snoring into late morning. When I grabbed consciousness long enough to realize that there was probably news waiting in my email, I pried myself out of bed.

Forcing myself awake, I slurped down coffee. When I connected to the internet, I watched over a hundred emails pour in. I scanned the subject lines, looking for something from Dafne, and found a request to call her when I was back in Amsterdam. I wasted no time. Relief flooded over me when she told me there was another project role waiting. The project was under a different manager at another Dutch utility. She gave me his details and asked me to contact him directly. My new manager's name sounded like "eel," but I didn't catch the rest.

Still looking for my business brain, I showered and tried to function. All Dafne said was that she had granted my earlier request for a lead role on my next project. I couldn't imagine why they would be interested in me leading a project at a Dutch energy provider, but I was game. They could have told me that I'd be climbing poles to repair faulty electricity lines in a thunderstorm and I would have said yes, so I could stay with David.

I didn't reach "eel" (which, I later found out was "Eelco") on my first attempt, so I left a voicemail and went about getting my apartment and myself organized to return to work. While I was sorting laundry, Eelco called back with details on the position, which would last two months. If I accepted, I would be working in a city south of Amsterdam called S'Hertogenbosch. When he heard me struggle to say the name, he told me the modern name of the city was Den Bosch. This time I knew to ask more questions. In the Netherlands, location is key. According to him, the project location was easily reachable by train from Amsterdam in about thirty minutes without any bus connections.

Next, Eelco described the work. I was to lead a team of client personnel through the selection of a document archiving system. This software would have to integrate with the organization-wide system also being implemented currently by my company. The company-wide software was the same as the one I'd worked with on Dafne's project and in Germany.

As he spoke, I realized that this was the same client where David worked, and alarm drowned out most of what he said next. I did catch the line that the role was open, as the previous project manager had been asked to leave. That didn't do much to quiet the alarm bells. Regardless, I told Eelco I'd think it over and phone him back within a day. Even as I said the words, I knew I would accept the job. Based on my last project experience, I had to ask some questions from a trusted source before committing.

David returned to my apartment, tired after a long day. With my mental time zone advantage, I pounced on him anyway. A wide smile came over his face when I said I'd been asked to stay. He took in every detail. His immediate reply was that while his project was the same client, it was in a different building. Apparently it was a big company with sites all over the country, from Friesland in the far North, to Zeeland at its southernmost point. Considering his own responsibilities, he said he didn't see how our roles would intersect.

On hearing this, I relaxed for the first time since speaking with Eelco. That was the one thing I could not cope with, the collision of our work lives. The scenario was complicated enough navigating the two nationalities, and my unhappiness with my less than perfect life so far in the Netherlands, without being forced to have a working relationship as well.

David told me more about the project and the various projects going on at this client. I knew some of the details about the company from my time in Germany. I had been the central point of contact for the firm's projects worldwide, so I'd met several of my European colleagues over the phone. Groundbreaking work was happening at the Dutch energy firm and this move fit my plan perfectly. The position had leadership responsibility and the project had a good reputation.

I learned during my German days that sometimes, large-scale software implementations are known as "death marches." This happens when the company sells a project that they can't bring an adequate number of staff on board for fear of losing money. A project might also be known as a death march when the original estimates of the work were grossly inadequate. Fault can lie with the contractor or the client, depending on whether something was left out of the original design or whether the client requested enhancements beyond the original specifications.

The Devil Wears Clogs

The undesirable projects were known only by word of mouth between colleagues. If you weren't plugged in to an informal network in your region, you could land in a very bad situation. I would be the last to call my luck fantastic, but it could have been much worse. Several colleagues I knew had been stuck working sixty to eighty-hour weeks for several consecutive months. Often, the project manager would not allow them to report any overtime either. I knew I had to be very careful not to land in such a situation. I've never been opposed to hard work, but I am definitely opposed to slave labor.

I called Eelco the next day and accepted the Den Bosch assignment, starting the week after. He seemed nice enough, but he was all business. I knew he'd just finished a large project in my specialty area, customer relationship management software, and I had high hopes that I could learn something from my new boss. Fifteen months of experience had shown me that the Dutch and Germans had a very different approach to their customers than I was used to in America. I wanted to know why.

* * *

Taking Dafne's advice, I also called the Amsterdam office to make an appointment with the executive responsible for my business unit. The subject of the meeting was a possible transfer from Cleveland to Amsterdam. If I managed to pull it off, that would be one less worry. It would no longer be possible for the company to yank me back to Ohio if they felt like it. Meeting scheduled, I took a deep breath and steadied myself for the road ahead. So far, avoiding the potholes had been difficult. Had I been religious, I would have prayed for this path to be smoother.

Despite having one successful Dutch project under my belt, I didn't relish the idea of working in the Amsterdam office for even a day. The only good thing about it was the half-hour walk from my apartment through the Vondelpark. Amsterdam's largest park is sprawling, and I had no idea which exit to use, but I was always early at the office so I didn't worry about it. Being a little bit lost made me feel free and I got a kick out of finding my way when I didn't have strict time constraints. My meeting at the office wasn't until 11a.m., so I could afford a good long stroll.

Expecting the park to be nearly empty at seven in the morning, I was in for a shock. It was anything but quiet. Entering through the imposing black-and-gold iron gates, I began my first rush-hour walk. Within minutes, the shrill ring of bicycle bells was at my back, demanding that I move from the path. Hundreds of bicycles, manned by frowning guys in business suits sped past, their front baskets weighed down with laptop bags.

I tended to avoid this office because, like everywhere else in Holland, it is intensely crowded. When I did go, I arrived early enough to snatch a desk by the window, so that in between tasks I could look onto the city streets and pretend I was somewhere else. All our offices had a "just in time" policy, which meant that no one had an assigned work location. You had to make a desk reservation for the days you planned to be in the office. Of course, management hoped that you would *not* be in the office because this meant that you, as a consultant, were not at a chargeable client location. Probably as a deterrent, desks were scarce after 8:30 a.m.

Spotting my favorite seat, I tried to slide in unnoticed. Most of my colleagues didn't love speaking English, and I wasn't in the mood to struggle through the little Dutch that I knew to answer the first, and generally only, question, "How is your Dutch going?" *Poorly*. Too bad I didn't think through my strategy, because it's difficult to blend in when you don't understand even the words on the coffee machine.

I had a few hours before I was to meet with Adriaan, the executive who I hoped would support my transfer application, instead of crushing my European dreams under his foot. No matter what you wanted to achieve at this enormous company, if you didn't have anyone senior behind you, you could forget it. I needed an Amsterdam executive supporting me for it to become reality.

A few weeks after my move to the Netherlands, I had floated the subject with Dafne and she had informed me, in typical blunt Dutch fashion, that performance was everything. Translation, "Until we've seen what you can do, you should drop it."

While I waited, I looked up information on my new client and contacted my home office. I gave them the details on my next assignment, which was to begin the first week of February and last until March or April, depending on how things went. At least I could count on one thing, as long as I was working for a client, Cleveland management wouldn't have any issue with me staying. Thank God there weren't two battles to fight.

At the appointed hour, I walked to the office where Adriaan was working that day. We did not know each other beyond a few brief exchanges, so the conversation was stilted. I didn't know who was supposed to lead this dance. He was the senior employee and I was the lowly consultant, but the meeting was at my request. After fumbling through a few words on how much I was enjoying working in Holland and hoping that my nose did not suddenly begin to grow at an alarming rate, I got to the point.

Without mincing words, Adriaan said Dafne had delivered a positive review of my performance and that I was welcome to stay in Holland. I nearly leapt from my seat to bear hug this serious man. Ecstatic to be released from the constant nagging threat of returning to a dull Ohio life, I'm sure I was far too effusive for this practical Dutchman.

I didn't hug him, as this culture prizes even-keeled demeanor in all respects. Merely saying I was happy was probably over the top. I shut my mouth and he continued talking about the practicalities of the transfer, and told me I needed to wait for the HR paperwork that would finalize the process. Walking on air out of his office, my only thought was how much fun it was going to be to give David the news.

That night we celebrated with a decadent meal close to the scene of the morning's chaos. In the Vondelpark, there is a snazzy dungeon-like restaurant called Vertigo. I did feel dizzy as I sipped silky champagne with the handsome man who had helped steady me in the torrent of Dutchness. The soft candlelight between us worked its magic. Savoring my triumph, I couldn't help but indulge in the illusion that this development proved I was meant to be here and the more dangerous illusion—that I was welcome.

CHAPTER 20
INTERVIEW WITH THE DEVIL

Following Eelco's directions, I exited the Den Bosch train station on a frosty February morning and headed for my new office. According to him, getting there without a cab or a bike was only a few minutes' walk, so I squinted at the building numbers in the bright morning light and tried to walk quickly. Fifteen minutes later, I was still walking, not fun in pumps and a skirt. I thought for sure I'd missed it. Always underestimating the logistics piece of this puzzle, I arrived at the building after another five minutes. For a guy wearing a warm coat and loafers, twenty minutes *is* an easy walk. Changing one or two of those variables alters the equation.

My new client's campus, a trio of non-descript office buildings, presented the next challenge. I walked toward a guard, who seemed to fancy himself more Secret Service agent than a door guard at an energy company. Understanding now that smiling a greeting to an unknown person is taboo in Dutch culture, I launched straight into my story. His non-smile became a distinct frown when the guard realized it was the English language coming out of my mouth. Without a word, he pointed a large hairy finger toward what looked like a concierge desk where I repeated my story. The expressionless woman behind the desk managed not to frown, but instead sighed audibly and walked over to collect the visitor registration book. Clearly, I should have known before I entered this establishment what the rules were because every Dutch person knows what they are. How unfortunate that I'd been born elsewhere because, at least during my time in the Netherlands, I would have to pay the price.

Maintaining a weak smile plastered on my own face throughout this unpleasant interaction was key. Who knew what kind of power this grumpy duo may wield over mere mortals? I had to make my initial impression a good one, or at least non-threatening. The realization that I would always be somebody's burden in this country had been slowly creeping in from the back of my mind since I arrived. Whenever I joined a team, they had to make at least one excruciating extra step to explain how to get a user ID for the client network or access to the project documentation archives, tasks that were de riguer for everyone who could read the instructions in Dutch.

I shouldn't forget that they would also be forced to speak ten or twelve English words to point me to my office. No matter how much I tried to use in my limited Dutch, the party I was speaking to never failed to immediately switch to English. It must have had something to do with that pained, squinty look that took over every Dutch face when I spoke. You know the look. The one people get when there's an intense build-up of gas in their intestines? That look followed me everywhere in the Netherlands, and these two were no exception.

Sign-In Lady managed an enthusiastic farewell when Eelco appeared and led me away through a maze of hallways to my desk. It was relief to see that she was capable of experiencing happiness at something, even if that something was my departure. My clacking heels echoed throughout the silent corridor, announcing my arrival to everyone. Heads turned in doorways as we made our way to the third floor office where I would be working.

Meeting Eelco for the first time was unremarkable. He had dark-brown curly hair and his cappuccino-colored Italian leather shoes were polished to a high shine. He spoke English well and maintained the European suit-and-tie demeanor. Everything about that first meeting was bland. I was introduced to others. I was shown around the building. I was given a summary of my project responsibilities and deadlines. Honestly, there was nothing to it.

The morning passed with routine business matters and client-specific procedures and soon I was clacking down those same stairs to have lunch in the canteen en masse. Fifteen of my Dutch colleagues worked in this building and the protocol seemed to be to eat lunch together daily. As someone who enjoys eating solo, while reading the paper or responding to email, I didn't quite get the need for daily lunchtime togetherness.

Relieved at having conquered the unknown landscape of a Dutch cafeteria at Dafne's project, I took a seat at the table across from Eelco. Everyone was speaking in Dutch when I sat down, so I assumed my usual routine of pretending to pay attention. Just my luck, the conversation switched to English to cover the familiar stomping ground of President Bush and the looming Iraq invasion. I couldn't say for certain whether it's the renowned Dutch bluntness or their limited English vocabulary which makes small talk painful, but it was immediately clear that the "Getting to Know You" dance had ended and we had begun, without a net, the double trapeze acts of "What Are Your Most Controversial Opinions?" and "How Do They Differ from Ours?"

As I had traveled this road more than I cared to in recent months, I kept my comments light and hoped they wouldn't sense my irritation at listening to the same tirade on the wrongness of U.S. action. When they failed to rile me into a heated debate, the conversation eventually turned. I didn't need to justify my opinions to the group of men sitting at the table, but as a bonus, my silence annoyed them more than laying my cards on the table. Regardless of the usual frustration on my first day of the new project, I survived. There were nice people working on other projects, and not everyone wanted to ram their limited worldview down my throat. At first, it seemed like an adequate working environment, and I eagerly embraced my new challenge.

The beginning stage of any new project is the most exciting part. This role was no exception. It would take a while before the quiet voice in the back of my mind began to whisper that things didn't seem quite right. It would be even longer before that same voice started shouting.

The first thing I wanted to do was to meet the client personnel who would be my team members, and get their views on the best ways to work together. The previous project manager, whose disappearance was never fully explained, had left notes, but I wasn't going to base my efforts on the work of someone I'd never met. I prefer to get my information straight from the horse's mouth. As it turned out, these horses roamed the entire country.

* * *

My knowledge of Holland's geography was sketchy. It was news to me that the Netherlands included a foreign country within its borders where the people speak funny and act very differently from other *Nederlanders*. It is known as Friesland, a rural province in the far north. While there are big differences in dialect between the north and the south of Holland, this is the only province where people speak a different language. Called *Frisian*, it sounds markedly different. Friesland consists of a pocket of mainland and five beautiful North Sea islands called the Wadden Islands.

My investigation of the region began immediately, as I had to pay a visit to a facility in north Friesland where the employees had critical background knowledge. Four hours on the train across the frosted Dutch countryside had me arriving to meet them in the flesh. Phone meetings with multiple accents and varying degrees of proficiency in English are a last resort.

Accompanied by two of my clients, Dan and Eize, I was given a tour of the mail processing center, which would be implementing the solution my team was to select. It was located in a city called Sneek, which cracked me up because it is literally pronounced "snake."

Eager to show off their unique heritage to the foreigner, my new teammates told me that the Frisian language is derived from English and German. This immediately made sense because, despite the crazy accent, I understood the spoken Frisian better than I understood what was spoken in Amsterdam.

Maybe because I had been warned about these "weird" Frisians, or possibly because we were all considered outsiders in this country, I felt at ease with these two from the moment they picked me up. I saw they would be knowledgeable advocates for the project. What a major relief! It was my job to lead the team to the best possible solution, but input and participation from people who didn't report to me was crucial. When I saw how much effort they made at our first meeting, I was sure my new team would be a big improvement over my last.

The Devil Wears Clogs

* * *

By the time I met everyone, it was almost Valentine's Day. In 2003, it was a Friday. It was a touchy subject to ask for a day off when I was only scheduled to work at this client for two months, but I was buoyed by the positive interaction I'd had with them. Cautiously, I broached the subject with Eelco, expecting the answer to be "no." Surprisingly, he didn't hesitate in saying yes. Celebrating Valentine's Day isn't common for Europeans. The no-nonsense thrifty Dutch are not whipped into a frenzy by any holiday that requires buying presents, unless it is for children at Sinterklaas. Even then, the celebrations are subdued. In comparison, Americans look materialistic.

With a sly smile, Eelco asked me if my day off was for Valentine's Day, and I admitted that it was. The creepy grin on his face told me I didn't want to know what he was thinking.

Looking to trade my air miles for escape, I studied the map of Europe. David was keen to get away for a few days, so we decided on Vienna. He had never been there and I'd found it terribly romantic when I visited the year before. The flight was under two hours and there was plenty to keep us occupied for a weekend.

Having seen most of the tourist hot spots in Vienna, this trip was all about indulgence. We wandered through a Karntnerstrasse boutique, which glittered floor to ceiling with antique crystal chandeliers, and lounged in coffee houses with the intelligentsia. We photographed the exceptional Vienna Opera House, and talked about what we wanted from life. It was how I had always pictured my life in Europe would be, until reality ruined it.

We spent the frozen mornings lounging in our hotel room and warmed our afternoons in luxurious cafés and museums. To me, Vienna is as beautiful as she is understated. It is not a city that loudly shouts what it has to offer, she's too refined for that.

Easy to please, David would have been happy with the *weiner schnitzel* alone, but the pastries and deep chocolate cake were absolutely sinful. If you add the immense pride of the Austrians to have produced Wolfgang Amadeus Mozart, his music filling the air, then you have an idea of what you would find. It doesn't matter that Mozart was born in

Salzburg, because he achieved fame in Vienna. The entire country has claimed a piece of his legacy and his work is performed throughout. What amused me the most was not the young boys wearing powdered wigs and knee-length velvet dress coats while hawking concert tickets, but the numerous boxes of foil wrapped chocolates bearing his likeness. I wonder if he would approve.

One afternoon, just after we left St. Stephen's Cathedral, and were headed for a *Sacher torte* and a *weiner mélange*, I saw them. A rumpled mass of protesters was gathered in the middle of Vienna's historic center. At least fifty people of various races and ages stood clustered together. I tried to read the signs, but few were in English. One with angry blood-red brush strokes leapt out at me, "Take Bush to the Hague!" My heart skipped a beat as the meaning sunk in.

"Convict Bush!" someone shouted, thinking he belonged on trial at the International Court of Criminal Justice. "Put him on trial!" yelled another.

Pushing past them, I felt like they could tell I was American, which was impossible. I was numb. I hadn't voted for the man, but I didn't believe he belonged in prison either. This was the President of the United States we were talking about. Like a knife to the chest, I finally understood how heated the conflict between the U.S. and Europe was becoming. Despite the fact that I had been listening to my Dutch colleagues rant for months on the topic, I hadn't realized how many Europeans passionately believed that President Bush deserved severe punishment for his advance toward an Iraq invasion.

I had no way of knowing that the shadow of the controversial U.S. president would follow me across Europe, creeping into places I never expected. I certainly couldn't have foreseen that the election of President Bush for a second term in 2004 would lead Europeans to seriously question the judgment of Americans. Growing up American, I believed in fighting for democracy worldwide. I was educated and liberal enough to understand the downside of this mission when it was perpetuated by zealots, but I believed that we were in this to fight the good fight, and that America's allies would be behind us as we'd stood with them. I couldn't have predicted how deeply divided Europeans and Americans would become.

CHAPTER 21
ALTERED STATES

Having gotten our fill of Viennese culture and cuisine, David and I went back to work. Both working in Den Bosch, we could ride together most days. My train misadventures were piling up, and I was grateful to be rescued from the icy train platforms. Once I took a train in the wrong direction because I rushed into the station and didn't hear the platform change announcement.

Another time, I just barely missed arriving in the wrong city. Squinting at the fluorescent sign above my head and trying to read the last Dutch line felt like deciphering hieroglyphics. I understood parts of the words, but not the entire meaning. It looked like it said the last car of the train was going to another destination, but how was that possible? Frustrated, I finally asked the man standing next to me, who looked like a local. He confirmed that yes, the train, except for the last car, was going to Den Bosch. *Insanity!* As long as I didn't choose that car, I'd end up where I was planning to go. This concept was foreign to a non-train-educated American. For an hour each morning, David drove to the office while I stared out the window. February had begun to show signs of occasional warmth and the Dutch countryside was no longer thick with ice. There were patches of brown wet ground, which hadn't re-frozen overnight. Somehow, this gave me hope that my life in the Netherlands would thaw out too.

Just like the snags of the train system, undesirable aspects of my new project were rearing their ugly little heads. Eelco had gladly shared the background and history on the client and their personnel, but he was closed-mouthed when it came to previous project manager. As I got to know my client contacts, we formulated our analysis approach for the two main types of software under consideration, I also learned more about the context in which our software decision was to be made. It seemed that my predecessor had not been fired after all, but had chosen to leave.

To add to the fun, corporate politics was a major factor in the software decision. One team member, Peter, demanded information on all of our activities and meetings, but refused to make even the smallest effort for his department, a critical one for the project. "I have already chosen a system for this department," he declared, end of discussion.

"I understand that you have a preference, but your team isn't the only one affected," I pushed.

"We are the only one that matters."

Because Peter was a client, I had no way to influence him other than to present the information and consensus of the other team members. As we progressed, he then refused to speak or write any English. It became clear that someone intended to win the game by any means possible. When the Dutch language became a weapon, my desire to learn it waned considerably.

My ability to land in unwinnable situations was depressing. I started feeling like a lamb being led to slaughter on every drive to work. The more I learned about the client factions, who had dug their heels in on their side of the argument, the more it appeared that I was expected to recommend the—in my opinion—less appropriate system. My silent-but-deadly team member had strong ties to this manufacturer and had likely already promised them the business.

There was over a million euro at stake for the winner, but I wanted no part of this shady business. The rest of the team, who would be stuck with a very complex implementation of an inferior software product, didn't want it either. Their road would be hard enough. The more complex the implementation, the more work involved and the longer it would take to have a running system that enhanced productivity.

Faced with this subtext of ridiculous game playing, I began to see why the Dutch office gave this assignment to me and not to one of their own. I was expendable. What I said or did would not reflect poorly on the Amsterdam leadership, as I was still not one of them. The transfer was verbally approved, but the paperwork hadn't reached me yet. I wasn't going to play favorites and allow one rogue manager to interfere with my above-board approach, so I had to move forward carefully.

Every meeting and discussion was documented without leaving an inch–or should I say centimeter?–for false interpretation. Four out of five team members were behind me on the strategy. We didn't openly discuss our wayward member in meetings, but all of us were well aware of his influence on the decision at hand.

* * *

After wading through a ton of independent industry data and creating an initial draft of the client's needs, it was time to pay visits to the two software manufacturers. My intention was to uncover the smoking gun hidden in the marketing rhetoric, which would render one firm unsuitable. One company sent a detailed implementation strategy document and the other plied me with a fancy-lunch-and-red-carpet treatment.

The company favored by my silent team member, who thought they already had the business, considered me an obstacle–and rightly so. In earlier emails and telephone conversations, they were openly hostile about providing information, claiming it had already been given to the former project manager. When they realized I wasn't going to be brushed off, they switched to the sweet-talk-a-woman approach: "Once you see our system, you will know it is the right decision. We would be honored to have you as our special guest for the afternoon. We will have a very nice lunch."

Obviously, since I was female, I wasn't intelligent or experienced enough to see through it. It was insulting that they would bother with such an obvious sexist ploy. During the meal, where absolutely nothing of substance was discussed, I played the game. Afterwards, my continued insistence on missing crucial details was met with surprise. They turned visibly pale when I demanded dates when the information would be available, since they could not provide it today. I was relentless. Leaving their office seething, I documented the discussion verbatim on my three-hour ride back to Den Bosch. If the information had "already been provided," why was it so difficult to resend it?

My second manufacturer visit took me to South Holland, to a city called Sittard. Close to the Belgian border, I started to get the picture that the further south you travel in Europe, the looser the business protocol becomes. At this meeting, the manufacturer tried to figure out what I wanted in return for allowing them to win the deal. *Seriously? A kickback?*

In less than an hour, I was flying furiously over the rails again, deep in dilemma. Ultimately, the answer was simple: stick to the facts. There was no reason to go into the gritty details of the meetings or my bully of a team member. I found it disturbing that this kind of bullshit was still happening in the post-Enron era. Anyone who thought they were going to get a biased, unsupported decision from me on something so important clearly didn't know who they were dealing with.

For the next week, I documented all the facts and reviewed them numerous times with my team. With their feedback, I revised the summary presentation on our findings. The immense amount of detail involved in a proper software selection analysis is rarely interesting to high-level executives, so I stuck to the highlights and recommendations with the supporting data in an appendix in the back of the report.

After numerous revisions, I submitted it to Eelco for review. When he was satisfied, I would convene a final meeting to finalize our recommendation, and it would be submitted to an executive committee for approval. To me, it was a very straightforward process. Eelco thought differently. "What am I supposed to do with this?" he fumed, calling me the next day.

I was caught completely off guard. "I'm sorry, what do you mean?"

"Didn't you learn to create a proper presentation when you started at this company?" he demanded. "You are jumping all over the place. The presentation must tell a story!" He was irate.

I was speechless. I'd just spent a year developing presentations for Hanna, and writing a complex software implementation strategy document in Germany for which I had received outstanding reviews. After that, I spent three months learning software conversion techniques and running a successful data migration. Now, suddenly, I was incapable of putting facts together in a presentation? I would have

The Devil Wears Clogs

thought that his reaction was a joke, except that he was definitely not laughing.

At the same time, I found his irrational behavior utterly disproportionate to the facts at hand. It was an electronic format that no one but he and I had seen. It could easily be changed to a style that would be better understood by the executive committee. What was there to get so riled up about? If your manager wants something changed, they tell you and you do it. Simple. Except, nothing in the Netherlands is simple.

I slunk out of the office. With the standard amount of coaching that the Dutch management provides, zero, I had worked hard to sort out a complicated situation, and I was proud of my team. Otherwise, I would never have given the draft to a superior. I was approaching three years with the firm and I had never been on the receiving end of such a blistering attack on my work. It was devastating. I didn't even want to discuss it with David on the way home, because it felt too personal. I'd spent years defining myself by my career. If I was a poor performer at work, what did that make me as a person? I went over the facts again and again, but couldn't make sense of Eelco's reaction.

In a cosmic joke, the transfer paperwork from human resources was in the mail when I got home. Eagerly, I ripped open the envelope to read the details. For four months I had labored under the impression that an approved transfer was the answer to my prayers. Being shipped back to the United States at the drop of a hat would no longer be a concern. I would be a member of this new, albeit strange, community in the Amsterdam office, and I could focus on developing advanced skills, rather than accepting any assignment that came my way just to stay close to David.

The illusion dissipated the moment my eyes focused on the letter I held in trembling hands. The company *was* willing to allow the transfer if *I* was willing to give up over twenty thousand U.S. dollars of my compensation to do it. Prior to this, David had carefully explained the basics of the Dutch tax code to me, and that if I made over fifty thousand euro per year, I would sacrifice 52% of my income to the Dutch government in taxes. *Yes, 52%!* During my wait for the paperwork, I had already been worrying about how I could survive on less than half of my income, and now the Dutch office wanted to take another huge chunk out of it. No matter how much I loved David, I couldn't fathom it. I immediately called and declined the offer. I would keep working in the country on a temporary basis, but remain part of the office staff in Cleveland. As soon as word got around that I had refused the offer, things went from bad to worse.

* * *

If Eelco was going to demolish my reputation by stating that I was unable to create a coherent presentation, then I was going to demand that he prove it. I scheduled a meeting to review the document page by page, "error" by so-called error. We agreed on a date in our Amsterdam office, rather than using the client office. The day I met with Eelco coincided with a meeting for all Dutch staff. With only one office in the Netherlands, people traveled from all over the country to attend. I barely managed to secure a conference room for my showdown with Eelco.

These all-hands-on-deck meetings were designed to foster networking between employees. Outside of large engagements, which are teams of fifty to one-hundred consultants at the same location, the majority are farmed out to far-flung client sites and rarely see coworkers from our own office. These meetings showcase the achievements of the collective Dutch team. The formula is a quarterly staff update, followed by breakout sessions, which discuss more detailed topics like CRM, Customer Relationship Management, software and then drinks.

Despite my current opinion of Eelco, I'd agreed to join his team, partially based on his rumored experience leading projects in my specialty area. From what I could tell, wide-scale adoption of this software hadn't been triggered in Europe. I wanted to understand why, so who better to answer the question than an experienced manager who had just completed a large CRM implementation? The day we met at the Amsterdam office for my scheduled lecture on how to create a "proper" PowerPoint presentation, Eelco was facilitating a group discussion on exactly that topic. When I heard about it, I immediately registered.

The Devil Wears Clogs

I arrived at the office very early, to avoid fighting for a workspace. With the time I had left, I planned to review my work for the umpteenth time to look for the missing magic ingredient that would make it acceptable to Eelco.

The tension spread like wildfire throughout my body as soon as I walked through the office doors. Though it was early, it was crowded and I was forced to cram into non-existent space at a table already overcrowded with disapproving coworkers. By the time I finally got situated, it was time to meet Eelco in the conference room. While I waited for His Majesty to arrive, I mentally listed the places I would rather be. Copenhagen, Barcelona, Edinburgh, Sicily, Rome. The list was nowhere near finished when he showed up, twenty minutes late.

When I asked for the meeting, I'd explained its objective. I had no intention of doing so again for fear I might explode. In comparison, Eelco was very calm. It was a significant departure from the hothead who had attacked me the week before. He and his shiny leather shoes sauntered in as casually as can be, and he fired up his laptop before going for coffee. Why should he be deprived of caffeine just because he'd already wasted thirty minutes of my time?

I assumed that we would go over my presentation for him to critique it. Well, it's high time that this International Business Woman stop making assumptions–because she is never right.

No, we didn't go over my presentation so that I could discover the error of my ways. What happened next is that Eelco pulled out a training presentation on how to enter content into a template in PowerPoint. What happened next was that he spoke to me like a naughty child who needed an afternoon nap. What happened next is that he said absolutely *nothing* specific on where my written content was so spectacularly wrong. He went through each slide of the training pack and read verbatim from the pages of something that was designed for the firm's entry-level employees. The material was clearly beneath a woman with over ten years of business experience. I found it so insulting that I was at a complete loss for words.

He continued his elementary school teacher nattering until the demeaning ordeal came to an end. If I didn't have the confidence to speak up and call him on his bullshit, I certainly would not give him the satisfaction of asking questions so that he could fix me with that snide smile and provide the wisdom of the ages. *No way.* I plastered a look of bored indifference on my face until the teacher-student routine was over. When he was finished with his self-important display, I delivered the most insincere, but profuse, appreciation I could muster and made a dash for the door. The last thing I saw before walking out was Eelco's smug look. For the first, and only, time in my life I wanted to punch a colleague in the face.

* * *

Before I could fully process what had just transpired, ten o'clock had arrived and the entire office was stampeding into the main conference room. David was around, but we tried not to make our situation completely obvious by being glued to one another. It was uncomfortable because I had few friends in Amsterdam, but since it was a lecture format I didn't care where I sat.

Late again, the speaker took his place at the podium and covered the agenda—in Dutch. It's relevant to mention that my firm is American. The organization operates globally, and speaking a reasonable level of English is a pre-requisite for hire. Therefore (my turn to look down my nose and assume a teacher's tone), we can say with a high degree of certainty that the entire assembly of more than two hundred people spoke English. So, when the comedian with the microphone continued to prattle on in Dutch for twenty minutes before asking, "Does everyone here speak Dutch?" you understand my hesitation of being the sole person raising her hand to say, "No." While in the midst of asking myself, should I or shouldn't I?, someone else spoke up. A British voice came from the crowd, a guest at the CRM meeting that afternoon, asked if the speaker would please switch to English. I spoke up to second the request.

Now even *you* would assume that since more than one person had now indicated that they weren't up to speed on the Dutch language that the egomaniac with the microphone would take the hint and switch with little or no further discussion. *Wrong!* The U.K. guy received no reply to his request, but I was singled out. This pillar of the community

The Devil Wears Clogs

told me, in front of two hundred coworkers, that if I planned to continue attending these meetings, I'd better improve my Dutch. Before now, I'd never been one to subscribe to conspiracy theories, but at that moment I considered getting a subscription ASAP. Mr. Congeniality finally switched to English and moved on. We reviewed the earnings statistics for the Dutch office for the previous quarter and then went on to review the performance of the region, which included France, Belgium, and the Netherlands.

After sitting in that room for two hours, listening to dull statistics, we broke for lunch. I would rather have made a break for it, than push my way into another crowded hostile table of people I didn't know, but after the beating my ego had already taken, I didn't want to give anyone further reason to criticize. Filling my plate with smoked mackerel and salad, I made for the most harmless-looking crowd—the table full of total IT nerds. Little chitchat from the geek contingent came my way, but for once I wasn't pummeled with opinions about the situation in Iraq either. I ate quickly and then excused myself to retreat to a corner where I checked email and phone messages before the next fun-filled event.

The last session that afternoon was the customer management software discussion starring The One and Only Eelco. I had booked into this meeting before he'd decided to humiliate me earlier in the day, and was told it was too late to change to another group. With no choice, I took a seat at the back of the room and waited for my second opportunity of the day to assume the role of student. I was fairly sure that this session would prove as useless as the first, but a little part of me wanted to hear what kind of bullshit was going to come out of his mouth in round two.

Because everyone loves a recurring theme, Eelco launched his presentation with a complaint that since two non-Dutch speakers were in the room, he would be *forced* to give the talk in English. Those were his exact words. When Mr. U.K. joked in return that it was equally painful for us having to listen to his English, Eelco couldn't conceal his annoyance. Already knowing that Mr. U.K. would get more respect than me, I kept my mouth firmly shut, and tried not to laugh. The thought of being scolded like an unruly child for the third time that day was not appealing.

Roughly fifty people were in attendance, but no one asked questions or commented on Eelco's points. For a crowd of Know It All management consultants, this is highly unusual. I didn't know if they were asleep or uninterested, but I came bearing specific questions and thought others would also join the conversation. Having received an in-depth tutorial of Eelco's so-called knowledge, I wanted to hear what the other participants could offer. The silence in the room was disappointing, but in hindsight, it was also revealing.

Sadly, silence isn't my strong suit. Bracing for a nasty reply, I finally asked the question I'd been dying to ask, "Eelco, why are there so few CRM implementations in Europe?" If looks could kill, my body would have slumped to the ground. The reason I now had a bullseye on my forehead probably had something to do with the answer that Eelco was forced to give.

There are more consulting firms per capita in the Netherlands than in any other country in the world. The Dutch have an opinion on absolutely everything, and there isn't a single one alive who would willingly speak the words, "I don't know." Unfortunately, that is exactly what I forced Eelco to say in response to my question. Later, I would uncover this charming cultural trait when I recognized David's own ability to make up a load of almost-believable bullshit before admitting the simple fact that he didn't know the answer.

At this point, I realized none of this. So, stupidly, I continued: "The reason I am asking is because, in the United States and Canada, we are seeing an increase in the adoption of customer management systems in the utilities industry, due to gas and energy market liberalization. Clients who could have cared less about efficient customer service in the past have realized that their lack of service can translate into customer loss when they have the ability to choose where their energy comes from. Since Europe is on the cusp of energy liberalization, do you see any increase in utility client interest in CRM?"

Here is where I made my career-limiting move without knowing it. First is the reason that I already mentioned, no Nederlander wants to be caught dead answering "I don't know" to a question, ever. This is especially true when the questioner is a subordinate. I also learned later that in Dutch society it is considered a big deal when a person fails or makes a mistake. It's the opposite in the United States, where we are taught that making a mistake is often how you learn to succeed the next time.

My second faux pas was more subtle. It is considered poor form in the Netherlands for an individual to stand out, hence all the other good little kids in the classroom maintaining their respectful silence. No one will look especially good or bad if they don't say anything at all. Completely unaware I'd just made a huge spectacle of myself, by forcing my superior to admit that he didn't know the answer, and further trashed my reputation because they would think I was boasting about my previous experience and knowledge—which appeared, in this case, to outweigh my manager's.

Whenever I replay this scene in my head, even years later, I wonder if it would have turned out differently if I had just managed to shut the hell up. I would be lying if I said there wasn't a part of me that wanted to show him up. I wanted revenge for being refused the respect that a woman who had been successful in three other countries was entitled to.

There is no doubt that my anger was barely below the surface, but I am being honest when I say that at that moment I had no idea of the seriousness of my offenses, as seen by my Dutch manager. It was only after years of therapy, just kidding, years of reflection and education about the Dutch culture, that I began to make sense of what happened.

I'm sure no one was surprised to learn that Eelco didn't react well. He replied in a clipped manner that implied he didn't trust his own tongue. He said they had seen no increase in adoption, and that his former project had been at the smallest of all the energy providers in the Dutch utility market. They knew that with liberalization they would not survive if they did not become a more service-oriented company. That was it.

He seemed to have lost the last of his patience with yours truly and refused to meet my gaze for the duration of the meeting. Given that I was unaware of the gravity of my offenses, it was just as well. I could easily have dug my grave deeper by prolonging the discussion.

* * *

The hidden elements of Dutch culture only came in bits and pieces. David was a big help in deciphering the code, but honestly, you don't realize what is unique (God forbid, I say "peculiar") about your own cultural traits until you leave your country. Out there walking through the world, it becomes abundantly clear that there are as many ways of getting things done as there are countries to do them in. Entrenched in a new country, surrounded by its people, the minority for the first time in your life, it is impossible to continue believing that your way is the only way. You've hardly got a chance in hell of convincing a nation full of others that your way is the best way.

There are some nations whose people are confident that they are the Enlightened Ones, believing that they, and only they, have the right methods or the best products. The French come to mind first, secondly the Japanese, although that is hardly an exhaustive list. I adore French wine and all things Japanese. My opinion is that every nation excels at one thing or many. Unfortunately, for me and my fellow Americans, we are the worst offenders in this manner of thinking. We are brought up to believe that the sun rises and sets in the United States of America. "My way or the highway" describes it well, but I was uncovering a new philosophy. "If it ain't Dutch, it ain't much" was the worldview I was expected to adapt to.

David gave me a very funny, but somewhat frightening book, about the weirdness of Dutch culture called *The Undutchables*. He translated the language when we were out exploring his country. He briefed me on etiquette of new situations to save me awkwardness or embarrassment. In short, whenever it was obvious that he should fill me in, he did. The problem was that the deeper mysteries, the biggest points of potential conflict, were still hidden landmines.

Not having received any cultural education on Germany or Holland left me at a major disadvantage when it came to managing the politics of business. In every nation, in every business, politics exist. This in itself was not a newsflash. In my case, it became virtually impossible to manage the politics of a highly-political organization, because no one had written down the rules of the game.

Though I don't gossip, I'm a longtime believer that the most vital aspect of a successful career in my organization is your peer group, your informal network. This is where you'll get the heads-up before you land in quicksand. Not only was I outside my home country, but I also lacked any sort of business network whatsoever aside from David. He seemed to be part of the "in crowd," friendly with the people who controlled the Dutch practice, but he was also four years younger and a man.

Those last two items make a big difference in how you perceive the world, let alone the workplace. I knew I was on thin ice having no local support, and turning down the transfer offer; I also knew support would now be very difficult come by.

Eventually, it was the people in my U.S. network who found me a Dutch "coach." Your coach acts as a mentor, someone senior to whom you can turn for advice, but who is not your direct manager. I had been given his name and number just before The Day From Hell, but hadn't yet reached him. The present moment seemed like the perfect time to get that rolling.

The first time I met Martijn, my impression was positive. He was six feet tall with brown hair, and kind brown eyes behind his thick gold-rimmed glasses. His English was excellent and he was easy to talk to. He worked at the same client site that I did, but was so busy that I never ran into him at the office.

Martijn asked what I was working on, but not much else. He seemed to be on such a hectic schedule that if there was no immediate emergency, he had better things to do than to get to know me.

As I became more familiar with Dutch work habits, I understood that there was less emphasis—actually *no* emphasis—on the soft skills of people management, as they are referred to in the United States. In particular, the Dutch do not provide positive performance feedback outside of a formal review. You will be told if you are failing, but when you excel, you won't hear a peep. It is considered poor form to stand out in the Netherlands. An individual should be no better or worse than her peers. Sociologists call it Tall Poppy Syndrome and it is dominant in more than one culture. Moderation is the key to successful living in Holland. One who receives praise is apt to get a big head. When that head rises above the rest, it becomes an easy target for lopping off.

By this point in my Dutch timeline, it was a godsend that my project lasted only three months. The end of the road was approaching as I saw the first hints of spring in the Netherlands. After the Battle of PowerPoint finished without a victor, I continued finalizing the evaluation of the two different software applications with my team. The conclusion from my initial draft, the one I presented to Eelco, opting for the less politically desirable solution, did not change. The software we recommended would be easier to implement and offered more features and functions to the users.

Eelco barely uttered a word when I delivered my final copy. He also denied me the opportunity to attend the meeting where it would be presented to the client's executive committee. The excuse was, yet again, that the presentation had to be delivered in Dutch. I can't say with 100% certainty, but I don't believe my Dutch was the issue. I am quite sure it was my conclusion that would get lost in translation, because those in the room preferred a different one.

Later that afternoon, I walked out the office doors and was hit full force with the smell of cow shit. Den Bosch is not a large city. The outskirts, where our office sat, is surrounded by farmland. As sun eliminated the barrier of frost covering the fields, the overwhelming odor permeated the air. It was the perfect metaphor for my experience thus far in this lovely country called the Netherlands.

* * *

Since Vienna, David and I had been too busy to leave the country or spend much time together. We did, however, receive a welcome invitation to a black-tie Spring Party for everyone working at our client. Just under a hundred consultants were invited to a historic inn in Arnhem, somewhere I'd never been. Visions of romance bloomed when I learned that the company was paying for hotel rooms if we wanted to stay after the party. David and I planned to share a room and explore the city the day after.

The Devil Wears Clogs

The downside was finding a formal dress to wear to the engagement. I obviously had reason to be paranoid about my taste in clothing where my nearest and dearest was concerned. This would be a true test. I had never been a sorority girl and had missed all the black-tie events back in Cleveland due to traveling. There was no magic wardrobe full of dresses to choose from when living out of two huge suitcases. Normally I loved shopping, but I knew from past excursions finding something gorgeous would be a challenge. Just one more way that your informal network can make or break you. It would have been much easier if I had known where to look. I didn't. David was the last person I was going to have a conversation with on this subject.

I chose The Hague to start shopping, due its large volume of international traffic. When I got there, I discovered the choice was between couture houses full of thousand-euro Chanel dresses and bargain basements. My luck changed when I walked through the gleaming glass doors of Max Mara. Here, in an elegant rainbow of velvet and silk, were beautiful dresses. Slowly, I pushed back an off-the-shoulder black number to admire a long-sleeved navy one. Both were too somber for spring.

In a Chanel studio, I would expect to be treated like a nobody. But at Max Mara? Where clothes came in my size and budget? By now, I really should have known better. I should have expected the catty shop girls to have a laugh at my expense because I didn't speak their language or the language of formal dress.

"Wouldn't you like some shoes to try on with the dress?"

"No thanks," I mumbled through the door. High fashion was something I couldn't be bothered with. Obviously, I'd missed the memo which said to bring high heels when trying on dresses.

With the dress on, I opened to door to find the full-length mirror, still wearing the black thermal J Crew socks I wore to keep my feet warm in icy northern Europe.

"You want nylons!" The declaration came from a squinty sales girl, as though she couldn't bear to take in the full image of my awful socks with their beautiful dress.

"Yes!" said the other one.

"It doesn't matter. I already know what I will wear with it," I tried to reassure the panicked women. Socks or no socks, the dress looked amazing. Perhaps that was the real problem with these two.

I heard them snickering to one another while I changed in the dressing room. My face flushed red to match the scarlet-crepe dress. I tried to block them out. To end to the humiliation, I bought the drop-dead gorgeous dress. At the register, I delivered my best "go to hell" glare, but it didn't diminish my embarrassment.

Later, I was pleased at avoiding a potential party pitfall by finding a hot outfit that was elegant too. This time, it was David who screwed up. After rushing from the office to make it to Arnhem in time for the seven o'clock cocktail hour, he realized he'd forgotten the shoes that go with his tuxedo. He would be forced to wear regular brown loafers all night because it was way too late to run home and get the right ones.

Just as I was relaxing into the thought that *finally* someone else had made a mistake, he turned his attention to my cultural etiquette training. Much to my dismay, I was about to receive instruction on the European use of cutlery.

Now, I love David. I think he is a wonderful man who has turned my world upside down for the better. So I will forgive him for failing to realize my stress level at having to sit down to polite dinner conversation with the very people who had been making my life a living hell. He had no idea he was striking a match next to a pile of dynamite. I recognize that David was honestly trying to save me from embarrassment when he began a lesson in something I had successfully performed since I was six years old. As a lady, it is my duty to spare you the words I said to him at the time, so we will pretend that I accepted this wisdom and thanked him for his courage.

Truth be told, there was something to what he said. There is a system to Europeans use of forks and knives. Both are commonly used at once. In the U.S., the knife is often resting at the side of the plate when not used for cutting. Many Americans would laugh if you told them there is only one way to place your silverware to signal that you are finished with your meal. Essentially, David did not want me to be further embarrassed by my Americanness when it came to table manners. That is why he elected to give me a quick course in European dining etiquette. David's heart was in the right place but his timing needed serious work.

It's a miracle we made it to the event without one of us landing in the emergency room, but we entered the room hand-in-hand and made the best of it. I remained on high alert for Eelco sightings, so that I could disappear should he show up. I even managed a bit of conversation with David's teammates.

David did most of the talking and was clearly pleased to introduce me, the tall blonde American, as his date. I scanned the room to see what other women wore. I already knew Dutch women do not love dressing up, and that just sitting down to attend to their hair and slight makeup was a chore they disdained, so I wasn't terribly surprised to see that my dress was much more chic. When several of them openly stared at my fabulous dress, I smiled inside at my tiny victory.

Thirty minutes later, we were seated for dinner and I was less than thrilled to find my former manager, Dafne, seated next to me. Thankfully the formal speeches began within minutes, so I was saved from lengthy conversation for the time being. Later, it couldn't be avoided.

"How are you doing on the new project?" was her opening line.

Caught off guard, I am always stupidly honest. "Not great," was all I offered.

"Why don't you just leave and get a job somewhere else?" Dutch directness struck again. I was floored that this was the second thing out of her mouth, but that wasn't all she had to say. "Eelco talked to me about it. I think you would be better off to find another job."

I couldn't believe these people. Who says something like that to a colleague? Let alone the very person who told you less than two months ago that you were capable of outstanding performance.

Did I mention that this is taking place at an event that was intended to be fun? Caught by surprise, I told her I didn't want to leave the company just because things hadn't gone as expected in Holland. After that, she headed off to ruin someone else's evening and I turned my attention to others, putting up a wall of wine to insulate myself from further insult.

* * *

On Sunday, I was less enthusiastic about exploring Arnhem than I thought I would be. The intense throbbing in my head, caused by my less-than-conservative approach to wine, was not about to allow me to enjoy the day any time soon. Slowly, quietly walking through the beautiful city center, I was rattled when David headed directly to a herring stand for breakfast. I couldn't handle the smell or taste of anything that morning, let alone herring. Watching David devour several pickled herring with the heads lopped off, nearly pushed me over the edge. I turned on my heels and walked to a spot where the wind quickly carried off the smell, before I made a scene in the street that no one wanted to see.

Dafne's remarks the night before had cut deep. My new reality made it impossible to continue with the firm in the Netherlands. The directness of her comments and the swiftness with which she raised her bow and aimed her arrow made it obvious that she and Eelco were in cahoots. There were rumors that this Amsterdam Mafia protected their own. Everyone else was fair game. I just hadn't expected the tables to turn on me so quickly without what I considered sufficient provocation. This was about the time that I began referring to Eelco as the Antichrist.

Back at the office on Monday, I received a meeting request from Eelco to review my project performance. This mandatory meeting that takes place when a consultant finishes a project role, and my last day was to be the following week. I was a little surprised that he was ready so early, but given our contentious relationship, I assumed we were thinking the same thing: the sooner we part company, the better. Doomsday was scheduled for three days later.

The day the guillotine fell is not as clear in my memory as the rest of this dramatic sequence. It was a foregone conclusion that our collaboration had not been a spectacular success, so this was merely a formality to end our non-existent relationship. I expected the Devil to send the paperwork in advance, I would review and comment on it, and that would be that. I did not expect a guns-blazing Wild West showdown.

When I didn't receive the files via email in advance, however, my radar was immediately up. It was a company requirement that the employee being evaluated is provided with the information pertaining to their performance by the manager prior to the face-to-face meeting, although, as I have duly noted, all bets are off in Amsterdam.

I walked into Eelco's office and silently he handed me the form I've seen many times before. Its purpose is to measure performance in all areas of project contribution. The employee is assigned a number for each category and then the numbers are weighted to lend gravity to the most important criteria. You get the drill.

I scanned the paper and did a double take. My heart thumped in my chest. The Devil had given me an overall rating of "Needs Improvement." This form had passed through my hands no less than fifteen times in my career, and those words had never once been used to summarize my work. Once, I had been upset by receiving an evaluation that deemed me average, but never this.

My face grew hot, but I couldn't speak. I knew anything I said would be held against me in a court of Dutch law.

Looking him in the eye, I said, "I won't sign it." He had the gall to ask why and I said it was an inaccurate representation of my work. My client team had been more than pleased with the way that I'd run the project and, to my knowledge, the only point of contention was that my manager did not like my style of presentation. Nothing had ever been stated or written about the quality or content of my assignments, so how was he justified in saying that I hadn't met expectations? He shrugged off my question and mumbled that I would never understand how things worked in his country. End of discussion.

I asked for an emailed copy and left fuming. Normally, I have no cause to use the word hate, but in this case it was appropriate. I wouldn't make a fuss over how this so-called team ridiculed my country and government, but I wouldn't allow anyone to malign my professional reputation for no reason.

Returning to my desk, unable to speak, I considered my next move. If there were ever an emergency, a pressing need, to call on my "local support," this was it. I walked out of my shared office and found an empty meeting room where I left a voicemail for Martijn, asking for an immediate appointment. Afterwards, I sat in disbelief. It was impossible to imagine how I had taken a disparate group of client team members, cultural and language barriers aside, to come to a solid conclusion on the best software, complete with factual basis and supporting data, and I needed improvement? On what exactly?

Martijn took his time getting back to me, which should have been a signal to the outcome. He wasn't willing to meet until he had spoken to his tribe to get the details. When he finally called and agreed to discuss the evaluation, there were two days left before I was to finish the project. At an early-morning meeting, I pled my case. My initial impression of him as the kindly and wise colleague went straight out the window.

It was obvious he lacked the patience to listen, as he'd made up his mind at the secret tribe council meeting with Eelco. I hadn't even finished speaking before he said, "Eelco isn't going to change your evaluation." Not, "Eelco believes he is justified in his assessment because of this, this, and this." Not, "Eelco didn't think he made it clear that this, this, and this were factors in your evaluation." Just, "Eelco isn't going to change it." End of story, end of discussion, and end of *you*.

I was living in the *Twilight Zone*. Whatever I said or did, the opposite was taken from it. I didn't even know how to use silverware, so how did I think I could create a presentation? If I was unable to dress myself, how exactly did I think I could pull off a sophisticated technical software evaluation? But the fact is, I did manage all those tasks. Not only did I manage them, I pulled them off despite everything stacked against me.

Okay, so I wasn't culturally savvy, but seriously, there was *nothing* redeeming about my performance? I fell into a spiral of shame and confusion that I call PTDD, post-traumatic Dutch disorder. Symptoms appear in non-Dutch people who have given the best of their ability, only to have everything explode in their face. The victims are left to believe that their best is no longer good enough for anything.

Abruptly, I left the office. I didn't know where I was going, and couldn't have cared less what they thought. It was clear that nothing

The Devil Wears Clogs

I did made a damn bit of difference to these people. I had been tried, judged, and convicted based on circumstantial evidence. The jury was fixed and the murder weapon was a knife in my back. When I reached my Amsterdam penthouse, where I once thought my dreams would come true, I was devastated by the injustice of it all. I had to do something.

* * *

Checking my watch to calculate the time in Ohio, I phoned my HR advisor, Julie, and relayed the story. She was very understanding of my situation during my months in the Netherlands. All along, Julie had lobbied for my return to the U.S. to take advanced project management training and leadership development. When I kept landing project roles, however, she let me run my own course. Now, with full disclosure, she was outraged.

"Jennifer, I'm looking at your file with several copies of your evaluations and not a single one indicates that you have a fundamental performance problem. This is obviously an aberration," she said, indignant. "It's time for you to re-join the Cleveland team and we'll get to work developing your advanced project management skills."

Finally, I could breathe. All it took was this short conversation to know where I stood. After months of second guessing everyone's hidden motives, I was grateful for Americans and for the English language. It was clear that this bullshit story would have no bearing on my reputation with the company.

Then I told her about David.

"Ohhhhh... that's the reason you wanted to stay! I thought after your first project there that you would have had enough. Now I understand. It's your decision what happens next. You can stay and try to get another project role despite this review, but we would love you to come back home. There is plenty of work for you in the U.S., I am sure of that," she said.

Relief was short lived. She gave me a week to sort things out before she'd be hounding me to catch a flight back to Ohio. Now I had a real decision to make: choose David, or choose the firm. Simple as that. If I went back to Cleveland, our relationship was over. We simply hadn't known each other long enough to make long distance work. On the other hand, why would I leave the company that gave me my European dream? What else would I be sacrificing by doing so?

CHAPTER 22
THE ROAD LESS TRAVELED

I heard every tick of the clock for three hours, waiting for David to get home. He knew I needed to talk to him, but that was it. There was no need for both of us to be shaken by my possible abrupt departure. Solitude was a relief. I could think about the potential consequences without distraction. It's no revelation that I hadn't been happy in my job since arriving in the Netherlands. Having had a far smoother professional ride in Germany, the United States, and Canada for the same organization, it was clear that the problem had to be this office. But was my experience with this company comparable to every other Dutch company? I could hardly imagine that was true.

As I saw it, the finding a good job locally with limited Dutch skills and having a place to live were bigger worries than giving up my current position. My lack of fluent Dutch was a factor, but it was also obvious that many young people in Holland spoke English. My utility clients were older, ex-government types in an industry known worldwide to be conservative. Perhaps this was the obstacle to my success? If moved away from that breed of culture into a younger high-tech organization, surely I would be better off. Even now, I remained an optimist.

Next on the List of Worries was the question of living arrangements. There was no way I could afford the Penthouse sans employment, but were David and I ready to live together? Given my view down the double-barreled shotgun that was about to blow away my life, it had to be worth a shot. But what about David? He wasn't talkative to begin with, but on the emotional front, he must have taken a vow of silence that he forever feared breaking. We had exchanged the three big words only a month before and I doubted that my leaving the country was his preferred ending to our story. There was no avoiding it. We had to have The Talk.

The trip from utter despair to unadulterated joy within the span of an afternoon might be unusual for some, but this roller coaster was becoming routine. My personal life and passion for travel were reaching unexpected new heights while my career was circling the drain.

David was barely in the door when I launched into a blow-by-blow account. When I finished, he, in typical blunt Dutch fashion, said "so you will stay with me then," as if there were never any doubt. Feeling slightly ridiculous at his simple solution, I was ecstatic. When my sky had turned black, it became a clean slate for better weather to move in. Pun intended.

David was my number one reason for staying in Europe, but not the only one. Easy access to the continent was addictive. I couldn't stand for my adventure to end, scurrying back to the United States with my tail between my legs. Cleveland was practically a distant memory the moment the plane to Germany lifted its wheels. Living in Europe had changed me. The adversity had made me stronger, more determined. A gang of Amsterdam street thugs wasn't going to make my decisions for me. You could count on that.

"My plan" became "our plan" that night. I would keep looking for another project in the Netherlands with my week-long grace period from Julie. If nothing turned up, which we knew was the likeliest scenario, I'd move my things into his place before returning to the United States to deliver my resignation to Cleveland's human resources team.

On my last day working for the Devil, I informed him via email that I would work remotely. My final documentation was delivered. All that was left on my "to do" list was to transition my project knowledge to the new project manager from the Dutch office who was replacing me. He was to lead the implementation of the software system chosen by my team.

Yes, you read that right. The Devil's team was going to implement the system I'd recommended and, despite my experience and strong client relationships, I wasn't deemed worthy to lead it. I was to hand

The Devil Wears Clogs

over my documentation and let new guy run with it. This decision had apparently been made months earlier without my knowledge. I was only there to fill a gap until the person the Devil really wanted to dance with was available. As unfair as the situation was, I didn't care. I simply couldn't fathom another minute reporting to the antichrist of managers.

The next seven days were spent talking to every company connection I could think of. I chased *everyone*. The Amsterdam human resources department delivered a superb performance of pretending to look for assignments outside of the utilities. My former managers and German connections didn't have room for a non-German speaker. As a last ditch effort, I began looking for jobs online. Finally, I had to deliver the news to Julie that there was nowhere else to turn.

On my final day, in April 2003, I made one last appointment with my Dutch coach, Martijn. Regardless of the unethical behavior of this group, it was important to end the relationship professionally. I doubted that he cared and it surprised me that he accepted the meeting. Expecting an ounce of assistance from the management in the Netherlands was out of the question, but I wanted to make it absolutely clear that I wasn't beaten. Perhaps they had succeeded in making it impossible to work in one office in one company in the entire country, but I wouldn't be banished to the United States, as I am certain they expected. No, I'd make my way just fine, thank you. *I don't need you either.*

Even though the day I met with the Devil to review my performance is hazy, a defense mechanism against a harsh reality, my memory of the last meeting with Martijn, is one I'll never forget. Maybe he expected me to come in, kiss his feet, and grovel for support. He might have even thought I'd ask for a new role, or lament the error of my ways. When I didn't, shock was unmistakable on the face of a man who was otherwise very sure of himself.

"Well, Martijn, the reason I wanted to talk to you," I began with a smile, "is because I'm leaving the company." This piqued his interest, so I continued, "I have learned so much working with all of you, but I've decided that it is time for me to move on."

"You are leaving the Netherlands." It was more statement than question.

"No, I'm leaving the firm, but I'm staying here." This was fun now.

Eyebrows raised behind those gold wire rims, he said "You are going to *leave* the firm and *stay* in the Netherlands? Now that's interesting." He spoke slowly, as though it were a concept he was having difficulty with. Even I couldn't mistake the implication of his statement: There *is* no other organization worth working for in this country.

I gave an even bigger grin, thanked him for his support acting as an intermediary between myself and the Devil. Sarcasm dripped from every syllable. This is the *one* situation that being a native speaker of English provides a distinct advantage. Until you know the language and intonation, sarcasm is undetectable. The irony was that he was clearly mocking me, but I couldn't have proven it. On the surface, it was a polite, civilized conversation. In reality, only 2% of what was happening involved the words spoken.

My last Dutch showdown behind me, I owed no explanation to anyone. I practically danced out the office doors. Let them wonder! Let them judge! *Who cares?* There was one weekend left in the Penthouse. My consolation prize was the upcoming Queen's Day, the most celebrated Dutch holiday of the year.

The actual name of this celebration is *konninginendag,* which takes a lot of practice, and beer, to pronounce. I wouldn't try it without the aid of alcoholic beverages. Colleagues and clients alike had been talking about it for weeks and the message was consistent: this is one party you don't want to miss.

For the two days before, I packed and sorted my worldly belongings into boxes. I didn't think David knew what he was getting into because my two huge suitcases had ballooned into large boxes. David's Ijsselstein living room, the biggest room in his house, would barely fit them. How could I my whole life fit into such tiny dimensions? It didn't matter, my fate was sealed. Nothing had been easy in Holland, but I was still alive and kicking. Living space was the least of our worries.

* * *

There was no festive air on the morning of my first Queen's Day in the Netherlands. Normal Dutch weather prevailed. The skies were gray and rain pounded on the roof. Even the weather conspired against me. Fingers crossed, the weatherman promised improvement in the afternoon.

Waiting for the sun to fight her way through the gloom, we watched the day's events on TV. Queen's Day honors the birthday of the Queen and three females had reigned in succession. Queen Beatrix, the present queen, has a January birthday but has wisely chosen to celebrate on her Queen Mother's April 30th birthday. An outdoor party in January would be punishment, even for the sturdy Dutch.

All members of the royal family participate on the day. One carefully-selected city or village receives the honor of a visit from the royal clan and the villagers perform to kick off the festivities. A favorite spectator sport is to review and judge the outfits worn by the Queen and her three daughters-in-law. These photos always make the papers and the comments are not necessarily kind. Watching this unfold on television was like a 1950's American sitcom. It was so hokey that my attention wandered minutes after turning it on.

When he noticed how bored I was, David decided the city events might be more interesting. All the large Dutch cities have special events, but according to David, we were in the capital of All Things Fun. His blue eyes lit up when he told me that the city turns into a large flea market. Sellers claim their territory with chalk outlines in the Vondelpark the day before to hawk their junk to the revelers. What an odd way to celebrate, I thought, but I liked the enthusiasm in his voice. I realized I had never seen a garage sale in Europe. It simply wasn't done. Maybe that's what made it interesting.

For me, the appeal was the list of twenty different bands performing in outdoor venues throughout Amsterdam, each one playing different music. I also liked the idea of Heineken stands magically appearing on every corner and beer flowing freely in the streets. Alcohol consumption outdoors was the norm, not the exception. The pubs would be jammed, but many sat in groups laughing and drinking on sidewalks. I prayed for the rain to subside.

I couldn't remember ever drinking alcohol outside in the United States in a place that wasn't roped-off and heavily patrolled by cops.

I found it weird that, while all other aspects of Dutch society are governed by an invisible rulebook, the entire city can party without restriction. I guess it's possible because moderation is so ingrained in the Dutch culture that force is rarely necessary to make them behave. In Americans, the dislike of rules is also ingrained. That must be the reason why, when alcohol is involved, that dislike is accompanied by a total disregard for those whose job it is to enforce the rules. Hence, we need to be corralled.

Eventually, the rain stopped and we hit the streets. It was immediately obvious was that the rain did not deter many and the party had been going on for hours without us. Living in the Land of Perpetual Precipitation must make you oblivious to it. If rain spoils your fun, you won't have any. The Leidseplein was a sea of orange; wearing the national color is the uniform of konninginendag. A green cup, bottle, or can with the word Heineken on it is the required accessory.

A twenty-foot stage sat in the square's center and, judging by the mad scurrying around it, something big was about to begin. I started laughing when the announcer introduced Adam Curry. I couldn't believe that one of MTV's original v-jays was right in front of me. I had no idea he was Dutch and married to a model here, who, impossibly, has more perfect hair than he does. Somehow this small link to the familiar gave me a lift. I didn't care he addressed the crowd in Dutch. For once, I understood something going on around me.

Just like the Oktoberfest crowd, I was struck by how friendly everyone was. The belligerent attitude that often rides side-saddle at large parties in the United States didn't show its face. I didn't see men fist-fighting because one of them had looked at the other wrong or hit on the wrong woman. When someone knocked into you, spilling beer all over you, they actually apologized. It was in second place for the friendliest party ever. The fun-loving crowd contradicted everything I'd experienced so far in this country. No wonder tourists continue to have a love affair with Amsterdam even after visiting several times. You never see beneath the surface unless you live here.

Three Heinekens and an orange-feather boa later, I was in the swing of things. If rock music didn't appeal, you could walk another ten minutes and find a different scene. The sun held out and, for the rest of the afternoon, we sat at a café on the Prinsengracht canal munching on *bitterballen* and *worst* to soak up the beer.

By then, we'd covered most of town. That only left appreciating the weirdness that cruised the canals. It was the best part. Every imaginable contraption, from the posh to the terrifically trashy floated by. Each vessel was full to maximum capacity with outrageously-dressed partygoers. Orange balloons, orange wigs, orange boats, and *lots* of beer made their way past our canal-side spot. Mostly, it was men who put on singing performances for the crowd, but women were mixed in too. I didn't know the words, but the theatrics cracked me up.

My camera was busy on Queen's Day. Whether it was Adam Curry or the floating parade, I clung to the moments. If I held them tight enough, maybe the rest of the awfulness would fade. Maybe I could go back to being the happy adventurous girl who just wanted to work hard and see the world, rather than a pariah.

This was far from the only day that happiness came with depression. After a while, I learned to expect it. You wouldn't know it from looking at the photos of David and me, grinning under huge orange crown balloon hats, but there was a dark side to the picture.

* * *

Sunday morning came far too early. Clearly, we had not thought the plan through when we decided that this was Moving Day. We had to carry all the boxes from the Penthouse to David's car and then unpack in Ijsselstein. The Stairs of Death laughed as we dragged our hung-over bodies up and down the four steep flights to cram ten heavy boxes into his car.

I was an emotional wreck. As much as I loved David, leaving the firm was severing the link to my home, my family, and all of my friends. The future was far from certain. If I based my guess on past experience, my new life looked woefully bleak. It must have been extremely confusing for David that I couldn't view our future together with more enthusiasm, but it just wasn't there.

Finally, the car was loaded. The Penthouse was emptied. There was nothing left to do but drive off into the sunset. The natural optimist was silent as we hit the highway entrance ramp and drove toward Ijsselstein.

David read my mood and tried to keep things upbeat by pointing out landmarks and giving me information about my new home during the hour drive. For David, love is demonstrated in taking action. He may not be a wordsmith or a chatterbox, but if he thought of something to alleviate my concerns and take the worried look off my face, he wouldn't hesitate. Unfortunately, there nothing he could do. He couldn't give me a new job, or a car, or a way to find my independence in his country.

In normal circumstances, it would have been an exciting moment when David and I shared our first night at his place, but my temperament was flat. My actions were automatic and without emotion. I unloaded. I unpacked. I said little.

David cooked for me and was very affectionate. He must have been hoping I would open up and tell him how he could help me deal with whatever was going on in my head, but I didn't. Faced with extreme emotional distress, I went numb. I'm not the type to talk about my troubles—not even to close friends. I am the one who is always "in control." I am the one who takes care of business and does what's expected, even in the worst of times. When the worst of times comes looking for me, I shut down.

CHAPTER 23
HOW TO LIVE IN A DORP

Monday's buzzing alarm clock was a slap in the face. I was on leave from the company until I tendered my resignation, but David couldn't hang around and hold my hand. As soon as he left for the office, I looked at my unfamiliar surroundings and wondered what the hell I was doing. What does a city girl know of words like "township" or "village"?

My European dream lay shattered at my feet. Actually, it lay in hastily-packed cardboard boxes. Everything I'd worked for, and dreamt of, was crushed until I found a way to be independent again.

Looking for the bright side, I put on a fake smile and took my first tentative steps into the great unknown. Since "city" is far too big of a word to describe Ijsselstein, I will use village. In Dutch, a village is a *dorp*. It was definitely a dorp.

Ijsselstein and its surrounds have a population of thousands, but David's apartment was in the old town center. This was the original area, walled off for protection in medieval times, so everything the townspeople need can be found within less than a mile of David's place. After my endless battle with the Amsterdam trams, I was excited by the convenience. It was quickly snuffed out.

David had taken me to town many times. We went to a local restaurant for dinner or grabbed the ingredients from the supermarket to make dinner at home, but I'd never ventured out alone. Probably because I knew this would be a very different affair than shopping in Amsterdam where English fluency is common. Here, in the land that time forgot, I couldn't read a single street sign.

Determined to make this town and its people like me, I went in search of basic necessities. That was my excuse. In reality, it was a reconnaissance mission to see who lived in this Petri dish and examine how things worked. Walking out David's front door, the magnetic pull of the windmill was irresistible. Finally, I could get a close up of one of these curious structures. That was far more interesting than bread and milk.

With my good-luck Nikon tucked safely in my pocket, I walked towards the mythical beast. I kept my fingers curled tightly around it as I put one foot in front of the other on the carved stone wall. This beast, which is friendly on closer examination, had a name. Time flew by as I stood watching the giant sails swoop overhead, but fascination rooted me to the spot.

The Windotter, built in 1837, is a working a flour mill. Restored in the 1980s, the *molenaar* lives with his family in a stone house a few meters away. Before now, he'd remained elusive, but today I was in luck. He was working outside, broad shoulders and broad smile, greeting the passers-by in his dark green work shirt, tan leather gloves, and wooden shoes. Yes, wooden shoes. Europeans call them "clogs," which is also a euphemism for a Dutch person. In Dutch, they are *klompen*. Either way, to see a forty-year-old man walking around in wooden shoes in 2003 was an unusual sight.

For a minute, I forgot my woes to consider what his life was like. I pictured tiny blue-eyed children with white-blonde hair running at his heels and a wife who took hearty meals steaming from the oven every evening. He raised brightly-colored sails on the windmill blades to mark special occasions and gave a friendly laugh along with his goods to those who came to buy. He waved as I passed by, and I waved back, smiling.

Next to the windmill is a lush green park. The canal, which runs behind our house, winds around the park to where giant weeping willows guard its banks. To say it is beautiful is to undersell. The glossy red tulips and golden daffodils of spring completed the quintessential Dutch landscape. To put the final touches on the still life, add the molenaar with his wooden klompen and ruddy-faced grin and you have the full picture. This is as far from Amsterdam as you can get.

The Devil Wears Clogs

Walking through the park brought me to a woman running a clothing repair and alterations shop. Past her, bent over her sewing machine is Ijsselstein's main thoroughfare. A small bridge covers the moat, canal in modern times, this part of town is a pedestrian zone. You cannot drive up to the cheese shop or the bakery and park, as you would in the United States. As much as this can be inconvenient on icy January mornings, I found it quaint that people still lived this way.

As I walked down the street, the spell was broken. No one here spoke a word of English. After I had taken my windmill and park photos, not brave enough to photograph Mr. Windmill himself, I had intended to shop.

The tantalizing smells which crept from the fleeting opening and closing of doors made it impossible to resist the shops. All Europe's goodness was available within three or four steps. Fat olives, stuffed with everything imaginable, sat in row after row of ceramic pots. Giant yellow wheels of Dutch cheese, revered for centuries, were stacked high, triangular wedges masterfully carved to reveal creamy insides. Belgian Trappist beer crafted lovingly by monks, sat side-by-side with wine perfected by Italians. French croissants colluded with other equally delicious pastry friends, tempting me to succumb.

The dream became a nightmare when I realized that none of these merchants understood my freaky style of accented Dutch. I was reduced to the Five Finger Pointing System, which left a massive gap for miscommunication. In order to obtain just one taste of these luscious treats, I had to point and hold up my fingers like a second-grader, indicating the quantity I wanted to purchase. I, Ms. Foreigner, had entered another dimension.

Here, the moment I stepped out my front door, a flashing-red light on my forehead indicating my alien status, switched on. Even though I wasn't here illegally, people did not warm to my unusual behavior, so unlike what they were used to. Before long, I gave up the game and the charming street-merchants and started going to the supermarket. In its familiar fluorescent safety, I could pick up anything I wanted with my own two hands and read the cash register display, which told me what to pay. If it was going to be a matter of trial and error with more of the latter, I'd take conversation-free shopping, thank you. Now, if I could only read the labels...

* * *

Operation Resignation would be executed within the week and David was accompanying me to the United States. Was he joining me for moral support, or was he afraid that if I went on my own I might not come back? He wouldn't be far wrong on the latter. Had I stuck around in Ijsselstein any longer, getting a better glimpse of my future, I doubt I would have wanted to return. Unfortunately, we couldn't expect smooth sailing in America either. David's first meeting with my parents and, more frightening, my friends, were in the cards. The coast wasn't clear of drama in any direction.

This was David's second trip to the States. His first was to Chicago for training, so he'd had no experience of life outside a corporate-insulated environment. My guess was that the characters I listed as friends and family were slightly different than the television versions. To call us dysfunctional would be to say that the Titanic had a wee problem with an iceberg. As a diversion, I included four days in New York City, a dose of excitement for us both.

Merely landing in New York quickens my pulse. I couldn't wait to experience my favorite place on Earth through the eyes of a foreigner. *Surprise!* His reaction was not what I expected. He was underwhelmed by the Big Apple.

Before I accuse David of having zero culture or taste, I must admit that I did manage to get a smile on his face a few times in America's most impressive city. Cheap American shopping at Macy's appealed to his frugal Dutchness. The free trip on the Staten Island Ferry by night, which reveals the magnificent Manhattan skyline, impressed. Literally running into Dan Aykroyd at Rockefeller Center was a cool addition to the agenda, even better when Tyra Banks lunched at the same Japanese restaurant as we did. At that, a little bit of awe snuck across his somber face.

It was the typical the New York characteristics which failed to impress, of course the things I love best. Central Park was cold and windy. The Met was nothing compared to the Louvre. The lowbrow Greenwich Village dives, where I'd spent many great nights in my twenties, did not meet his standards. Getting zero reaction on my

The Devil Wears Clogs

precious people watching spots, I was relieved to find one thing we agreed on: dinner in Little Italy should be repeated as often as possible.

If my favorite American city, let alone global city, didn't excite David, what would he think of *Cleveland*? I had given up my bachelorette pad in the city, and my parents lived forty-five minutes west of any potential fun. There was no alternative to using their place as a base while I took care of business and got my overdue taxes completed. I was watching my wallet and decent hotels were scarce.

Things between my parents had become strained. It was impossible not to feel the tension, and the prospect of staying under their roof while figuring out my life with my new boyfriend was daunting. Could our relationship withstand drama on both sides of the Atlantic? How the hell would I know?

Thankfully, David blended in. He went with the flow, and if he was nervous about meeting my family, he didn't show it. They liked him immediately. In fact, they seemed to prefer him over me, but I'm getting to that.

My mother said she was happy for me and now understood the drastic changes I was making after meeting him. My father didn't say much, but that was normal. That is, until the Memorial Day family barbeque where he suddenly had a lot to say. Alcohol has a way of helping that along.

"David, you sure are a great guy. A real peach," he gushed, slapping him on the back.

Am I hearing this right? Immediately, my radar was up. Compliments are not my father's native language. When things took a turn for the nasty, I was in the line of fire. My father continued his line of reasoning about why he thought so much of David after knowing him less than forty-eight hours: "He'd have to be to put up with you."

His brother, once my favorite uncle, echoed, "Yep, he must be a saint."

Excuse me? My eyes were wild as I looked at David to see if the comments registered. He didn't seem to take notice of their offensive banter, but I was livid.

I have just flown eight hours across the Atlantic to introduce the man I love to my family, and while they embrace him, they insult me?

With the house full of people, I had no interest in making a scene. I reminded myself that there were only two days left before we escaped. Defending myself had only proven to make matters worse in the past and what exactly had I done that required defending? As I saw it, now I was not only unwelcome in my choice of profession, but in my own family as well. Where the hell did I belong?

The last thing David and I did before leaving Ohio was meet my oldest friends at a downtown Cleveland restaurant. My best friend Karla recently gotten engaged, and we were meeting to get our wedding "assignments." My friends are like family. In difficult times, I knew who I could count on.

David meeting my friends for the first time carried more weight than anything my parents might have said. Should my oldest friends give David the thumbs down, I'd have a lot of thinking to do. Having just quit my job, I didn't relish rethinking my relationship or my life. Allison had already voiced her approval after meeting him in Germany, but this is a tough crowd. They'd known me since I was five years old. There would be no hiding.

Why I spent any time worrying is beyond me. Karla and Kirsten, who happen to be cousins, embraced David with open arms. I had run amok alongside these two in our small town and they had known about David since we went to Venice. They were beyond curious about the man who was turning my life upside down. They wanted every detail on the guy who changed my plan from a twelve-month assignment in Germany to a Dutch residency.

Our noisy table of ten that night must have sounded like twenty. After so long apart, there were many tales to tell. Laughter was contagious and David was clearly a hit.

It was a boost to my confidence. I felt better knowing we'd see each other again soon at Karla's Fort Lauderdale wedding. Even if the months ahead proved as difficult as I feared, there would be much fun on sunny Florida beaches in April 2004.

Happy occasions like these were the good luck totems that I held tight during my most difficult periods. As long as there was something good on the horizon, a trip to a new country or a visit with close friends,

The Devil Wears Clogs

I had a lifeline. Career achievement could no longer be counted on to lift my spirits.

On the last day, we drove around Ohio towns and I showed David the places I loved–just as we had done in Holland. The beautiful riverside home I grew up in, fifteen minutes from where my parents now lived, was empty. A 'for sale' sign had been hastily stuck in the front yard. I showed David the town on the great Lake Erie that had once held my favorite memories, but it seemed desolate. Another path closed off.

"You can't go home again," they always say. Whoever they are, they are right. It was completely devoid of all that once made it home.

My parents' new house would never my home. It was a house they lived in. Truthfully, the old neighborhood always made me feel like an alien anyway. International dreams were few and far between. Maybe my intense desire to travel was simple. I was looking for the place I belonged.

The day we left was so unpleasant that, as much as I was worried about the months ahead, I couldn't wait to flee Ohio. Driving us to the airport, my father got a speeding ticket from a police officer hidden by bushes, as rural Ohio policemen have a tendency to do. He had been speeding, so of course he was in the wrong, but the arrogance oozing from this cop made for a toxic combination. My father nearly ran over the officer's foot as he ripped the ticket from the guy's hand and tore off. So much for teary farewells.

* * *

The quick hop from Cleveland to Newark was a piece of cake. Heavily-armed cops and intense security were everywhere as the post 9/11 reality lived on, but soon we were holding hands over the Atlantic once again. The company had its laptop back and my complicated tax return was filed. A sliver of hope had appeared amidst the gloom, in the form of a large tax refund. *Hallelujah!* That would keep me solvent until I found a job in the Netherlands. I hadn't relied on financial help since leaving Ohio State ten years earlier, and I wasn't about to become dependent on David. Here I was, already making the rules I would force myself to live by. This one was deeply ingrained, the belief that

I, alone, would get myself through life. I wasn't accustomed to sharing that life with anyone and honestly didn't know how to.

Back in the dorp, life went on. David went to work, and I scoured the internet for jobs that didn't require Dutch fluency. There weren't many, so I was lucky to have a strong resume of experience at global companies. The names were easily recognizable in the Dutch business community, which made business conversations easier. They helped me get a toe in the door. Soon, I hoped I would get an entire foot in, to push it wide open.

Within a month, I had my first interviews with recruitment firms. Usually, this is all it takes. I'd always been successful career-wise with the exception of the last three months and I didn't expect that to change now. When I received little communication from the recruiters, I began to suspect that something was amiss. By this time, it was June.

In my early Dutch interviews, I missed a few things. Number one, interviewing style is considerably different and number two, Europeans are more interested in planning four-week summer holidays than hiring. That person needs a replacement? That deadline is around the corner? Don't worry, we're off to the south of France! Work can, and will, wait. The Great European Migration begins well before August.

After ten years of working and living life at ninety miles an hour, I suddenly had nothing but time. I wasn't enjoying it. The future was too scary to relax. Not knowing what else to do, I contacted and met numerous professional people during this time and tried to understand the employment market.

The waters of communication were murky. The interviewing game has different rules in Europe. In America, you must sing your praises, toot your own horn, and generally demonstrate why you are the best one for the job–a poker game, in which bluffing is king. This is one reason people of little competence can fall into positions of authority. It isn't necessarily all based on skill, but he who has the best strategy.

When interviewing in Europe, facts are the only currency. Potential employers and recruiters want concrete examples of what you've done and where you've done it. No legislation exists to prevent them from asking your age and marital status. This appeared especially relevant in my case as I was female, in my early thirties, and had no children. Maternal leave granted in most European countries is substantially longer than in the United States, an average of six months.

There is no question that more than one employer looked at my age and imagined me, once hired, running off to get pregnant. I'm being sarcastic, but sadly, there *are* women who would take a job just to get their pregnancy paid for and would quit when the benefits ran out. Had one of these people looked closely at my employment history, it would have been glaringly obvious that I wasn't the settling-down type, but in the early days, no one did.

I doubt it takes a nuclear physicist to understand why I wasn't in a rush to perfect the language of this nation. It's like water torture, each drop is yet another thing that you haven't done right. When your torturers insist that there is only one way to do something, you rebel against that one way with all you've got. Yes, I knew it would make my life easier. Yes, I understood it would improve my career opportunities in the Netherlands.

One thing remained that I couldn't get past. Even if I studied for the next five years, I still wouldn't be able to have a technical business conversation in fluent Dutch. It wasn't going to happen. Aside from that, why should I make such an investment in a country that had thus far been openly hostile to me?

It hasn't escaped me that this is the wrong attitude. I knew I couldn't avoid language instruction forever and time was running out. At the very least, it would allow me to have real conversations with David's family. My measuring stick was maximum impact in the minimum amount of time.

Besides language, other sharks circled. I needed a work and residence permit to stay in the Netherlands. Without it, I couldn't work anywhere. It was huge relief that you don't have to be married to your Dutch partner to apply. Since we lived together, David had to support my application by proving his income and committing to pay to return me to my homeland if I became a problem. No joke. Since I was American, they would let me stay as long as I didn't claim state benefits. Why was everyone in this nation so paranoid about money?

Landing in Germany and then the Netherlands, I was initially under the protective wing of a giant corporation. All residency permits and work visas had been arranged by company representatives with very little action on my part. Initiating the process for my own personal permit, I discovered the swampy depths of European bureaucracy. Should your head sink below the surface, you will most certainly drown. Your best bet is to tread water as long as possible, hoping to tire out your opponent.

This wasn't my first time around the block. I had provided all the documentation for my work visas in Canada, Germany, and the Netherlands and knew what they wanted to see. What I didn't have experience with was the direct contact with government personnel who were only interested in job security. Every time I posed a question, I received a different response. The nasty attitude directed at anyone who wasn't Dutch also caught me off guard. Lurking beneath the surface of immigration laws in the Netherlands was the friction created by groups of thieves proven to be immigrants, and others who refused to assimilate to the Dutch government's satisfaction.

Without fail, there was a document I hadn't filed, requiring an additional appointment several weeks into the future. Too bad no one had mentioned this document before. Or a process appeared from nowhere that had to be completed before the step I was working on. If I had figured out the game earlier, repeating back everything I was told to verify each conversation, I would have finished the process in record time, but I didn't. For now, my future was at the mercy of the IND, *Immigratie Naturalizatie Dienst*.

* * *

The Netherlands doesn't allow you to work while your residency application is in process, so there was more time to fill. I was eager to see the few friends I had in Europe. Marlena lived near Amsterdam with her Dutch boyfriend. Via email, she said she'd also left the company. From our long conversations when I first arrived in Holland, I knew that her life here hadn't been easy. I was anxious to see a friendly face and to hear how her story had ended so abruptly. I suspected our stories would be similar.

The Devil Wears Clogs

A smiling Marlena bounced into the sunny café where I sat with my book. It was a relief to see her under happy circumstances for once. It might not have been obvious from the outside, but I felt beaten down by this place. Marlena, on the other hand, looked terrific. Her buoyancy lifted me up too. She and Anthony had been happily living together for the last three months. We were in the same boat, fighting with the IND over the details of our residency permits and unanimously agreed that it was a nightmare.

As expected, our stories were similar. Unfortunately for Marlena, her status as a South African national made her road tougher. South Africa doesn't have a reputation as a wealthy peaceful nation. During her application process, the Dutch government was convinced that she was fleeing the violence and poverty of her former country. They didn't grasp that she was a professional brought here by a global corporation, who now wanted to stay and make a life. No, being from such a poor nation, she was likely to put a burden on the Dutch state in some manner. Off she goes to *imburgerings curses*. Yes, it's as awful as it sounds.

The Dutch government had established citizenship courses for residency applicants. Popular opinion was that too many immigrants arrived and failed to assimilate to Dutch culture. Instead, they would continue to live in enclaves of their own ethnicity and speak their own language. What a strange notion when the Dutch culture was so welcoming.

It is in no way unreasonable for a person to be expected to learn about the country they intend to live in. What is unreasonable, in my opinion, is to mandate that the person spend four hours a day, five days a week for three months doing so. How exactly was a professional expected to earn a living during their enforced education? Rumors of this Dutch training camp had occasionally come my way, but I was too afraid it might be true to look into it. I avoided asking David about it, because I was afraid of my own reaction. The possibility that I could be forced into it made me feel faint. Just when you think things can't get any worse, someone or something appears to show you just how wrong you can be.

As if that appalling news wasn't enough, next we got into the details of Marlena's resignation. Originally, she had arrived with five other South Africans to work for the firm. In 2000, they signed up to work in the Netherlands for a three-year term. By the time Marlena's three years were up, she was the only one left. Everyone else had terminated their contracts and returned to South Africa.

When Marlena's contract came up for renewal, she decided that she too was finished. I knew the reasons, as her Dutch manager had probably been a relative of the Devil. Ironically, back then I'd considered myself lucky to only be dealing with gutless Hazel. I was the last person who would blame her for wanting to sever her relationship with the company, but the surprise ending was yet to come.

She had sent her resignation to my old friend, Dafne. In Marlena's case, she was even more vicious. After a positive three-year work record, Marlena told Dafne that she wasn't interested in renewing her contract, and would prefer to terminate the relationship, giving valid reasons. Delightful Dafne, knowing full well how important Marlena's relationship to her Dutch boyfriend, Anthony, was, remarked, "Oh, you don't want to work for us anymore? Well, I hope you will be allowed to remain in the country." *Bitch.* I thought it and said it simultaneously. Marlena, the soft-spoken kind-hearted South African, nodded her head in agreement.

We'd both received the same message when we chose to leave: "Without us, you are nothing." I simply couldn't believe the arrogance of these people. Who the hell did they think they were? God? You always hear about doctors with the God complex. Newsflash: It applies to Dutch management consultants as well.

Marlena and I sat laughing at the audacity of this crew who thought they ran the world. Both of us knew our lives, whatever directions they now took, would be a damn sight better without these people. We possessed educations and skills that were in demand. There was no question that the future would bring more positive working arrangements for each of us. While it is tragic that people in so-called positions of authority attempt to manipulate subordinates this way, the truth is it happens every day. The only difference is that in the

The Devil Wears Clogs

Netherlands, I suspect it happens several times daily.

Happily rid of the past, we chatted about our latest travels and future plans. I would have done anything for this not to have happened to my friend too, but when I left that afternoon, I felt a little lighter. It was now obvious that I wasn't the only target, I was part of a trend.

* * *

In July, I got to see Dora again. Not eager to return to the U.S., Dora had been working near Antwerp since leaving Germany. We had been in constant contact during the Dutch disaster, and she remained a well of strength that I drew from. She was still working for the firm and located at a Belgian utility project. I knew her experience hadn't been a bed of roses, but I also knew Dora was more determined than most. She isn't one to shy away from conflict. You'd better have your facts straight if you decide to take her on. She isn't a complainer either. If she's venting about something, it's likely more serious than she is letting on.

I took the four o'clock train from Utrecht to Antwerp, arriving shortly after five. Having the luxury of time, I made my way down a nearby street and checked out the café menus to find the best place for a long talk. With us, there was always more wine and conversation than eating. I hugged her tight, happy to see her face again and relive our German laughs. Eventually, I discovered that mine wasn't the only European dream going down in flames. Dora dealt with Belgian co-workers and clients. It's a globally-accepted fact that all clients are difficult. They want what they want, and when they're paying for your services, you must deliver. On Dora's project, it wasn't only the client being difficult, but the Belgians from our firm too. She'd listened many times to the peculiarities of dealing with the Dutch and we both knew about working with Germans. This was the first appearance of Belgians in our shared experiences.

Dora said Belgians were like the Geminis of European work astrology. They should be called the "twins" as Geminis are, because they often have two faces. One minute, you are praised for delivering the keys to the kingdom, the next, you are Eve biting the apple. She said it made her feel insane, because they truly have a talent for keeping the ground beneath you terminally unstable. It's like going out to sea in ten-foot waves. If you don't have good sea legs, you are going to hit the deck.

Dora had exceptional sea legs, professionally speaking of course, and even she was dragged down by the fierce undertow. I had always admired her strength. She had driven that Flintstone Fiat on par with the crazy Italians flying past us in Sicily. She spoke German like a native. Most of all, she was very successful professionally and highly regarded in our company. If these Belgians could rattle her, what chance in hell did I have of succeeding with the Dutch? I wasn't anxious to pursue the thought. Despite the daily work terror, it was still exciting to be part of the European experience. Maybe we were gluttons for punishment, but we also knew a good thing when we had it. If we could better understand the rules of the game, we could master it. That's what our conversations were very often about.

We agreed to meet again before she returned to the United States. She had less than a month left on this project. Though we were no longer lived in the same city, I would miss her tremendously when she left Europe. Long distance and six hours of time difference leave a lot to be desired.

Her fiancé, the American soldier based in Germany, was also returning to the U.S., so I couldn't blame her. She felt she was giving up because she hadn't won the war of client approval, but she had seen a tough assignment through and it had taken its toll. We all have our limits, and I could see that my friend had been pushed to hers. As sad as it was to see her go, I wanted her out of there.

* * *

Summer of 2003 charged like a lion on its prey, bringing temperatures high above average. Southern Europe is hot in July and August, but northern European countries are normally more temperate. August in Germany had been hot the year before, but peaks came and went quickly. I remembered only a few uncomfortable nights sleeping without air-conditioning. This summer was looking like a very different beast. By July, we'd already had several days over 100° Fahrenheit in Holland. In France and Spain, the heat was relentless.

Having learned that summer was not hiring season and to escape our tiny, claustrophobic, Ijsselstein hothouse, I registered for an intensive, two-week Dutch language course. Classes were held in the outskirts of Brussels, and began the first week of August. I had to live in the hotel where instruction would be given for two weeks. Personally, I thought my strategy for avoiding the intense summer weather was excellent. I continued thinking I was brilliant until I arrived in Sint Peter Leeuw.

The day David drove me to the hotel, thirty minutes away, we tested his new GPS system. They hadn't been on the market long and I'd never had one. I used an atlas everywhere I needed to go, a challenge because few English maps are available in Germany. When I bought my first German road atlas, I didn't know whether to laugh or cry. Eventually I realized it wasn't that confusing if you knew where you were going, and actually it was helpful because the map names and the autobahn signs matched.

So, here we were, rolling out of big-city Brussels in David's Audi with a fancy new device to guide us. David had never heard of this town and we assumed it was a Brussels suburb. Once again, I was reminded not to make assumptions.

As we got closer, the number of businesses and cafés dwindled and the number of farms increased. I found it unnerving. Even more unnerving was the GPS directing us to follow a route that looked like a cow path to get to the hotel. Without another road in sight, we followed that narrow dirt path, which took us to a long gravel driveway in front of my hotel. By now, I was in a full-blown state of panic. I was being exiled to the hinterland for two full weeks, including a weekend, in this place?

I tried to stay calm as I approached the desk to check in. The chipper young man was pleasant enough to make me think I was overreacting. Because my stay was long, he upgraded my room. I didn't hear anything else he said. I was looking pleadingly at David, willing him to see that this was a huge mistake and he could not leave me here. No luck there. He patted my shoulder, telling me to be a good student and work hard, which wasn't the least bit reassuring. I was completely surrounded by farmland. Did he not recognize a fish out of water when he saw one?

When the clerk finished talking, he handed me the keys to my cell in solitary confinement, and David tore off in the Audi across the cow pasture. I told myself to relax. I would lie down in the air-conditioning for a minute, and this would all seem less disturbing. Lying to myself worked long enough for me to open the door and see that there *was* no air-conditioning. In Belgium. On a farm. During one of the hottest European summers ever recorded! Tears of relief welled up in my eyes when I saw the huge windows that appeared to open. I ordered myself to get a grip. Human beings have lived for centuries sans air-conditioning. I wasn't going to die in that hotel, and surely this heat would end soon. No one could remember anything like it.

Hoisting my suitcase onto the bed, I found a pair of shorts and quickly tore off my jeans. Class began the next morning, so I was free for the evening. Trying to relax, I hoped a hot bath would make the room feel cooler when I got out. It wasn't a huge success, but I was able to fall asleep for a little while afterwards. The sun was about to set when I woke up. I threw the windows open, allowing the cool evening breeze to fill the room. It was a terrible plan. The windows had no screens and evening breeze was thick with mosquitoes. They attacked overnight. The next morning, I was covered with bites because I had slept without covers and only minimal clothing. *Yay! First day of school! I can't wait!*

The class itself was better than the environment. My instructor, Jan, was stern but likeable. For two weeks, I had to speak entirely in Dutch from breakfast until the evening meal was finished. If someone had pointed out that this would require using Dutch to get my morning caffeine, I would have walked right out the door.

One of the first things that Jan explained was the difference between the Netherlands Dutch and Belgian Dutch, adding yet another hurdle to my overloaded obstacle course to success. I knew that parts of Belgium had formerly belonged to Holland and had heard the wildly different accents, but I had not realized that the two sometimes used different words to convey the same meaning.

The intense days of instruction were not easy, but I was delighted when I could suddenly understand some of what was said on television.

The Devil Wears Clogs

Little bits of enlightenment crept in from all directions. Jan stressed that because this was a rapid pace of learning, it was critical that I continued to practice speaking and learning on my own. If I didn't, I would forget everything I learned just as quickly.

Every night, I watched the Belgian news to increase my vocabulary. Jan found me the last black-market fan in Brussels, so I was at least sleeping at night without fear of attack. I could concentrate enough to understand the news reports about the heat wave affecting all of Europe.

Each night as I watched, the situation worsened. One major problem that was described in more detail than I would have liked was the overcrowding of French morgues. All of France was on holiday while the temperatures climbed to over 105° Fahrenheit, and it was normal for families to leave their elderly relatives home alone while they traveled.

Many French families opted not to interrupt their holidays to return home to the ugly business of claiming a body. Had they no sense of decency? Nearly fifteen thousand died in France that summer, most of them were elderly people who had never confronted such temperatures. They didn't know how to react and there was no one around to help. Ten percent of that number died in the Netherlands during the same period. After hearing this, the Netherlands didn't seem like the worst place to live after all.

David picked me up from my hotel when my sentence was over. I even managed the last afternoon off for good behavior. I was never so happy to see someone in my entire life. I rattled off Dutch sentences as we drove the hour and a half back to Ijsselstein and he was clearly impressed. Now that I could read billboards and road signs, it was as if I'd been in a very dark room for almost a year and someone had finally switched on the light.

It was a massive relief to have some understanding of what was happening around me and I scolded myself for waiting so long. Obviously I didn't become fluent in two weeks, but I understood the basic grammar structure and had a growing vocabulary. In other words, I was better equipped than ever before for my new life.

CHAPTER 24
OPPORTUNITY KNOCKS

To lull me into a sense of contentment, there were less bumps in the road of my Dutch life for a while. After eight weeks of limbo, my residence permit was approved. Now there were two fewer reasons for employers to dismiss me before I could get an interview. I could now work legally and had basic knowledge of Dutch. The apt expression would be that I knew enough to be dangerous.

Finally, my resume began to generate responses and my professional life was resurrected from the grave. I didn't know whether it was my increased confidence or because people had returned to work after The Summer from Hell, either way, I didn't care.

Initially, I felt like that coughing Fiat we'd rented in Sicily. It didn't move fast, and you never knew when it would give out. There were at least six interviews that went nowhere before a recruiter contacted me about a position that sounded perfect—Global Service Manager for an Amsterdam company that operated in thirty-five countries. If this didn't fit the bill for my fascination with people and cultures, nothing would.

So, interview I did. First, I met the recruiter who explained the position and the benefits. We agreed that the job matched my skills and experience well, and an interview was set up with the hiring manager, a Brit. I still had no car and Ijsselstein was an hour's drive from their office, but I didn't want this to be a deal-breaker. If everything went well, I could buy a car. In the beginning, I'd have to use public transport to get there each day.

Despite an attack of nerves before the interview, I liked my potential new boss immediately. Peter, the Global IT Manager, had an engaging personality and a ready laugh. It wasn't one of those painful panel interviews, just a conversation between the two of us. Actually, Peter did most of the talking, laying out his vision for what the job entailed.

I wouldn't call it a tough interview. I didn't sell myself, rather he seemed to be selling me on the position. The job didn't sound easy, but Peter was confident it could be done, so I saw no reason to question that. There was travel involved because the company had originated in Australia and spread across the globe. Amsterdam was recently named the new headquarters. The business was marketing, sales, and distribution of some of the world's most well-known wine and spirits brands. Trips to Australia? Employee discounts on booze? Where do I sign?

After meeting Peter, I felt confident that this was the right place to land. The position was perfect, a combination of everything I'd done up to this point in my career. When the recruiter called me with an offer of employment just two hours after the interview, I was thrilled.

Once he delivered that news, he began speaking a language I didn't understand. It was still English, but what he was saying made no sense. It turns out that obtaining a job in the Netherlands and becoming someone's employee is much more complicated than the 'hire and fire at will' mentality of corporate America.

First the recruiter told me the salary, which was equivalent to my U.S. salary and higher than my former company had offered me to transfer to Amsterdam. Negotiating didn't occur to me because I needed a job pronto. The offer was twenty thousand euro above the last one I'd received, so what was the point of asking for more?

Then, he told me being an expatriate allowed me to file my taxes under the "30% Ruling." *What?* This was a three-year grace period intended to allow expats to adjust to the drastic increase in Dutch tax rates by paying a lesser amount in their first years of work. That was good news too. I'd expected to pay 52% of what I earned. Then he had something less appealing to say. The company policy for all new hires was a one-year contract. Working on a temp contract, in my experience, was what one did in the United States when one wasn't skilled enough to do anything else. It held zero appeal. Did I really want to go through all this again in a year?

The Devil Wears Clogs

Of course, the smooth-talking recruiter had a ready reply for every concern. He assured me he had already brought several employees into the company, and all of them had been offered permanent contracts after their first year. His explanation was that it is more difficult to terminate employees in the Netherlands than in the United States, so this was a safeguard. As reasonable as it sounded, I didn't like it. I told the recruiter I would get back to him, and I called David to make plans for a celebratory dinner. I knew I would take the job, but I didn't appreciate the exasperation in the recruiter's voice when he was forced to answer my questions. Let him wait.

When David arrived home, he was all smiles. He knew how tense being unemployed made me, and it seemed that we would soon be putting an end to that chapter of our new life. I was smiling too, because I could count on receiving a good salary for at least a year.

David was nonchalant about the one-year contract. "Temporary contracts are becoming more normal in Holland. It's impossible to fire someone, so companies want to make sure the person is good before they offer permanent employment."

"How can it be impossible?" David might as well have been speaking Greek.

"The HR representative and the direct manager need records detailing poor performance for at least a year before they can consider letting someone go. Even then, the employee can take the employer to court and 99% of the time the terminated employee wins and gets paid unemployment. It's a stupid system." David shrugged.

Both stories were consistent, but that didn't mean I had to like it. It didn't matter that in the bizarre context of life in the Netherlands, it made perfect sense; I didn't want to be looking for a new job in a year. Not wanting to focus on the negative, I dropped it. We clinked champagne flutes to our good fortune and savored rare steak and the ever-present French fried potatoes. Better times were on the horizon.

In the morning, I called the recruiter and accepted Peter's offer, contingent on receiving everything in writing. No longer exasperated, he assured the contract would arrive the next day. My interview with Peter took place in early October, but we agreed on a start date of

November 1, because Dutch salaries are paid monthly. Now that I was certain I wouldn't be financially dependent on David, I could relax.

* * *

My first trip to the office didn't go as planned. The daily commute by public transport took twice as long as it took to reach Amsterdam by car—two hours one way. But after I met my new co-workers, my concern over the four hours I'd be spending on trains and trams faded. They were a friendly bunch from all over Europe. I shared an office with two IT guys, a chatterbox from Portugal and a more reserved one from Holland. On Peter's team, we also had a good-natured Malaysian woman, a serious German, and four other Dutch.

I heard about the cowboy software manager who was Australian, but out of town on business. There were two young women who ran reception, one American and one Irish. Everyone was laughing and gossiping about the Halloween gathering the weekend before, which sounded like a hell of a party. Everyone was supportive, offering help with any questions.

Peter took me to lunch to give me a more detailed lay of the land. He confirmed my suspicion that my mission wasn't easy, but he was confident we could do it together It was the honeymoon stage and everything was coming up roses. Late afternoon meetings were often punctuated with glasses of good wine. Initially, nothing seemed awry.

The new job tension passed mercifully quickly. There's nothing worse than not even knowing where the bathroom is on your first days of a new job. When the shiny-newness of it began to fade, I began digging beneath the surface of Peter's story about my assignment and the current situation. According to him, the foundation for my goal had already been laid—to document a service agreement, which defined the terms by which IT changes and issues faced by the business would be resolved.

I didn't need to dig very deep to see that the situation was not exactly as Peter described. The team didn't have a system in place to track the software problems being raised by the regional business units. If—and that was a big if—a problem or a system change was recorded, it was on a piece of paper. If you were really lucky, maybe an old spreadsheet existed. No dates or responsible parties were recorded. No follow-up actions were stated. In short, I was expected to build a luxury resort when the land hadn't even been cleared.

This wasn't the only problem. The team I worked with was brand new. They were skilled, highly-paid technical resources. These new additions, with their higher price tags, had caused a major rift with the sales and marketing business people who were paid less, despite their seniority. The-not-so-professional human resources team had leaked salary information, so it was known to be valid. The expression "conflict of interest" was woefully inadequate.

With battle already being waged between the team implementing the software system and the business people expected to utilize it, enter the Global Service Manager. She will solve our problems! Even if she hadn't been told what they were, or been provided with any information about them, surely the Wonder Woman of IT Service will save the day. All I needed were a cape and a tiara.

My first week on the job, I knew I'd made a mistake in accepting their offer. This was later confirmed when I was told by HR that I wasn't eligible for the 30% ruling because I was already living in the Netherlands. This rule only applied if you had been brought in from overseas to fill a position. Nice. *What exactly was true about this job?* Truths made a shorter list than the misrepresentations I'd already discovered.

I won't even mention the fact that this young company had no processes or procedures for anything, including the reporting of IT incidents and problems. It's just too painful. Wonder Woman has just left an organization of one hundred thousand employees with resources and global procedures galore to join Mass Chaos Inc. You would think that our eternally-optimistic heroine would catch a break, right? No. No breaks here. We reserve those for Dutch personnel only.

With the writing now in flaming-red letters on the wall, I dug deeper to see what other problems lie in wait before initiating a conversation with Peter. No matter what I said, our deal had been struck. I had to either leave or make the situation work. I had no desire to hit the streets and start my job search over again. I needed to find a way.

Considering the closet full of skeletons I'd discovered, it was going to be rough. My defining characteristic is blind optimism, no matter what comes. Naïve or not, I believed hard work could solve anything. If something was within my ability to fix, whether it was my responsibility or not, I would try to do so. This was a new company and I had the benefit of experience. Why shouldn't I put it to good use?

When I finally cornered Peter, he sheepishly admitted how much he had wanted me to join his team. In his haste to get me on board, he had embellished the status of his current strategy. His passion and sense of humor had won me over to begin with, so of course he convinced me to stick around. We created a plan of attack to get the project a foundation I could live with, and went on with the show.

Step one was implementing a tracking system for the help desk. I met the key players of each European business unit and learned the business of liquor sales and distribution. Had my progress continued this way, one phase of business improvement at a time, with each step expanding the available IT services and improving service quality to our internal customers, I would likely have stayed at the company for many years. But that isn't the way it turned out.

* * *

Peter took a long Christmas holiday in December 2003. To underscore his confidence, he named me as his replacement. It was a big compliment. Peter was the Global IT Manager of the company. It felt good that he trusted me to make the right decisions under pressure. We sat together while he listed the pending items and "to do's" I had to chase. We finished the meeting with a glass of beautiful Bordeaux and me wishing him a wonderful Christmas holiday in Mauritius.

Despite the growing list of Mass Chaos's problems, there was much cheer outside of work. David and I were about to share our first Christmas living together before going to Ohio for a short break. From where I sat, I had a lot to be thankful for. I was employed. I lived with a man who loved me. I had a challenging new business to learn. I would write a happy ending to this story if it killed me.

At work, I was busier than I ever thought possible. In Peter's absence, I became aware of more serious problems within his IT

The Devil Wears Clogs

department after I tripped over the office grapevine one day. I don't actively seek out information, good or bad, about what is happening in people's private lives or careers. For this reason, I am usually the last one to know anything. I go to the office to work, not socialize. I don't go there to make myself look better by befriending the "right" people. People who schmooze instead of work are, to me, one of the lowest forms of life.

Peter and I agreed that the days immediately surrounding Christmas would be dead in the office. I should go ahead with my plan to make a quick dash to the States to spend Christmas with my family. I felt guilty dragging David to boring Ohio for the second time in quick succession, but I also felt guilty that I never saw them. I just hoped it would be painless.

* * *

The Lake Erie shore received a record pounding of snowfall that year. David caught a virus on the plane that knocked him out for three of our five-day visit. He was barely functioning on Christmas day, and not at all interested in the martinis I was mixing in the kitchen in a desperate attempt to lighten the oppressive atmosphere.

My parents were at each other's throats the entire time. My brother dropped in briefly with his new girlfriend and paid no attention to anyone else. None of them cared what was going on with me, my new job, or my life abroad. It went down in my book as the worst Christmas ever, and this includes the Christmas we celebrated in a blackout, and any one after the crash of the U.S. economy in the 1980's.

Being so far away made it impossible to understand what was going on with my family. Everyone, aside from my brother, was miserable. The urge to escape was overwhelming.

Karla kept me sane. We couldn't see each other because of the massive snowdrifts covering the lakeshore roads, but at least I could share her excitement about her wedding, now just four months away, over the phone. Despite the cost and length of trips to the U.S., I couldn't imagine not being in Florida in April.

I counted my blessings that I couldn't stay longer, and had the perfect excuse to exit the country. Every time I went there, it became clearer that my decision to remain separated from my family by an enormous body of water was the right one. No matter how much work stress I had, it was better than dealing with the bottomless pit of despair that Ohio had become. There was no good news. Ever.

CHAPTER 25
CHOOSING SIDES

Traveling to the Amsterdam office on January 2, 2004, was not a joyride. A pile of problems demanded immediate attention. My Portuguese office pal laughed at me when he arrived a few days later for coming back the second day of January. According to him, it was a known fact that everyone returns to work irritable and impatient to finish whatever they left behind over the holidays. According to the Logic of Pablo, that week is best avoided all together.

His comments, along with his southern European enthusiasm, always made me laugh. No American I had ever worked with took vacations longer than a week. When someone took two weeks off, they often wondered if they would still have a job when they came back.

As much as I enjoyed sharing an office with the funny, gregarious Pablo, he was also the source of most of the company gossip that came my way, so I decided it was better not to share my experience with long vacations. I told him I'd be sure make a note for next year. Clues for the case of radically-different Dutch employment law were mounting. There was simply no comparison with what I was used to in the United States. The jury was still out, but more evidence appeared daily.

Taking care of the petty issues that had accumulated, and preparing for Peter's return the following Monday kept me on my toes. I had great ideas how to make progress on the help desk we desperately needed, and the global agreement for IT Services was taking shape.

In my first two months at the company, I'd had to spend a lot of time on busy work in preparation for the "big picture" of how we wanted the department to run. Learning how the business worked took longer than expected due to the many nuances and regulations surrounding the sale of alcohol. Understanding our newly implemented system design was critical to gauge the impact of complaints I was receiving. Every issue raised had to be classified as a glitch or an urgent problem. Once I figured that out, I could identify who in the business wanted bells and whistles and whose issues were serious, preventing them from working.

The last week that Peter was away, Pablo rattled on about the major power struggle underway at Mass Chaos. He placed bets on the winner while I half-listened. I wasn't on a first name basis with the business leadership. All I needed to know was that they didn't look favorably on the new and very expensive team built by Peter. From their point of view, we were unable to solve the smallest of system issues.

I should have let them in on a secret: with the monolith of German software they had purchased, life would never be easy again. I kept my head down and my cards close to the chest. Pablo's daily updates, I took with a grain of salt. Who cared whether the French guy or the Scotsman got their way in the end?

My ears were full to capacity when a new arrival appeared on the management team. Suspiciously, this Swede named Gustav was introduced with responsibilities that overlapped Peter's. The rumor mill theorized that he was a relative of one of the main shareholders of the company, which was part Swedish. Truth or not, it made sense because Gustav didn't seem to have any relevant experience for the position. He wasn't an IT specialist or a beverage-industry expert. The rest of the employees at Mass Chaos were one or the other.

When Peter didn't return as expected, I started worrying. I worried more when Gustav called an all hands meeting. My interactions with Gustav had been brief thus far, but I didn't harbor a great desire to know more. Pablo had kicked his suppositions into overdrive and eventually managed to pull me in too. We sat in the office all morning trying to figure out if our worst fears were being realized.

By that afternoon, words from the Swedish horse's mouth confirmed it. Peter wasn't coming back and Gustav was taking over the team. My mental health, already a punching bag for this country, took another hit. My boss, he of the supreme vision and passion, was to be replaced by a know-nothing who had gotten his job because of who, not what, he knew. Would I ever wake up from this nightmare?

Gustav told the team they could work from home resolving system issues as Peter had allowed, but the rule no longer applied to Pablo and me. As the IT services department, we were to be personally available to the business at all times. That eliminated the last perk I'd been promised when I took this job. I'd be forced to do the four-hour daily commute five days a week.

Gustav was much younger than Peter and didn't grasp the fact that employees were more efficient not sitting on a train for half the day. I did need to be in the office the majority of the time and planned to be. When working on a complex proposal or presentation, however, I am more productive away from constant interruption and I'd kept this option in my back pocket just in case. Being treated as a child made me rebel like one.

The man who hired me gave a false impression of the maturity of the IT organization, along with the amount of senior management support for the work he tasked me with. The human resources department denied my right to a tax adjustment of 30% over three years, so I would now have to get used to paying 52% of my income to the Dutch government immediately. My boss, whom I liked despite his deliberate deception, was fired and replaced with the know-nothing relative of a higher up. The new boss, Gustav, was insecure and inexperienced, and equates managing people with adult baby-sitting. Add to the mix the stellar cultural experience of living in a tiny village where no one understands me and my family falling apart across the ocean. I was beginning to feel like the leading lady in a Lifetime mini-series.

I began to lose it. I could not run away from the fact that there was no way to win in this country, no matter what I did. The Reaper lurked around every corner and Depression moved in. I began to dream about death. I dreamt both awake and asleep of my own death, not that of Gustav, which might have been considered appropriate. It was simultaneously the weirdest and scariest feeling I have ever experienced.

Gustav's bombshell brought fallout from all directions. I laid low to avoid a direct hit. I didn't react to Gustav's nonsense or make claims of mutiny. I waited to see what would happen next. If Peter could disappear that quickly, surely Gustav could be eliminated too. Perhaps he was just a management stopgap? Maybe Peter had was fired for a severe breach of conduct? Pablo and I could only hope. As things stood, I only had a one-year contract with these people. I just needed to do my job until I could find a way out.

The reward for joining the mess of Mass Chaos was new friends. Karin, a Dutch woman who had lived for several years in Germany, and Lorena, a Malaysian woman who had recently moved to the Netherlands with her Dutch husband, became my confidants. The Australian program manager quickly became a friend and ally too. Stan had only landed in the Netherlands one month before we met and was struggling with the same things that drove me crazy when I had arrived in late 2002.

The thread woven through this eclectic group, each of us having a connection to another country, loosely bound us in this confusing land. We did things together socially and occasionally drowned our sorrows in drinks after work. Those with cars shared rides with me, and life delivered a brief reprieve under the leadership of the Swedish simpleton.

* * *

It was my responsibility to report the status and expected resolution date of system issues. In this capacity, I dealt with everyone in the organization: the business people who reported problems and the system specialists who solved them. One teammate, for lack of a better term, who I tried my hardest not to deal with was a technical specialist named Berndt. Berndt was Dutch. The team loner, he had a reputation of being difficult to deal with. Unless I absolutely had to make contact, I kept a wide berth.

Due to my position, avoiding anyone who had dealings with the system on either side was impossible for long. Regardless of what everyone said about his personality, Berndt was a technical expert. For weeks, he had been working on solving a particularly complex system issue. During that time, we were forced to engage in civil conversation.

Looking for any possible rapport with the guy, I tried to learn a little about him personally. This was not a wise move. He asked me point-blank whether I had to take the dreaded imburgerings curses. I replied honestly that I didn't think so. Two Dutch work permits had already been approved without a word about it from anyone in the immigration office.

Giving Berndt an honest answer to his question also gave him a concrete reason to dislike me. His Turkish girlfriend had to take the classes. "Why are you special?"

I thought about reminding him I had a job and was financially self-sufficient, but I didn't. Those things did not apply to his girlfriend, according to Pablo who knew everything. Rather than add fuel to the fire, I claimed I was late for a meeting and disappeared. The truth was I didn't know why I was playing by a different set of rules.

In Berndt's nastiness, I understood the flip side of the seemingly-positive iron-clad Dutch employment contracts that David mentioned. The way he had described it, it was virtually impossible to get fired in the Netherlands and the ever-present Mass Chaos grapevine said the company had wanted to fire Berndt for at least a year.

Maybe he was a technical genius, but his belligerence and rare appearances at work made him far from a model employee. Pablo relayed more than one ugly example of his behavior, but added that Berndt wasn't going anywhere in the near future. Putting a strong case together was difficult enough, but the incompetence of our HR staff made it almost impossible. The result? The entire team suffered because one man was allowed to behave as nastily and unreliably as he wanted, while the rest of us remained buried in an avalanche of technical issues.

Whatever I thought about Berndt personally, he had a fair point. Why were there two sets of rules for foreigners wanting to live and work in the Netherlands? I brought it up to David but even he, my source on all things Dutch, couldn't give me an answer. I turned to the internet. It was a sad state of affairs that I was now looking for the worst rather than laying my hopes on the possible best. I had to figure this out once and for all, or it would continue to give me heart failure every time it came up. I couldn't fathom spending half my day, for months, in a classroom full of newly-arrived immigrants answering questions about the freaky behavior of the Dutch after working in this country for over a year.

I spent hours searching through the information online regarding American residency in the Netherlands before I finally located the explanation I'd been looking for. The U.S. government had negotiated an exemption with the Dutch government. When this rule came into effect its citizens could not be forced to take the classes. For once, a Get Out of Jail Free card! One item that caused panic at its mere mention could be now struck from the list that previously done nothing but grow. *Take that, Berndt.*

* * *

I wish I could say that this good news was enough to create an attitude shift, but it wasn't. In the winter of 2004 and the following spring, depression ran me down like a freight train. I began worrying about my death from various forms of cancer and often saw myself flying through the windshield of a car. The visions were so real I heard the shattering of glass. As if it wasn't bad enough, it began to happen at work too.

I could hazard a guess that my subconscious was screaming not to relinquish every single familiar thing I've ever known. That's what transitioning to Dutch life felt like, that I was expected to renounce the way I did nearly everything and adopt the *Dutch* way. Why else would new immigrants be kept in a classroom for months, for four hours a day other than to force them into submission?

What made no sense was that I was considered to be a strong person by many. Who else picks up and moves to Europe knowing no one? I know for sure it isn't the weak. On the other hand, if I was so strong, why was this happening to me? Along with depression, regular tension headaches and the inability to sleep were invited to the party. I was barely hanging on.

David could see my mental state and suggested going to the town doctor to get something for my headaches. At last, a logical suggestion from a rational mind. I declined his offer to come with me on the grounds that it was unlikely that going to a doctor in the Netherlands was any different than going to one in the United States. As David

The Devil Wears Clogs

had explained, most university textbooks are in English, so anyone with a university degree most likely speaks English. I walked through Ijsselstein one morning to find the tiny doctor's office and was told to take a seat.

The doctor has open hours on specific days of the week and everyone who needs to see him just shows up at the designated start time. Then, it's first come, first served. I didn't realize this, of course, so I took a seat with everyone else in the waiting room and tried to figure out the sequence of events.

Each new person that entered said good morning to the people in the waiting room. *Oops.* I didn't know I was expected to greet strangers while feeling like hell. Ninety minutes later, it was my turn. The doctor hadn't used his English much since he'd left university. He barely got a word of what I was saying and I simply had no Dutch words for this situation to save me.

I also learned that the Dutch don't rely on medication, prescribed or otherwise. It's one of the only countries in the world where it is illegal to receive pain medication during childbirth. Thank God I was only talking about tension headaches. For most ailments, the suggested remedy is "go home and rest." When I could see that he had no idea what my problem was, I decided not to get into a discussion about depression. The fact that it was happening was embarrassing enough without having to spell it out to a complete stranger using the words of a fourth grader.

Physically exhausted and mentally defeated, I made my way to the office the next day. Gustav knew I wasn't coming in the day before due to a health issue. It was business as usual until I learned that Gustav had planned one-on-one sessions with "his new team." When I heard this, I immediately looked for a way out. Having not shown up the day before, I had no choice but to participate. I was assigned an afternoon time-slot and I prepped my arsenal of issues to overwhelm him with.

I had to make the best use of this moment, so I decided to show him that he needed me and not vice versa. I wasn't worried about my job, but I wanted agreement to extend my one-year contract into a permanent position. It simply didn't send the right message to have a temporary resource on the mission to overhaul IT service delivery. At least, it didn't make sense to me.

Lost in preparation, I checked the clock just in time to make my way to the conference room to meet Gustav. I wasn't intimidated by him in the least. I just didn't have time to deal with the new boss who came off more like a petulant child than an authority figure. I knew this wasn't the attitude to take to the meeting, but I couldn't help it. The rules had been changed and the rug was pulled out from under me yet again. Did I mention that Gustav was short and I am five foot ten? Maybe you've heard what they say about short men, that they are always trying to make up for their shortcomings by demanding respect? Well, Short Man Syndrome certainly applied to Gustav.

Not having been part of my hiring process, Gustav asked about my background and experience. As he could easily have prepared for this discussion by reading my resume, I found this tedious but tried not to show it. Upon learning that I had been part of one of the top management consulting firms in the world, he decided it was appropriate to talk about an article about consultants that he'd recently read. I pulled the ever popular "Oh really?" to see where he was going with this.

"Yes. The article stated that there are more cases of severe insecurity in consultants," Gustav stated with confidence, "than any other industry."

"I see. And how did they diagnose such a condition? I mean, what constitutes "severe" insecurity as opposed to just being plain old insecure?" I asked the insecure man with a severe case of Short Man Syndrome.

"Oh, I can't recall. I just know that the overall conclusion was that people who really have no idea of who they are often end up in that business."

"Right. So what is it that you wanted to talk about?" I asked, wanting to get the show on the road.

"I wanted to find out more about my team members and their strengths, so that I can finalize an organizational structure that is better integrated into that of the entire company."

"I see. Well, I can tell you where I've been and what I was hired to do, but honestly I would expect you to already know all that. I can also tell you about a number of outstanding issues, which are not exactly insignificant." And I went on to do so. While I listed problems with the network and the frequent failing of the servers in Copenhagen which supported our business software system, I watched his eyes get bigger and bigger. I was, in all honestly, thoroughly enjoying the moment, until he said:

"Jennifer, what should I *do*?"

You see, I had plotted to freak him out. I had planned exactly what effect my words would have on a man who was in over his head. These issues were what we call show-stoppers: items hand-picked by me to give a distinct impression of fragility in the IT infrastructure as it currently stood. With the business department heads already screaming about the failings of the software system, I demonstrated that his problems could actually be a hell of a lot bigger. To someone who doesn't know that there are processes and procedures to remedy these things, and mostly what it takes is an outlay of cash, it might appear that the sky was falling.

Sadly, Wonder Woman hadn't planned on his admission quite so quickly that he didn't have a clue at what needed to be done. I hadn't prepared a list of the possible solutions to combat the problems one by one.

I told him I would document potential options and get back to him. Then I asked about my one-year work contract. He gave the textbook management answer, "If it makes sense to renew your contract when it is up, then we will do so." I told him I needed to know what was happening before then, and he agreed to get back to me in June, which was eight months through my twelve.

I left the meeting thinking about how I was supposed to supply this little man, who earned a great deal more than I did, with answers that would make him look good to our senior executives. At the same time, I was receiving zero confirmation about my own place in the company and already knew that the mission had zero support from those same senior executives. It just happened to be that *my* limited understanding of their IT infrastructure was more than he had. What the hell had he said to get the job?

I had to weigh how badly I wanted the job and play my cards right. My ethics told me that giving this moron all the answers was not the right thing to do. My fear of pounding the pavement for a new job said, "Do whatever it takes!" I was torn.

Once Gustav's one-on-one meetings were finished, I had a few one-on-one powwows of my own. Stan agreed that this guy didn't know which way was up. Karin, said she really missed Peter and didn't think Gustav had the strength to carry the team. Lorena, hated him and didn't waste time saying anything else. Pablo told me there was another player in the game to watch out for whose name was Bert.

Bert, it seemed, was as ambitious as they come. Conveniently, he also had a complete lack of ethics. He was one of those slimy guys who cozy up to whoever has the best shot of winning the war. Bert knew that Gustav was in his position because he was favored, for whatever reason, by the executive team. It didn't matter that Bert had also been hired by Peter and was Peter's friend. Nope, it only mattered who curried favor with the "right" people.

I am not capable of operating that way. I would be lying if I said I wished it were a talent of mine. I have an equal amount of respect for a Bert as I do a Gustav who traded on family connections to get his job.

The obvious fact? The place was a hornet's nest. Not being someone "in the know" who avidly searches out gossip was a major disadvantage. Around every corner lurked another trap that I unwittingly fell straight into.

Being an employee of a company this small was a real eye-opener. Everything operated on rumor. They say that women are bigger gossips than men? *Fat chance!* These grown men sat around trading rumors more than they actually worked. I know because I was *working*.

My competitor, it seemed, for the right-hand position of the IT leader, was Bert. Bert didn't waste his time formulating real plans to fix our biggest issues. Bert liked poking holes in the plans that I came up with instead. Over time, I didn't even hate Gustav. Like a fly, he was simply a nuisance who didn't know enough to be malicious. I did, on the other hand, come to hate Bert.

CHAPTER 26
BREAK IN THE CLOUDS

The fun and games of life at Mass Chaos continued throughout winter and spring. I clung to my routine of exploring Europe in bits and pieces whenever possible, to remind myself why I was putting up with this horrific professional life.

David took me to Ghent for a romantic Valentine's Day weekend, and in March, I surprised him with tickets to Barcelona to celebrate his thirtieth birthday. Milestone birthdays require a party, and no place parties like Barcelona.

I no longer considered myself a Barcelona amateur. I knew the Spanish custom was to dine late, whereas in the Netherlands, many families are seated at the dinner table by six o'clock. Trying to show off my local knowledge, I was pleased to get a much sought-after reservation at a trendy eatery at half-past nine. La Gracia sits in the Barceloneta district, with several clubs and pubs just steps away. It was the perfect spot to mark David's big birthday.

I was stunned when we discovered that even 9:30 reservations made us part of the dreaded tourist seating. Locals didn't arrive until we were nearly finished at eleven! The afternoon siesta must work wonders because ladies and gents in their fifties and sixties quickly filled the recently-emptied tables of tourists.

April brought the U.S. trip for Karla's Fort Lauderdale wedding. Wanting to make the most David's first trip to Florida, we took two weeks off. We planned the week after the wedding in the Keys and a quick stop in South Beach before flying out of Miami.

I was eager to see my friends, but I was in a fragile state of mind. Insomnia was a frequent uninvited guest and sleep deprivation often robbed me of common sense. With my parents also attending Karla's wedding, we rented two condos at the same Key Largo complex for the week after it. I hoped that getting them out of Ohio would lighten the oppressive mood that smothered Christmas, another item added to my list of worries. All I wanted was some fun with my closest friends, without the family tension that put a stranglehold on our every meeting.

The best days were the ones leading up to the wedding. I ran into many old friends for the first time since leaving for Germany. Most of the guests and wedding party stayed at the same hotel near the beach, making me feel immediately sorry for the rest of the vacationers staying there. We tumbled into piano bars and shared fluorescent cocktails out of fish bowls, overlooking the ocean. Reminiscing about the good old days, we laughed until tears rolled down our cheeks.

Without the adrenaline of dearly missed lunatic friends to combat the jetlag, David crashed earlier than I did most nights. For me, it was non-negotiable to squeeze in as much time as possible with people I knew and trusted. I never knew when I'd see them again. When I finally did go to bed, I never slept. Depression, fatigue, and sleep deprivation had dragged me to the point that I was afraid to fall asleep for fear I wouldn't wake up. Karla, the centerpiece of the happy occasion, was under extreme stress. I had to hold it together for her sake.

Although being in it felt like pushing a boulder up a mountain, the wedding turned out beautifully. As the twenty-person wedding party, we were gathered in front of a white gingerbread gazebo on the edge of the Intracoastal Waterway. The blushing bride and handsome groom were picture perfect saying their "I do's" in front of 150 smiling guests, while palm trees swayed in the ocean breeze. Crystal flutes clinked minutes afterward and the party rolled on until dawn. I wasn't the only one who wanted to cling to the moment.

We booked one last night at the beach for recovery. Karla and I hugged fiercely when we couldn't put off our goodbyes any longer. I was happy for her new life to begin, but I was terribly sad to leave her.

The next morning, David managed to restore my smile by picking up a cherry-red convertible Ford Mustang to drive to the Keys. I couldn't wait to show him South Florida, but leaving my close friends cut little pieces from me every time I had to do it.

The Devil Wears Clogs

* * *

Dressed in Florida's uniform of shorts and shades, we cruised south past Miami to Key Largo in comfortable silence. Nothing needed to be said. I was relieved to be in familiar surroundings, with David behind the wheel and sunshine warming my face.

When we arrived at the condo, all I wanted to do was get groceries and collapse next to the pool. I made dinner plans with my parents for the following evening. David and I discussed the pros and cons of different activities for our week of freedom in the tropics. It felt good to be the knowledgeable one for a change. We reserved one day for Key West. The Everglades National Park couldn't be missed and we could do that with my parents. My dad wanted to rent a boat to show David the local scenery. The rest of the days were easily filled with poolside reading and barbeques. Relaxation was a high priority, but I kept to myself how badly I needed it.

It was funny to see David so far removed from his natural surroundings. My family vacationed in Florida every year and made several trips to the Caribbean. I was at home in the ocean and on board any type of boat. Flippers and snorkeling gear had lived in our home for many years, so I didn't think twice about strapping on a mask and diving in. This was not the case for David. I could see that the idea was somewhat intimidating. After being forced to comply with Dutch social order in every aspect of my life, I admit to finding this amusing.

On our second day, we boarded a tourist boat jammed with other first-time snorkelers. The company eased his apprehension enough to have a good time. Before now, it had never occurred to me how little David knew of my American life because all our time was spent in his territory. A two-hour snorkeling trip might not seem like a critical life experience for anyone else, but I'd lived on the water my entire life. I couldn't let go of this passion because it makes me calm. Was it the idea that one could always escape across a large body of water? Was it the tranquilizing effect of gentle rolling waves? All I knew was that I instantly felt better on or near water and David would have to get used to it. It was his turn to adjust.

The restaurant that night was a nearby waterside favorite, serving seafood of course. We went early so we could watch the sun setting over the ocean before. It was a balmy night as only April in South Florida can be. Tiki torches flared when darkness fell. David and I shared the tale of our snorkeling adventure, laughing the whole time at his awkward first time in a wet suit. It had every ingredient for a great night, but it wasn't.

A happy couple in their thirties near us made a special request, telling the band they were celebrating their ten-year wedding anniversary. Rather than toasting them, my mother ripped in to my father, "It's not like they've been married for *forty* years!"

I wanted to crawl under the table. Her behavior completely embarrassed me and I was mortified that David had to witness this ugly display. For the life of me, I couldn't figure out what the hell was going on. Who would say such a thing? It shortened the night considerably. My father paid our bill and we were out of there. Saying goodnight, I told them that we were driving to Key West the following morning, and wouldn't be around during the day. David, the man of few words, said nothing about the evening except how much he enjoyed the fresh grouper. He probably didn't know what to say. I didn't either.

* * *

Bright sunlight poked through the gaps in our Venetian blinds early the next morning to nudge us awake. *Key West!* I was so ready for this. It's more exciting than sleepy Key Largo and I was anxious to have some fun alone with David. I slathered on sunscreen while David pulled the Mustang's black ragtop down. Along the way, I pointed out landmarks and told the same stories my father had told me over the years–gunrunning, drug smugglers, and infamous cocaine busts. We arrived before noon, so it was easy to find a cheap all-day parking garage. Before we knew it, we were swallowed by the craziness of Duval Street.

Key West is the tourist and party capital of South Florida. There are a thousand t-shirt and seashell shops within a five-mile radius. What isn't saturated with shops, to sell you everything you don't need, is designed to fill you up with far too much drink.

I wanted to show David every place I loved, spots where fishbowls were *not* on the menu. I desperately needed to re-live the good old days. My first stop on every Key West excursion is Papa Joe's. Given its name by a famous patron, Ernest Hemingway, it's been an institution since the 1930's. As Florida's southernmost outpost, the walls are jammed with photos of its colorful history and locals continue to flock to it eighty years later.

Afterward, we went for burgers at Hog's Breath Tavern before grabbing bar stools at Fat Tuesday's for their deadly daiquiris. Feeling lighter, like the weight of the world might be lifting, I had a great time. Even so, it was impossible to ignore that David grew more and more preoccupied as the day wore on.

Knowing we couldn't turn up in shorts and t-shirts at any decent restaurant, the six-foot-five David and I had a challenging change of clothes in the Mustang. On any given night in Key West, the main event is the Mallory Square sunset party. The word "party" loosely describes the uncoordinated noisy mix of tourists and locals at a traditional nightly gathering point. Most revelers begin their night with a clear view of the ocean to watch sun take her nightly bow on fine evenings. In the Keys, the evenings are very often fine.

Walking towards the square, David started acting weirder. He was obviously in a snit about something, but wouldn't say what. We stopped at one more place for appetizers, and I finally had to walk away. My excuse was taking a few quick photos. Fifteen minutes later, I was relieved to return to our table and see the beginnings of a smile. He claimed he was worried about missing the sunset, so we made our way to the square.

Fate reserved the perfect ocean-side table, so we took our seats to enjoy the show. David grabbed my hand and I gave him a grin, relieved that whatever was bothering him had dissipated. A triple-masted white sloop sailed in our direction across purple-pink waves, and the fiery-orange sun sank slowly into the sea. It ranks high on my list of favorite sunsets.

Salt breezes blew softly and David squeezed my hand to get my attention. Turning to look at him, I saw his blue eyes sparkling with mischief. He stared into my eyes for a few minutes before he asked if I would spend the rest of my life with him. I went numb. I had to ask him to repeat himself because the world had gone quiet. The hundred unruly tourists behind us disappeared, and life went into slow motion.

Once more, he asked if I would be his wife, and I squeaked out, "Yes, of course!" before he hugged me tight. I was paralyzed with shock and disbelief.

David took my hand and led me out of the crowd. "Let's go get some champagne," he said.

I grinned in return and pointed toward a chic restaurant a few steps away.

David became the Man of the Hour, taking control. He ordered a bottle champagne and a huge pile of fat strawberries to celebrate his fiancée. I was still quiet, my eyes brimming with happy tears. I kept squeezing his hand, so he knew how excited I was. He must have been wondering if I'd say no when he was acting so odd earlier. Or maybe he was looking for just the right words. It wouldn't have mattered. Not for a second did I consider saying anything but yes.

After dinner, we drove back to Key Largo. David had drunk little throughout the night. The evening's events had sobered me up, too. I wanted to shout the news from the rooftops, but the right thing to do was tell my parents first. I called to organize a barbeque with them the following night, having already forgotten about their argument the night before. I couldn't wait to share our happy news. David was obviously happy too, and we celebrated that night in the privacy of our Key Largo condo.

Wishing I could stop the world right there, I fell into my best sleep in months. Maybe I would get my happy ending after all.

CHAPTER 27
FAIRYTALE

The night after I got the shock of my life, we spent the next day relaxing at the pool. The sun was merciless for April and we couldn't be bothered to move more than a few steps from the water. David sped through a novel while I dozed, and floated in the water, lost in thought.

That afternoon, we went to a huge grocery store to pick up fat Gulf shrimp and thick steaks. As we roamed the aisles, a disoriented English tourist approached to ask pitifully if we'd seen the cold medications. David pointed towards the aisle we'd just walked through. I realized how confusing it must be for Europeans to find anything in warehouse-style American supermarkets. Then, once you finally locate it, you must choose from fifty similar products. The man was visibly relieved, and I giggled to myself after he walked away. If supermarkets were a cause for international confusion, what did that imply about life's more crucial elements?

Sharing the news with my mom and dad was harder than I expected. I actually had to say out loud that I was getting married. It didn't seem real. It felt like I was playing house with the neighbor boy. My parents actually smiled when we finished the big announcement. They knew how much I loved David. The fact that I had rearranged my entire life around our relationship left no doubts. No other boyfriend had gotten such a reaction, so they knew he was special. I called my brother too and he sounded happy for us.

Immediate family duly informed, I was free to tell anyone I wanted– and happily did. Late that night in Florida, David also called his parents, who gave their blessings too. I couldn't wipe the smile off my face for days. Shouts of excitement came from Kirsten, my closest friend *not* on her honeymoon. I didn't think it was possible to be happier.

I took David to the Everglades so he could see live alligators for the first time without barriers. Wildlife isn't accessible in Europe anymore. Most of it was killed off centuries ago, and what remains is far from the Netherlands. David loved getting close-up shots of the many colorful birds and, of course, the sneaky snarling gators. He nearly choked with laughter at the sign asking visitors to please keep a safe distance from the animals.

David found it ironic that Americans put warning signs on a cup of coffee at a fast food outlet saying "Beware this beverage is hot!" and create labels for plastic bags that tell the owner it's possible for a child to suffocate using it, yet we leave it to the individual's discretion to watch himself around deadly wild animals. In Europe, Americans have a reputation for paranoia and overreaction. It was too much for him that this didn't apply to something that could eat you, if it felt like it.

The rest of our days in the Keys went too quickly. When we left, I hugged my parents and tried not let my impatience show. I thought they'd understand why David and I might want privacy, but this didn't seem to supercede their need for our company. My mother had knocked on my door and phoned, no matter what time of the morning or evening. I was glad to be parting company for our last few days in Florida. I loved them, but I was eager to be alone with my fiancé.

David and I were bound for South Beach. With its famous nightclubs and wild cabaret scene, this was no place for anyone's parents. I had chosen the hotel with extreme care. On one side was a gorgeous swimming pool in front of the ocean beach and on the other was the famous South Beach Strip. Everything was at our doorstep.

When we were finally alone, time evaporated. We shopped in Miami's designer malls and took a peek at Tiffany engagement rings. I thought David would faint when he saw the price tags, so I had a good joke at the expense of my frugal Dutchman. David's preference was that I pick a ring that I loved, so we took our time finding it.

We drank martinis on the beach every evening with live music filling the soft salt air. Both the days and nights were happy with sparks flying between us. A new chapter had begun, bringing much to look forward to in the months ahead. The depression and insomnia, which had plagued me, abated slightly during the last Florida week. I could think clearly again.

All was well until the day we drove to Miami International Airport to board the flight to Amsterdam. My world went black. I didn't want to go back, and I was a pain in the ass to deal with. It took every ounce of my willpower not to run away—to save myself.

Most transatlantic flights from the eastern United States are overnight flights and I could never get comfortable enough to sleep. David's height made sleeping impossible for him too. Holding hands, we watched movies until the plane touched down on the spaghetti bowl of runways known as Schiphol Airport.

Arriving at the first light of dawn, we taxied for what felt like an eternity before reaching the airport and exiting the jet way. My heart sank at the sight of the familiar blue-and-yellow signs for baggage claim and ground transportation. For the next thirty minutes, while waiting for our bags, the wet wool blanket of depression closed in and smothered me. Dutiful David loaded our suitcases on a cart, and we walked toward the car park. Thankful for our one day at home before we returned to work, we tossed our bags aside and slept heavily into the afternoon.

Having made the mistake of telling my mother the actual time and date I would be home, the phone's shrill ring dragged me out of a sleep too deep for dreaming. It took me a minute to remember where I was and realize what had woken me, but I caught the phone before it stopped ringing. "He left me," were the words that greeted me.

I didn't know what she was talking about, "Who left you?" I stammered.

"Your *father!*" came the tearful reply.

"What do you mean?" I said. Either a sleep-induced coma was preventing my brain from functioning, or it was something else. Perhaps it was the icy fingers of fear tightening their grip on my heart.

"He said he was going to be with his *girlfriend* and he left me!" she shrieked.

"What girlfriend? I don't understand what is going on?" The incoming data would not compute.

"Your father has decided that after forty years of marriage we are no longer going to be together and he has moved out."

The fog of what had been going on between them in Florida began to lift. The off-the-wall comments and dark shadow that followed them from Ohio were indicative of what had likely been brewing for a very long time. I'd known there was Trouble in Paradise, but why *now*? It seemed to me that your sixth decade is the time to settle in to your life, not the time to run off and start a new one, but I didn't get a vote. I only had to figure out how I was going to handle the raw pain coming through the phone line.

Luckily for me, she did the majority of the talking. I sat there listening while reality sunk in. Telling her I'd call her back the following day, I relayed the news to David. As I was over thirty, tears seemed inappropriate. The familiar numbness returned. *Don't I deserve one week of happiness?*

* * *

May 2004 was a complete blur. For four hours a day, I rode public transport to and from Amsterdam, to and from a job I couldn't stand. I created presentations and drafted documentation for a boss I had no respect for. My ideas were ridiculed by a colleague I hated. My mother made every weekend miserable by calling David and me before we were even out of bed in the mornings. My life was a bottomless black pit. What should have been the happiest time in my life had turned into a nightmare I couldn't wake up from. I was just going through the motions.

The colleague anxious to beat me out for the open position of Gustav's Right Hand Man, Bert, slammed every idea I suggested in front of Gustav the Confused. At the end of my proverbial rope, I tore him to shreds one day, also in front of Gustav. Consequently, I was immediately branded with the scarlet letter "D" for *difficult,* deemed an unsuitable role model for "teamwork."

I made little attempt to undo the damage. When I finally forced information about my temporary contract out of Gustav, the fact that

The Devil Wears Clogs

Mass Chaos Inc. had chosen not to offer me permanent employment was not exactly a surprise.

During that same conversation, I gave Gustav my resignation with the obligatory one-month notice period. For all I cared, they could pay me to plan my wedding for the next month. There was no way in hell I was going to deliver all the answers to a company that didn't want me to see it through. Pride wouldn't allow Bert to claim my hard work as his own. My feelings were confirmed when I heard that Mass Chaos was paying for his master's degree, and this was the likely reason I no longer had a position at the company. Thanks, Pablo, for adding insult to injury, now please tell that grapevine to shut the hell up.

June was a farce. Concealing my ill regard for the circus that Gustav had turned the place into took every ounce of my effort. In return, I was rewarded by being kept out of every meeting worth attending. Never have I contributed so little to a place that paid me a salary.

With work no longer consuming my life, David and I began discussing ideas for the wedding. Our visions, it seemed, were at opposite ends of the wedding spectrum. I wanted to be barefoot on the beach with only close friends and family. David's said that if we were going to have a wedding, we were going to make it the big deal it ought to be. How could I not have seen this coming?

Trying to picture myself as a bride for the first time in my life was no simple task. I didn't grow up dreaming about being the girl in the white poufy dress. Even at thirty-four, the idea of being the center of attention filled me with dread. The only thing that offered any solace was that a wedding in Holland would lessen the crowd considerably. If I got married in Ohio, I would feel obligated to include more people. Getting married across the Atlantic was suddenly very appealing.

There was also great appeal in my newest Dutch discovery; Holland has a high density of beautiful castles that have been converted into special occasion venues. *Bullseye!* If I was going to be talked into dressing like a princess, I would play the part.

* * *

After my last day of work at Mass Chaos in June, I took up the reigns of managing our wedding. Without any reason to wait, David and I began the search for our fairytale castle. Looking at glossy photos of one gorgeous palace after another was almost as much fun as the day we chose my engagement ring. Almost.

Emerald cut diamonds are uncommon in the Netherlands, at least at the ten jewelry shops where we looked. To increase the probability of finding one, we went to the Amsterdam Diamond Center in Dam Square, which sold loose diamonds of all shapes and sizes. Seated in soft Italian black-leather armchairs sipping cappuccino, we gave our requirements to the cheeriest Dutch girl I've ever seen, and she went to collect diamonds of different carat, cut, and clarity. We received a lesson on three C's that day, which was far more enjoyable than any other lesson in my life so far! David and I smirked while sporting ocular pieces that allowed us to see the interior and the tiniest detail in each diamond. It was as surreal as it was thrilling. David bought me the most beautiful diamond I have ever seen.

After the crashing and burning of my life in May, summer was a big improvement. Moving at full speed, we narrowed the venue choices to three castles, all within an hour of our house, and made appointments to check them out. One castle was as big as Versailles, but the snooty attitude of the people who ran it ruined its beauty. The second was a stone fortress, evoking images of knights and fair maidens, complete with a surrounding moat. The drawback was the likelihood of several functions happening at once. We had no intention of sharing our castle with anyone, thank you very much.

After ruling these out, we found a place we felt immediately comfortable with the competent staff. The female director and her professional crew assisted with every detail, recommending the best photographers and florists. They also knew how to manage a crowd of international guests. They had handled every nationality imaginable, so I wouldn't have to worry about our guests being uncomfortable on the big day. They also gave us the name of the local celebrant who could officiate our uncommon ceremony. She had done it many times in English and Dutch. With my parents' nightmare divorce and the rapidly escalating illness of my grandfather, my hands were full without worrying whether the staff would speak English and be American-friendly.

The Devil Wears Clogs

The selected one was a stately manor house in a divine wooded setting. It was available on the twenty-ninth of October, but not again until six months later. Autumn is my favorite season, and neither of us wanted to wait until spring, so the decision was made. The loved ones we invited to our storybook wedding were shocked at the news that would marry just six months after our engagement.

* * *

In August, I traveled to both Ohio and Florida. I had no hope of finding a wedding dress I loved in Holland, where custom dictates the bride should wear a *hat*. I also had to assess the family situation prior to their invasion of Amsterdam in two months. My father and I hadn't spoken and I wanted nothing to do with the girlfriend who had suddenly appeared.

I stayed with my mother for the two weeks I was in Ohio. It wasn't pleasant. My search for another job in the Netherlands made me tense and she was in a pit of despair. The five minutes I spent in my father's company on that visit ended with the words: "The family no longer exists," as if he were it.

My only intelligent decision was choosing to visit Ohio before spending a week in Florida with Karla. She, better than anyone, understood the situation. The biggest dramas of her life had also played out in the days and weeks leading up to her own wedding in Fort Lauderdale. With Karla, I could relax completely and not have to handle everyone else's problems in addition to my own.

I flew back to Amsterdam with an elegant cream-satin wedding gown, a gift from my mother. I adored it and Karla said it looked great on me. In September we chose of flowers and a photographer. RSVPs for the wedding of "Lady Jennifer" and "Sir David" began to flood in. We struggled with whom to seat where, and the big question of walking down the aisle.

A little secret of getting married in another country is that you can abolish any traditions of your own country's wedding ceremony that you don't care for. I didn't have to choose bridesmaids from amongst my closest friends, because they are not part of the Dutch wedding tradition. The tacky tossing of the garter and throwing of the bouquet?

History! Most importantly, David and I would enter the ceremony hand-in-hand and walk down the aisle together. I didn't even know if my father would show up. David's presence would give me strength as I dealt with my paranoid fear of being the center of attention.

While I worked on the details of our fairytale extravaganza, I kept one eye on the Dutch job market. Within days of each other, I interviewed with two very different companies. One was a giant American computer hardware firm beginning a new service platform in Amsterdam. The other was with the European headquarters of a much smaller American company in Eindhoven, in the south of the Netherlands.

During my interview session with the Amsterdam firm, I met with three people. The first two interviews went smoothly and I was impressed, until the man who would be my boss stepped out of the elevator. He was a clone of Gustav the Confused and displayed a Short Man Syndrome-esque attitude. I listened to what he had to say and answered his questions, knowing I would only take this job if I had no other option. The experience reminded me of the firm that had brought me to Europe to begin with. The boss was ego-driven and full of himself. *Next!*

My interview in Eindhoven couldn't have been a greater contrast. People actually smiled in this office. I had begun to think it was illegal in Holland. I met with several people on my first trip to that office, all of whom were relaxed and friendly. The European team consisted of eighty people responsible for the sales, service, and repair of American-made mobile and wireless devices throughout EMEA, Europe Middle East and Africa. They had recently taken on a large German project whose magnitude had rattled the company foundations.

They were looking for an experienced project manager to effectively manage the manufacturing, delivery, and deployment of their hardware units while reducing the shockwaves that large projects had on the organization. Not having a hardware background, it sounded like a challenge. The fact that I would be required to travel throughout Europe to work other local teams and meet clients made it irresistible.

Cyril, the man who would be my boss if I joined Main Street

The Devil Wears Clogs

Hardware, was a Brit. He seemed kind, and that was about all I initially noticed. Well, that and the fact that he had a stutter. It wasn't immediately apparent, but it showed up in the second or third conversation we had. That's when I had the first inkling that maybe I was intimidating to him, but I squashed that little voice like a bug.

Cyril said he was looking for extensive IT project management experience. He also said he had recently taken on responsibility for building the project management team. From the way he spoke, I knew he had a higher technical aptitude than I did–speaking with his British accent which, minus the stutter, always makes Americans feel that they are the lesser intelligent of any pair. I had no reason to suspect that he was incompetent or mean, the two red flags I'd already run into in my previous Dutch offices.

Responses to our wedding invitations continued to arrive and travel plans were checked and double-checked. David and I chose Scotland as our honeymoon destination. We hired a bus to drive our foreign wedding guests from Amsterdam to the wedding venue in Tiel. An avalanche of email questions arrived daily. David and I sampled champagne, and I made a trip to the Amsterdam bloemenmarkt for roses to show our florist what color "peach" was. We spied on other weddings to evaluate which band would get our guests on their feet. It was a crazy exciting period. I couldn't believe that everyone I loved would be in the same room on my side of the ocean for the first time.

Along with all the good news, came bad. My grandfather, ill for years with cancer, passed away the week before David and I were to say "I do." I never imagined the impossible position of having to choose whether or not to postpone my wedding. My mothers' sisters had already decided not to join us, but I couldn't imagine asking twenty-five other people to incur the expense of re-planning their travel. Not to mention what David and I would have to go through to save the money again that we would lose on deposits.

It was clear that the show had to go on. I was never able to apologize enough for not being with my grandmother, Irene, during this time, but she didn't punish me for my decision. My happiest moments always had sadness in the background.

In the weeks before the wedding, I received two job offers: one from Slick American in Amsterdam and the other from Main Street Hardware. Even the way they were delivered couldn't have been more different. Slick American sent an employment contract with my offered salary and benefits. It was impressive. The salary was slightly lower than what was discussed, but a car allowance and stock options were included. The fact that they drew up and sent a contract we'd never discussed sent a clear message; there will be no negotiation. Who joins an organization that dictates the conditions with zero discussion?

Cyril called, "pleased to offer" me a salary that was moderately higher than what Slick American offered. I told him about the other offer and got him to bump it up further. When we agreed on a number, he asked Human Resources to put the contract together and I received it two days later.

I wasn't willing to disclose my reason for turning down the job with Slick American to the replica of Gustav the Confused, so declining their offer was not pleasant. Since working for them would be even less pleasant, I was confident it was the right decision.

My first day at the new company in Eindhoven would be mid-November, after David and I returned from our Scottish honeymoon. Formalities completed on both the wedding and job hunting fronts, I was ready to celebrate.

* * *

Guests began arriving in Holland a week before the wedding, so David and I were caught in a never-ending loop of entertaining and tour guiding. We tried to give my American friends and family a real taste of the Netherlands that included windmills, the Van Gogh Museum, Gouda cheese, and the red-light district of Amsterdam. Had the tulips been in bloom, it would have been a home run with bases loaded.

Even the Land of Perpetual Precipitation allowed the wedding festivities to carry on without a downpour and fall was in all her glory. The evening before our wedding, we took the whole crew on a canal boat tour of Amsterdam at nightfall. It was hilarious. Neither David nor I are height-challenged people and the majority of our friends and family are also tall. The beautiful teak hull of the boat cruised silently through the canals and the only noise we heard was the captain shouting "Get down!" every time we approached a low bridge and the peals of laughter that immediately followed. Amsterdam has a lot of bridges. Miraculously, even after a buffet of steaming hot dishes and a fully-stocked bar that had dulled our senses, no one was knocked unconscious.

As soon as the boat docked, David and I made our escape. We begged off because neither of us could stand for one more minute. It had taken every ounce of our combined strength and adrenaline to keep up with this crowd. My parents' drama continued with my mother dragging me out of this or that conversation to cry on my shoulder. My father managed to make it to the wedding, but I said nothing to him other than I was glad he came. My sanity hung by a thread, and I thanked God for my friends and my husband-to-be for keeping me afloat. Getting back to the Amsterdam hotel, I don't think David and I said two syllables before we collapsed.

On the last day of the wedding marathon, that eerie calm feeling returned. Lady Jennifer had issued an edict that no one was to be in the castle before the time printed on the invitation, which was 2 p.m. I knew my friends were dying of curiosity, but I needed a few hours of peace to pull off this show. I loved David and was thrilled to be marrying him, but crowds and being in front of them are not my forté.

The woman hired to do my hair and makeup arrived just after David and I put our things down in the castle wedding suite and he ran off to issue orders to his brother. The photographer knocked minutes after I put my dress on and took photos of me getting ready. Both of them were surprised that not a friend or family member was with me, but I silenced them with a look. I was far too nervous to dwell on it now.

Our castle, Kasteel Wijenberg, was gorgeous. Guests were served coffee and tea in the blue silk library before the ceremony. Afterward, we had the entire building for our personal use. There was a grand dining room, decked out with giant peach roses, autumn leaves and berries. David had designed cards naming each table for a city or place that held a special meaning. Brass candelabras were centered on each table and a knight in armor stood guard in the corner.

The ceremony was held in the Salon Blauw, both elegant and suitably official for the occasion. Our female *ambtenaar* officiated beautifully. She wove the tale of Lady Jennifer and Sir David alternating English and Dutch, so everyone felt included. When it was time, David gave the Dutch crowd a laugh by saying "Yes, please!" instead of a simple "I do," and our mothers signed as witnesses. I heard there wasn't a dry eye in the house, and that included mine.

David's brother led the jubilant crowd into the wine cellar after the ceremony and corks popped in the oldest room in the mansion. It had stood here since A.D. 1100. I hoped that bode well for the characters in our fairytale too.

As for me, I ended this day "happily ever after."

CHAPTER 28
KNIGHT IN SHINING ARMOR

My absolute joy at being David's wife was countered by the depth of my sadness when everyone left town. Having friends and family share our happiness was the greatest gift I could ask for. Being filled-up by their happiness left a gaping hole when they departed.

The wedding, which carried us all into the early morning hours, was better than I ever imagined. David's brother and my friend Dora gave thoughtful speeches that brought tears to my eyes. Wine flowed, and laughter echoed through our four-course dinner. Afterward, David and I were handed a four-foot gleaming sword that we struggled to jointly wield, to slice the deep-chocolate wedding cake. When no one lost a limb, the rowdy gang was herded into the double salon where a seven-piece band rocked the house. David's father danced with every woman in attendance, and happiness was contagious. It was an exquisite night.

David and I woke early in the castle tower room. The princess effect hadn't quite worn off and I peered out the turret window into the misty forest. It was beautifully silent. I felt like Rapunzel about to be rescued. I was allowed only two peaceful minutes before realizing we were expected for our private breakfast in the library. I have never been so tired in my life. Even with the help of strong Dutch coffee, a Polaroid of the happy new couple revealed that without a doubt.

We wanted to linger over breakfast, but the hired bus would be pulling out soon to take our guests back to Amsterdam. We had no choice but to say our final farewells. I hugged each of my friends fiercely and thanked them for coming. Before this moment, I had no idea it was possible to be so happy and so sad at once.

Finally, we waved them off and ran back to the castle. We had one free day before leaving for Scotland, so that we could rest a little. It was a wise decision as we were both running on fumes. At home, we tried to decide what to bring on our Scotland travels. Lastly, when we were lying in bed with no other distractions, we opened cards and gifts and read messages. Finally, we slept.

The Dutch have strange rules about the use of surnames. A woman isn't entitled to take her husband's last name when she marries, unless she is also a Dutch citizen. I couldn't take the citizenship exam yet because you are required to live in the Netherlands for five years, or be married to a Dutch national for three years before you are eligible. So, as David and I began our lives as man and wife, I began my own personal identity crisis.

The common method of an expatriate wife to write her name is the Dutch name first followed by a hyphen and her own name. In my case, the Dutch name was also difficult to pronounce so I was constantly explaining my name, including which one was mine and which was David's. Couldn't the Dutch make one thing simple for someone who wants to marry one of them?

But there we were, Mr. and Mrs. David, loading up the Audi to enjoy the Scottish adventure we had painstakingly planned. It was the 31st of October, Halloween in the United States. As my friends in the States donned creepy costumes and headed to parties, I assumed my Mrs. David identity and climbed aboard a vehicle ferry across the North Sea to the United Kingdom.

We were grateful for more rest in our luxury cabin on the overnight journey to Newcastle. The sea was unusually calm, and we were anxious to get there. Our best trips were always road trips and this was the longest so far. We were touring the Scottish Highlands, our ultimate destination was the beautiful Isle of Skye. Photos in a travel magazine had opened our eyes to its mysterious allure. Long forest walks and treks along rocky coastlines are activities that we both loved. David was becoming an avid photographer and I was in love with the tranquility of a region so sparsely populated.

Our good luck only got better when we saw the Scottish weather forecast for the weeks ahead. We knew it was a major risk to take this adventure in the month of November, which is normally quite wet, but the days were glorious. The deep reds and burnt oranges of fall lit the rolling landscape, and castles beckoned from the cliffs. Scotland gave us more days of sunshine and blue sky in our two-week adventure than we could have hoped for.

We took photos of ourselves in Stirling Castle and pronounced it Rainbow Day as we saw dozens in one afternoon. We investigated whisky distilleries and stayed in opulent historic inns. One night, still awake after an incredible gourmet dinner, we fed the swans that made a surprise visit to our lochside cottage. We walked hand-in-hand underneath tall pines and cozied up to the fireplace when it did rain.

There were still times when my emotions took control. When the hoopla of wedding planning died down, I came face to face with the shocking realization of being married to this man *for the rest of my life*. Most brides know they are entering into a lifelong contract and most will likely face some doubt before walking down the aisle, but when the music stops and you see only two chairs for your remaining days, it's daunting.

I loved David. That was never in doubt. My concern was whether I was built for the marriage game. Watching my parents self-destruct weeks before my wedding, I was angry with my father for his callous behavior. In the six months of planning and activity, I felt that anger. I'd stuff it back down and go on with the show. In quieter times, it escaped its steel cage and attacked the wrong person: David.

If I ever had doubts about whether David was the man for me, all I had to do was look at how he stood by me without fail through years of terrible uncertainty. The awful adjustment to Holland, the miserable misadventure with the Devil and his co-pilot Dafne, the pain and destruction of my family—all of it. He was there every minute and never did he allow me to think that he was planning to book the next flight out of our relationship.

If it had not been for Sir David, my knight in shining armor, I wouldn't have made it. There's no question about that. Throughout the years after Germany, David was my hero. While I was whining about why I couldn't have a little happiness, I should have taken a good hard look at Mr. Nice Guy, who appeared from nowhere and held my hand while my life burned to the ground. For that, I will love him for the rest of my life.

Aside from a few rocky days when we didn't see eye to eye, or when the BBC announced President Bush was elected for a second term at two in the morning U.K. time, our Scottish honeymoon was a dream come true. Who knew that sheep have the right of way in the Highlands, and will staunchly refuse to move out of the way of an oncoming car? Or that silvery Loch Ness shines like the sun when the late afternoon makes a mirror of its surface? We also learned about the Scottish sense of humor when we chose an "uncomplicated little walk" from a book of walking trips, and ended up fearing for our lives along a jagged-shale path on the Isle of Skye.

The biggest surprise of all was the last stop of the journey: Glasgow. Its modernity and striking contrast to stodgy Edinburgh couldn't be more pronounced. It is a city with electricity coursing through its veins. It is charming and romantic in ways we honeymooners never imagined. Our last gorgeous hotel, 1 Devonshire, and the nearby delicious restaurants full of joking red-cheeked Scots, provided the perfect ending to our journey in the middle of November 2004.

CHAPTER 29
SWITCHING TEAMS

Far too soon, our feet touched ground again. Streamers and balloons of congratulations posted on our front door by the neighbors and packages stuffed with photos from friends welcomed us back. Doing my best to find some semblance of order in the tiny Ijsselstein canal house, my mind wandered to my first day at Main Street Hardware, which was rapidly approaching. I wondered if I could trust my gut feeling about the happy employees and Cyril as a decent boss.

I decided it was best to wait and see, rather than speculate on a future I couldn't possibly predict. I chose my outfit for my first day with care, feeling like a schoolgirl. I double-checked the train and bus schedules and prepared myself for the long commute. The office was in the opposite direction from my last two work locations. Ijsselstein lies close to the center of Holland. Eindhoven, where Main Street Hardware was located, is south in the province of Brabant.

When two Dutch people meet for the first time, they usually talk about being from *"boven ou beneden het rivière,"* the river being the Maas, which cuts across the country. Those above the Maas, as in Noord Holland where Amsterdam lies, have the classic traits of northern Europe, more aloof than those below in the friendly south. I'd heard this phrase ever since arriving in the Netherlands, but didn't fully understand it. From the moment I walked into my new office, I understood.

Marina greeted me at the reception desk. Since I was still not a fantastic Dutch speaker, she quickly switched to English and offered me a cup of coffee while I waited for Cyril. I gratefully accepted it after the chilly train ride, and we chatted in which she asked for my life story. After my previous interactions with Dutch receptionists who wanted me and my bad Dutch to quickly disappear, I was so surprised that I offered details I would never normally share with a person I met five minutes before.

Soon, Cyril arrived with Esther, the human resources manager whom I'd spoken to over the phone but hadn't met. We went into the canteen to "have a chat" and "get to know one another." It was a greeting from another planet. Get to know one another? Surely they expected to talk about what I needed to get busy doing. I hid my surprise and stumbled through the polite conversation that I wasn't used to having in this country. Esther and Cyril couldn't have been nicer. They asked about my wedding and my new husband before launching into weightier topics. Even when we did get around to the subject of work a few coffees later, the conversation was light.

When we were finished with preliminaries, Cyril took me on a tour of the building and introduced me to colleagues in each department. I did my best to remember the myriad of new and complicated Dutch names. There were at least four that started with the letter "m" and seemed to be slight but critical variations of the same name. And that was only the women. Moving from sales to finance to service and repair in short order was a little confusing, but one fact was clear: no one seemed bothered by speaking English. That alone made the start-up process much easier than every other team I had been introduced to in this country.

Finishing a short meeting with the female-dominated sales office, our next stop was the service department where the mobile computers were worked on. Cyril held the door for me while I walked into a cavernous bustling room, which went silent the moment we entered. Talking the whole way, Cyril took me over to the desk where I was introduced to Colin as the new EMEA project manager.

Colin, a tall red-headed Scot, welcomed me in his booming voice, and told Cyril it was about time he included a woman on his team. At least, that's what I thought he said. It could have been something entirely different as Colin's Glasgow accent was thick. I smiled as he then introduced the members of his service team who also seemed

The Devil Wears Clogs

surprised to see a woman in their midst. We joked and chatted a little before Cyril and I departed for our next stop. For the first time, I saw I was the lone woman on the project management team and one of the few women working outside the usual places women are found: reception, phone sales, and HR.

Leaving Colin's department, Cyril took me to the desk he used when he was in town from the U.K. and showed me the one I would be using, next to his. He told me more about the structure of Main Street, adding that it was a flat organization that didn't pay homage to the hierarchical structure of most American firms. I was told to feel free to bring my ideas to anyone in the company and expected to be direct with my coworkers.

Cyril said that the American senior management in upstate New York had declared that the project management team was responsible for enforcing change and being the champion for the customer, whatever it took. The team, led by Cyril and reporting to the director of professional services, a Frenchman named Bernard, was new. They needed to implement processes and controls on their large European customer projects, some of which had gone off track.

Cyril concluded his mission statement on an ominous note: the American CEO could be aggressive when things aren't done to his satisfaction. I considered this, thinking at least if the aggressive ones came from my side of the Atlantic we would be speaking the same language. If something did go wrong, I could make myself understood for the first time in years.

Cyril and I continued meeting daily, and I was introduced next to the technical experts who worked in Eindhoven. There was a team-lead from technical support and two solution architects who focused on the inner workings of Main Street's devices.

After spending hours with the techies, I admitted to Cyril that my brain was short circuiting. The units, manufactured in New York rather than in Asia like our competitors, were more sophisticated than I had realized. The learning curve was steep, but no more so than any position before this. I thrive on challenge, but I wouldn't be running my own show as quickly as I thought.

During my first week, Cyril mentioned two topics that were more fun to talk about than technical procedures and hardware manufacturing. First, he said that our European headquarters held an annual kick-off meeting to discuss the previous year's progress and the goals for the year ahead. The meeting was held in an off-site location every other year, and this year, the event was to take place in Andalucía in January. All eighty European personnel would attend, and hotel and airfare were paid for by the company. The words were music to my ears. Though the three-day program was work, I was going to Spain! Andalucía conjured up many romantic images with rolling hills covered in olive trees and elegant horses. I would join the team there less than six weeks after joining the company. This couldn't be a bad sign, I was sure of it.

Cyril's second order of business was better. In the interest of promoting and integrating project management techniques, his team was taking formal certification courses and exams in the U.K. As a girl who loved school, I happily agreed to anything that boosted my resume. A week in England to do it only added more fuel to my European fantasy engine.

The picture began to lose its rosy tint when my new boss said that the American project management team was following a different certification path. The courses were popular in America, but not up to English standards as Cyril saw it. I didn't understand why we would actively choose an opposite course of action from the more experienced project management team, but I kept my opinion to myself. I was the new girl on the block. The new girl wanted to go to England.

As I learned more about the company and my responsibilities, Cyril and I agreed that spending three hours a day on public transport five days a week wasn't necessary. I agreed to be in the office three days a week, and the other days I would either be traveling or working from my home office, which I guaranteed him was technically well-connected.

* * *

The latter half of November and December flew. I learned about the company and its products and got to know my new colleagues. David

The Devil Wears Clogs

and I attended a company Christmas party at an indoor ski park in Holland, and there I met several members of the U.K. office. Everyone was easy-going and we agreed that it seemed I had a nice group of people to work with.

In January, I met several more people from the French and Italian offices at the kickoff event in Andalucía. On the last day of the event, I met Carlo, whose apartment in Milan was our Italian office. Carlo told Cyril and me about a project in Italy that he was working on. Cyril asked if it was something I wanted to work on. Without hesitation, I said yes. Carlo gave me a big smile and, from that moment, we were friends.

The line-up of projects I would run took shape quickly. I was working with Alan from the U.K. team on a British retail project. Carlo and I traveled to Perugia to put together the project. There were further talks about my background in French and my level of fluency, and Cyril decided that I would take on additional projects in Paris with a French salesman, Christophe. Suddenly I was very busy and thoroughly immersed in what appeared to be a dream job.

Every week, I flew from Amsterdam's Schiphol airport to Heathrow or Charles de Gaulle or Milan Linate. Sometimes, looking out at the white fluffy clouds high above the earth, I felt like pinching myself to see if this was real. Flying to Germany years before, I never imagined being the star of my own fairytale wedding or having a jet-setting career in Europe. Main Street Hardware was small, friendly, and informal. Rapidly growing, the company had a bright future in which I was a star player. Finally, I had found my way.

In my first months on the job, I was fascinated by the new clients and countries. For the most part, I worked with great local colleagues who gladly showed me the ropes of business in their countries. Flying in and out of a new country in a few days was exceedingly less stressful than moving to one.

For my first U.K. client, a large retailer, I stayed a night in Southampton before boarding a corporate jet to the Isle of Guernsey where their office was. Alan, my colleague, was a perfect gentleman. I wasn't used to men carrying my bag and opening doors, but it occurred to me that the Dutch could learn a thing or two from these guys.

At first, I was just happy to be working with someone whose first language was English, but I quickly discovered that American English and the variety spoken in the United Kingdom are different languages entirely. On one of my customer visits, my contact Tom greeted me with, "Are you all right?" rather than "How are you?" and I thought I must look ill. As three more people entered and asked me the same question, I figured it was the common greeting.

Another time, I was at a loss when someone asked me whether I wanted black or white coffee. Black coffee was obvious, but was white with cream and sugar or just cream?

When I flew into Perugia to meet with Carlo and visit his customer's site, he suggested that I stay in the city of Assisi. Assisi, which had its first settlers in 1100 BC, was the most amazing example of a medieval village I'd seen yet. It is famous for its Franciscan order of monks and a beautiful cliff top basilica. From the moment I arrived until the time my flight took off two days later, it was a marathon of meet, greet, and eat. My hosts wanted to show me all the best that Italy had to offer, and didn't waste a minute. It was on this trip that I was instructed cappuccino is a morning drink and one does not order anything but espresso after noon. Duly noted.

One evening, on our way to meet a large group for dinner, I asked Carlo how long it would take to get to the restaurant and his simple reply said it all, "It depends what happens on the way." I smiled and thought about how nice it would be to live in a country where one's interactions with friends and business partners are not dictated strictly by the clock. After several stops to greet Carlo's friends, we ate the most delicious *antipasti* and *scallopini* at a simple outdoor restaurant. Chianti flowed, and we laughed a lot.

Working in Paris was completely different. I spoke French reasonably well, but that made no difference in my interactions with my colleagues or hotel staff. Christophe, in particular, was determined to be difficult. Having visited Paris twice before I began working there regularly, I revered it as the epitome of beauty and chic sophistication. I had heard much about the rudeness of the Parisians, but I hadn't personally experienced it on my earlier visits. Christophe changed all that.

He made it clear that he was Christophe XIV, and my peasant

processes and methods were worthless. He did this by making an agreement with me face-to-face and then disregarding it the minute I turned my back. Insult to injury was the bakery girl laughing at my French, and discovering that getting from Charles de Gaulle to our office across Paris could easily take two hours in midday traffic. My mammoth government French client was no joyride either. Instead of informing us of technical issues in a normal direct manner, they sent certified letters threatening legal action. *Magnifique!*

* * *

In the summer of 2005, Cyril decided that I should meet the team in New York. Traveling back to the United States on business was a bonus, because I could sneak in personal downtime and it didn't cost me a fortune.

I was looking forward to working with people with whom I'd be able to relate. My hometown wasn't that far from this office, so I assumed it would be easy to find common ground with my fellow Americans. It was a big surprise when, not only did we fail to see things the same way, but they seemed to have very little time for me whatsoever. Until then, I hadn't realized how much I'd actually changed. I wasn't living on American soil and therefore could be pushed aside and told what to do, like the rest of the Europeans. I was appalled that the only interest they seemed to have in me or my point of view, as an American who had lived abroad for nearly four years now, was whether or not I was going to do things their way. Talk about déjà vu!

It was a deeply depressing visit, but I now understood why my European teammates complained endlessly about "the Americans." They were tired of being treated like idiots because English wasn't their first language, or because they resisted The American Way. My advantage was that I could see the viewpoints of both sides: the Americans wanted things done their way and the Europeans wanted things to done according to local practice. No one was winning the war, and I was now squarely in the middle of a debate that had been going on for years. Another battlefield, just different warriors.

At the beginning, I went wherever my colleagues shouted for help. That is, until I realized that there really did need to be some more formal procedures in place, or these complex projects would go haywire in a hurry. Six months at the company now, I tried to address this with Cyril. His very reason for hiring me was for my experience with large projects, so I expected him to be open to my suggestions. I had now passed my formal project management certification in England and understood the company products, so it never occurred to me that Cyril wouldn't appreciate my views. At first, he did. At first, he gave me free rein to do what I thought needed to be done to enforce control in technical project delivery. Then, ever so slightly, the picture began to change. The more confident I became, the more controlling he became. He wanted me on the phone constantly, to know my whereabouts every minute. He implemented a new project review system based on completely subjective information, and used it to criticize my performance. Somewhere along the line, I became a threat to be controlled.

During one of Cyril's team meetings in which we discussed the same list of "lessons learned" we'd discussed for two hours in the last meeting, I suggested that we devise a list of project management tasks to be completed and each take a few. Cyril wasn't working on any of his own customer projects, with the exception of one that was a giant mess (he had been politely asked to leave the customer's office), so I decided it was time he started acting like the leader he was supposed to be.

I grabbed the tasks I thought would help alleviate pressure from the leadership in the United States, by giving them more visibility to our work. If it was clear that the methods we used in Europe were producing the desired results, I was sure the Americans would stop assuming we were incompetent. Not only did the U.S. project managers like the idea I had come up with, they decided to take it, and the credit for its implementation, as their own. Cyril was lost in a fog. I was furious.

The situation between me and Cyril deteriorated rapidly. He was primarily based in the U.K., but when he was in the Eindhoven office, we avoided each other. I spent months attaining a second project management certification, the same one that the American project management team had. I couldn't be discounted for being female or

THE DEVIL WEARS CLOGS

living in another country when the letters behind my name were the same as theirs.

The war between the U.S. management and the EMEA team showed itself in many ways and at all levels of the organization. Suddenly, I was in the undesirable position of being an American having to explain to a team of Americans why their ideas would not fly in Europe. They wanted to gain new and impressive customers by showing up on our shores with the CEO and a bunch of touchy-feely tactics. They didn't understand that in Europe, business relationships are built on years of trust, and that he who arrives with the biggest display of insincere affection rarely wins. I took on more complex assignments. I found out that the EMEA management knew something that I hadn't been clued in on initially: Cyril was incompetent. I had been so blinded by all the travel and a challenging new work situation, not to mention one where the people were *nice*, that I hadn't taken a good hard look at Cyril as a boss and leader.

Every day, more information seeped from cracks in the walls. Colin, the service and repair manager, was the one who finally told me about Cyril's problems with his failed project, and Christophe's long reputation for the same bullshit games he was playing with me. Carlo said he was thrilled when I had taken over the Italian projects because Cyril was no help whatsoever. For the third time, I was in a no-win corporate game. I wasn't a member of the Boys Club, even though Colin claimed I had bigger *cojónes* than any of them on this side of the Atlantic or the other.

Knowing that I could work harder than anyone and still not be able to change the politics, the battle faded into the background of my life in 2006. David and I bought a beautiful new home in Rotterdam. I grabbed every training opportunity available and handled more diverse clients. My team and I went to Johannesburg for a wild client visit where we overviewed the processes at both a bank and a cash transport company, the most dangerous business in Africa. While we were there, we visited Sun City and went on a safari in Pilanesburg National Park. Taking photos of giraffes and rhinos in the wild was the most unbelievable business trip so far.

In the middle of that year, we were told our project management team would start reporting in to a boss in New York. As I had been placed in the unenviable position of being the spokesperson for everything that was wrong with the Americans' approach for the past two years, I knew this was the unofficial end of my career with the company. A few months later, we received the news that the company was being sold to a giant multinational. Many careers would soon be over.

In September of 2007, on a vacation in Tuscany, David received a call from his office. We had rented a villa with several American friends, and I was busy showing them what Carlo had taught me about how beautiful life in Italy can be. All of us were lounging at the infinity pool that overlooked the rolling Tuscan countryside when David asked me to come with him for a minute. His hushed tone told me it was important. Inside the villa, he went into our bedroom and motioned me in before shutting the door. "I have a question for you."

"Okay. I don't know what you couldn't ask me in front of my best friends, but I'm all ears," I replied.

"Would you be interested in moving to Singapore?" David said, grinning.

"What?" I was sure I did not just hear what I thought I'd heard.

"I said, would you be interested in moving to *Singapore*?"

"Are you kidding me?" I nearly shouted, which is why he'd pulled me into a confined space to begin with.

He wasn't. David's company had asked him to manage a large project team for a client in Singapore. The assignment was for three to five years. He wanted to do it. Hell *yes*, I was interested! The timing couldn't have been better. After six years, I knew immediately it was time to wave the white flag and surrender. My job wasn't worth fighting for. My lessons on European culture were invaluable, but Asia was completely unknown. We'd never even taken a vacation there.

As we hugged each other tight, I asked if I could tell my friends, and David replied by throwing the door open wide. Hand-in-hand, we gave our friends the unbelievable news. The look of shock on their faces was well worth it. A celebration was called for. Soon, we were scrambling to break out the Chianti along with the *prosciutto* and *pecorino* we had purchased at the local markets. The barbeque was heating up for an outdoor feast and glasses were filled and raised and filled again.

At our magical Tuscan villa in the countryside, the setting sun put a fiery-orange exclamation point on our news, red wine flowed, and we laughed.

About The Author

I live in a peaceful bush suburb north of Brisbane after 30 years in the United States, a year in Germany, five years in Holland, and four years in Singapore. The Lake Erie shores, west of Cleveland were my first chapter in life. A proud Buckeye, I graduated from Ohio State University in 1994.

Early in life, I was consumed with the idea of living in Europe. Joining a global technology firm in 2000 allowed me to realize my dream. When the door opened in 2001—I never expected Germany to be on the other side! Meeting the man of my dreams turned that one year assignment in Heidelberg into six years in Europe. During that time, I worked in the Netherlands, France, Belgium, Italy, Denmark, the UK, and South Africa.

My husband and I relocated to Singapore in 2007 and fumbled through the subtle complexities of Asian culture. Here I followed through on my longstanding desire to write. I began my first memoir in 2009, still working as an IT contractor. Southeast Asia at my doorstep made travel writing a natural choice. *The Guide* magazine published several of my articles in 2009 & 2010. Travel writing became an addiction as I explored China, Thailand, Malaysia, Australia, New Zealand, Cambodia, Laos, Hong Kong, & Borneo.

2011 brought me to Australia where I briefly returned to consulting. In 2012, I made the leap into writing full-time. In 2013, I launched my Facebook page, www.fb.me/worldwiseJen. My European memoir, ***The Devil Wears Clogs*** was first published in 2014.

The second book in my memoir series about life in Asia, ***Singapore Salvation***, was published in 2015. Now I am focused on the wonders and oddities of Australian life for my third book due in 2017. I am also speaking about world destinations and cultures and writing about my further adventures at www.WorldwisePublications.com.

Please join me on Twitter @JenniferBurge or Instagram @JenBurge and share your stories about the weirdness where you live.

www.ingramcontent.com/pod-product-compliance
Lightning Source LLC
Chambersburg PA
CBHW031411290426
44110CB00011B/338